# A PATIENT'S RIGHT TO KNOW

For Mum and Dad, not forgetting
Alvin and Cara

## Medico-Legal Series

**Legal Issues in Human Reproduction**
*Sheila A. M. McLean*

**New Reproductive Techniques: A Legal Perspective**
*Douglas J. Cusine*

**A Patient's Right to Know: Information Disclosure, the Doctor and the Law**
*Sheila A. M. McLean*

**Medico-Legal Aspects of Reproduction and Parenthood**
*J. K. Mason*

**Law Reform and Human Reproduction**
Edited by *Sheila A. M. McLean*

**Legal and Ethical Issues in the Management of the Dementing Elderly**
*Mary Gilhooley*

**Mental Health Law in Context: Doctors' Orders?**
*M. Cavadino*

**Discrimination and Mental Illness**
*Tom Campbell* and *Chris Heginbotham*

**Pharmaceuticals in the European Community**
*Ken Collins* and *Sheila A. M. McLean*

**Pregnancy at Work**
*Noreen Burrows*

**Changing People: The Law and Ethics of Behaviour Modification**
*Alexander McCall Smith*

**Patients, Practitioners and Data Protection**
*R. Irvine*

**The Law and Economics of Health Care Allocation**
*R. Lee*

**Surrogacy and the Moral Economy**
*Derek Morgan*

**Family Planning and the Law**
*Kenneth Norrie*

**The Right to Reproduce and the Right to Found a Family**
*Athena Liu*

# A PATIENT'S RIGHT TO KNOW

Information disclosure, the doctor and the law

SHEILA A. M. McLEAN
*Director, Institute of Law and Ethics in Medicine,*
*University of Glasgow*

Dartmouth

**Medico Legal Series**

Published by
Dartmouth Publishing Company
Gower House
Croft Road
Aldershot
Hants GU11 3HR
England

Gower Publishing Company
Old Post Road
Brookfield
Vermont 05036
USA

**British Library Cataloguing in Publication Data**

McLean, Sheila A. M.
   A patient's right to know (Medico-legal series)
   1. Great Britain. Medical information.
   Disclosure to patients. Legal aspects
   I. Title   II. Series
   344.104'41

**Library of Congress Cataloging-in-Publication Data**

McLean, Sheila.
   A patient's right to know: information disclosure, the doctor and the law/Sheila A. M. McLean.
      p.      cm. — (Medico-legal)
   Includes index.
   1. Informed consent (Medical law)—Great Britain.   I. Title.
II. Series.
   [DNLM: 1. Informed Consent.   2. Legislation. Medical—Great Britain.   3. Patient Advocacy.   W 32.5 FA1 M4p]
KD3410.I54M35   1989
344.41'0412—dc19
[344.104412]
DNLM/DLC

ISBN 1 85521 010 x
     1 85521 021 5 (pbk)

Phototypeset by Input Typesetting Ltd, London.
Printed and bound in Great Britain at
The Camelot Press plc, Southampton

# Contents

# Acknowledgements

I wanted to be able to think of something incredibly witty to say in the acknowledgements. However, I am thrown back on the boring, but nonetheless real, 'thank you'.

There are a large number of people who have contributed their time, interest, energy, cooking and affection to ensuring that this manuscript finally was completed. In no particular order, but with real gratitude to all of them, my thanks to Prof. A. A. Watson, Prof. D. M. Walker, Prof. K. C. Calman, Tom Campbell, Noreen Burrows, David Fergus, Beth and Bill Black, Alvin and Cara McLean, Paolo Cortini and Peter Beharrell. A special mention must go to the secretaries in the Department of Forensic Medicine and Science, Glasgow University, and in particular to Liz Doherty who was her usual, unfailingly helpful, competent, charming and unflappable self – thanks Liz!

Finally, the staff at Gower have been most considerate, and particular thanks are due to Margaret O'Reilly and John Irwin.

I have been able to take account of the law up to January 1988.

*Sheila A. M. McLean*
*The University, Glasgow*
*30th May 1988*

vii

# 1 Introduction

Over the last few decades, the practices and aspirations of orthodox medicine have come under scrutiny as never before.[1] The individual doctor is seen less as a favoured friend and a devoted healer, and more as a specialized participant in a system whose impressive battery of weapons will serve the health of the world.[2] Orthodox medicine has a wide variety of sophisticated tools – routinely paraded before an awestruck public – with which to decide who is ill, to provide diagnosis and prognosis and to cure (or at least alleviate) many of these conditions. Of course, nothing is perfect and perhaps not every illness can be cured, but medicine can at least make the symptoms less difficult to endure.

Moreover, the rapid growth of associated industries – notably the pharmaceutical industry – has also changed the face of medicine.[3] Physician-like uncertainty and joint consideration of a given problem have often given way to the apparent clinical certainty of drugs and sophisticated equipment. As medicine and its related industries have become more and more subtle in their capacity to assess the mechanics of ill health, so the cures and the palliatives have become more specifically targeted, more chemically refined. Medicine has become more than an 'art' (or perhaps less than one) – it is seen as a science, technically based, technologically equipped and distanced in terms of knowledge and comprehension from a public increasingly baffled, but none the less impressed by its sophistication.

Moreover, orthodox medicine in its struggle for professionalism, notably throughout the nineteenth century, significantly affected many aspects of the life of every citizen. It is widely believed, for example, that the rise of professionalism in medicine, made an important, if not determinative, impact on laws relating to abortion.[4] Orthodox medicine played a major role in the downgrading of what is now known as alternative medicine,[5] with the implication that it is fringe medicine – not the real thing at all. But, perhaps even more significantly, orthodox medicine seemed to have adopted a

1

particular posture – namely interventionist rather than preventive. This trend has not been substantially reversed, ensuring (or at least contributing to the fact) that the vast majority of people in countries with orthodox medicine turn to it to cure or alleviate illness rather than to prevent it. In this way, and perhaps partially for this reason, the range of medical skills is significantly weighted towards sophisticated diagnostic techniques, and expensive high technology equipment, and medicine has looked to the pharmaceutical industry to provide many of its cures and palliatives.[6]

These points are significant within the context of this discussion, since it will be necessary to conclude that without challenging the absolute 'good' of orthodox medicine, without exploring the concepts of health and illness, and without a healthy scepticism of orthodox medicine's health care monopoly, autonomy reducing practices may more readily be justified. Moreover, the technical nature of much of modern medicine should not be underestimated as a factor in at least some of the problems currently confronting the doctor/patient relationship in many countries. In particular, the increasing sophistication of medicine may cause communication problems between doctors and patients, and might suggest that technical skills dominate the entire enterprise.

In those so-called developed countries in which orthodox medicine has a virtual monopoly of health care, the phenomenon of challenge through complaint or litigation is increasingly common.[7] The doctor in some jurisdictions may find him or herself constantly afraid of legal challenge while the patient may find that his or her status as patient can be used to minimize personal autonomy. If, as is routinely said, trust is essential to a 'good' relationship between doctor and patient then a 'good' medical act can only follow where such trust genuinely exists.[8] Indeed, one of the major reasons to fear the 'American disease' of litigation explosion is precisely that its impact on the beneficent relationship between doctor and patient is so dramatic as effectively to reduce the potential for trust, and therefore for a 'good' medical act, which should be the aim of both parties to the interaction. Kennedy,[9] among others, has criticized what he calls the engineer/scientist model of medicine, seeing it as both personally unsatisfactory for the patient (perhaps also for the doctor) and therapeutically of limited value. What is claimed here is that the nature of the medical enterprise is greater than merely its technological capacity, and extends into more personal and less easily measured realms of morality – in particular respect for persons.[10] Achieving a level of trust in any relationship depends on respect between the parties, and whereas the patient routinely respects at least the technical skills of the physician (otherwise why seek him or her out), respect must also be shown by the doctor to the patient.

Viewed in this way, medicine is not simply an exercise of purely clinical skills. It transcends the technical to reach the level of morality by the sharing of respect. Indeed, medicine has long been concerned with questions of ethics, and has long shown a commitment to morality in dealing with the patient – however incomplete it might seem to be. Much of this commitment stems from recognition of the need to view the patient as an autonomous human being, with rights and interests which are identifiable independently of medicine. Recent codes of practice, for example those promulgated by the World Medical Association,[11] have explicitly dealt with the human subject in terms which leave no doubt as to the status to be accorded to the patient. Although this commitment is traditionally more clear in cases where the likely nature of the interaction is experimental,[12] it remains sound and appropriate in whatever situation the doctor exercises his or her professional skills.

Medicine's response to its patients is not merely an academic question, since at one time or another (and in some cases frequently) each of us will have some contact with orthodox medicine. Indeed the increased longevity to which many people in the developed world can aspire, will likely have a significant effect on our experience of medicine. This is primarily because – whatever our life-expectancy – age brings with it apparently inevitable problems. High technology may be able to provide pain relief for the chronic conditions associated with the elderly, such as arthritis, but it seems neither able to prevent nor cure it. The increasing number of elderly in the community is likely therefore to mean that – as a community of nations – the per capita contact with medicine will increase.

Moreover, increased media attention, increased publicity by doctors themselves and the political capital that can be made by being ahead in the race for better cures, more exciting surgical techniques, control over life and death and so on, meant that medicine was constantly paraded before the public in dress uniform. Its successes were trumpeted – its failures often ignored. This apparent imbalance may have represented no more than a desire to view only the positive, perhaps for a variety of reasons, but it also resulted, whatever its motivation, in an exaggerated and potentially problematic perception of medicine as something that is not only always good and well-motivated, but also always successful, or at least always showing enterprise, awe-inspiring skills and an understanding that goes beyond that which could be expected of ordinary mortals. The current trend, identified by some commentators, of parading medicine's failures has further dramatized the practice and capabilities of medicine in a manner which is scarcely helpful.[13]

This proliferation of claims about orthodox medicine, and there-fore by implication about the doctor, may result in a number of phenomena, many of which are inimical to the morally good prac-tice of medicine. Patients may become humble, undemanding and uninvolved with their treatment. Indeed it has been said that:

> Although scholars have proposed various models to describe or prescribe the distribution of power within the doctor patient relation-ship, for a number of years one view dominated professional ideology and customary practice. Under that view, the patient was seen as making only one key decision, to place herself in a given doctor's care, thereby delegating all subsequent authority to the doctor. Such a model assumed that the patient lacked the technical ability to make medical decisions and their expertise justified the doctors making decisions on the patients' behalf.[14]

Since much treatment is enhanced by the active mental co-operation of the patient (indeed it is now becoming part of accepted wisdom that the positive involvement of the patient can be beneficial),[15] patient participation is very significant, but is unlikely to be achieved in a relationship between a masterful doctor and a cowed patient. Further, the doctor may increasingly come to regard his or her skills as so far removed from the ordinary patient's under-standing and experience as to forget that the use of these skills results in human and not solely technical consequences. The former of these the patient not only *can* understand but also must live with.

The technical revolution has also had further significant conse-quences for doctors and patients. As the gap in technical skills widens, so the difficulties of communication inevitably increase.[16] Equally, however, the expectations of the patient are increased, resulting in disaffection with a medical act which does not succeed – a disaffection which is likely to be all the greater if not canvassed in advance as a possibility. In other words, communication may seem paradoxically to have become more difficult and yet more significant. Patients may be more impressed by the range of medical technology, but people in general are equally more aware of their civil rights. Challenge can lead to hostility, and yet is more likely in a rights conscious community. Moreover, it is more likely where explanations, communication and discussion are sparse or absent.

This is not, however, to suggest that the exercise of purely tech-nical skills is not highly important. Indeed, perceived failure adequately to exercise professional skills probably remains the major source of challenge in medicine, as in other disciplines.

However, the expectations generated by the technical claims of orthodox medicine are merely one set of expectations which the patient may have. Rights consciousness also raises expectations of involvement and of dialogue, and the fact that it is the patient and not the physician whose health is in issue makes it reasonable to presume that the patient will, or should, be intimately involved in the therapy.

Medicine as currently practised is a high risk enterprise. No drug, for example, is entirely safe, and risks attach to many diagnostic and therapeutic techniques. Even the most technically proficient medical act cannot guarantee complete success, nor can it be assured that unsought side effects will not occur. Communication, therefore, becomes important at a further level. Not merely does it permit of the establishing of a therapeutic bond between doctor and patient, but it allows the patient to have a reasonable awareness of the possible outcome of therapy or of diagnosis. Thus, not only does it facilitate free decision making on the part of the patient as to whether or not to become involved in the medical enterprise, but it can also serve to minimize the disappointment and ill-feeling that can result from a short-fall between expectations and results.

Recognizing the significance of communication between doctor and patient is a fundamental step in generating a therapeutic atmosphere capable of respecting the rights of the individual patient. The doctor who ignores or minimizes the importance of patient involvement places his or her position at risk. The number of actions raised against the medical profession continues to rise,[17] and the impact of this on medical care cannot be underestimated. It has been said that the raising of an action against a doctor is the archetypal expression of patient dissatisfaction.[18] However, this dissatisfaction may be with the way in which agreement was obtained or with the unavoidable outcome of the medical act rather than with the technical skill demonstrated by the particular doctor. Thus, many challenges may stem as much from a failure to explain known risks as from the doctor's operational mistakes or negligence. Moreover, failure of communication denigrates the patient's status as an autonomous individual and represents an insult at the abstract, but highly significant, level of morality. A 'good' medical act – the desired outcome of all consultation and treatment – is inconceivable if it is not consensual. It is here that the willing involvement of the patient, only possible if based on adequate information, becomes most significant. Medicine must be encouraged both to practise its skills to a high standard and to deal with patients at a morally acceptable level.

## Medicine and technical skills

As with most groups in the community, challenges against the medical profession have traditionally arisen through a perceived failure on the part of individual professionals to exercise their skill at the expected standard. This standard is higher where, as with doctors, the individual holds him or herself out as having special skills and a high level of expertise.[19] Each group in the community practising a trade or profession is expected to show a reasonable level of care and attention when carrying out its art or science. When the enterprise is particularly risky, then a higher standard of care is expected by law and by the consumer.[20] Thus expectations (both legal and personal) of medicine are particularly high – at least in theory. This results not merely from the risk element but also from the value placed on health – the guardians of which, in the developed world at least, are routinely perceived to be orthodox medicine and its practitioners.

The status of the individual as healthy or ill is not value free - indeed it can be highly significant.[21] Thus, the diagnosis of ill-health (which again is generally the monopoly of orthodox medicine) may have a profound effect on the individual at a number of levels. At one level, the individual's self-perception is altered by the fact of illness, his or her personal and social capacities can be severely limited by the knowledge of the illness and its nature. At another, certain forms of illness can have even more dramatic results. The diagnosis of mental illness, for example, which has been described by some as highly speculative,[22] may result in loss of freedom, loss of opportunity to form relationships (particularly sexual relationships), loss of capacity to enter into legally binding agreements and, perhaps more significantly, in extreme circumstances may result in the person so diagnosed being precluded from participation in the democratic process. Medicine, therefore, plays a political as well as a personal role and its importance is thereby enhanced. The person who seeks medical advice may as a result place him or herself in a situation of vulnerability beyond that which is generated by the mere fact of illness. While this does not mean that contact with medicine is dangerous *in se*, it does suggest that the morality of the medical act and the appropriate use of skills within it, have significance beyond the narrowly technical.

## Information disclosure

There are, therefore, a number of interlinking characteristics to the debate about information disclosure in medicine. A number of them may appear to conflict with each other, thus presenting a confused and internally inconsistent picture.

Undoubtedly, medicine is seen as a valued social good. The law and society, therefore, might not unreasonably be expected to protect this good from unnecessary or inappropriate challenge. On the other hand, the rights of the individual are valued by law and society, and their vindication can also represent a social good. Balance may consequently be difficult to achieve. However, it is argued here that it is unhelpful to characterize what is going on as a conflict between individual rights and collective beneficence. A collective 'good' is the sum of its constituent parts – in this case, the respect accorded to patients by their medical advisers is the core element in the general beneficence of the medical enterprise. Inevitably, as states are currently organized, if this assertion is to be accorded any real weight it can be achieved only, or substantially, through its recognition by law. The value of legal process is not doubted, but its limitations must also be recognized and if necessary exposed. As Harris has said:

> If individual and collective freedoms and genuine equality between sections of the population are to be pressed for and protected, then the law has an important part to play. Its use as an ideological weapon must be exposed, but its force as a limitation upon power must be recognized.[23]

The interest at stake – that is, the autonomy of the patient – is one which is clearly of considerable importance and one, therefore, which the law could choose to protect in a manner consistent with, and appropriate to, its inherent value. This could be achieved through recognition of the need for adequate information disclosure – adequate, that is, in a moral rather than a strictly professional sense.

Appropriate information disclosure and recognition of the patient's right to accept or reject therapy, or particular courses of therapy, are the only mechanisms available to redress the apparent imbalance between doctor and patient; the only ways to facilitate the provision of a real and meaningful consent to treatment or to validate its withholding. The patient is thereby placed in a position to become an active participant in choices about his or her health care. The duty to make disclosures is placed on doctors because they are, by the nature of their professional skills, in possession of the relevant information. But this does not minimize the input of the would-be autonomous patient, and demands that '[m]edical personnel are not justified in substituting their best medical judgements for patients' informed decisions'.[24] A commitment to patient participation, however, does not answer the question as to the extent of information which must be disclosed.

If information disclosure is genuinely to protect patient autonomy, then obviously *all* relevant information should be disclosed. Thus, every known risk – whatever its statistical probability – should be made known to the patient, since every risk might have a significant effect on that individual. Patient autonomy is only adequately protected where a standard is set by law – a standard for disclosure which prioritizes the rights of the patient. Taken to its logical conclusion, this would require two types of information disclosure.

*Disclosure of therapeutic alternatives*

As has been seen, doctors exercise their professional skills both in diagnosis and in selecting appropriate therapy. However, in some – perhaps many – situations there are alternatives in therapy, each carrying their own risks and their own benefits. Patient autonomy is as importantly protected by the capacity to participate in knowing choices about the type of therapy, as it is by having the capacity to decide whether or not to accept the recommended therapy. This is not to suggest that the patient has the technical skills to know the available choices, but merely, and more reasonably, to indicate that where alternatives exist the patient must be put in a position to evaluate the relative risks and benefits of these choices. As has been said, '[e]very human being of adult years and sound mind has a right to determine what shall be done with his own body.'[25] It is not inconceivable that a patient may be prepared to accept the risks associated with one therapeutic option but not with another. This is because:

> In many circumstances patients can make adequate choices about medical treatment only when they consider non-medical benefits and harms in addition to the medical benefits and harms which may accrue from these choices.[26]

The availability of therapeutic alternatives is a not uncommon feature of medical practice. Moreover, doctors themselves may differ on diagnosis and appropriate therapy. As was noted in the case of *Hunter* v. *Hanley*, '[i]n the realm of diagnosis and treatment there is ample scope for genuine difference of opinion.'[27] If patient autonomy is to be offered adequate protection, however, it is for the patient – of course on medical advice – to select the therapy most suited to their emotional, personal or financial situation. When the law protects this freedom it offers more than a mere theoretical commitment to autonomy. However, in both the United States and the United Kingdom, concern has been expressed that such an attitude is not common, or at least not routine. As Shultz put it:

> The law's response to pressures for a greater recognition of patient autonomy has been ambivalent. Existing rules repudiate the view that the mere hiring of a doctor transfers all authority from patient to doctor. Yet full vindication of patient autonomy interests would necessitate placing final authority regarding important decisions in the hand of any patient, having the capacity and the desire to exercise it.[28]

Equally, in the United Kingdom, this 'vindication of patient autonomy' has not always been obvious in situations which involve therapeutic choice.[29]

## Disclosure of risks and benefits

It is not common for doctors to minimize the potential benefits of therapy, but it is equally not common for them to emphasize the risks. What has been called the 'therapeutic imperative' dictates much of medical practice. If medicine has a potential cure, then it makes medical sense to use the appropriate therapy in order to effect that cure, and not to deter the patient by explaining the potential risks. At a purely professional level, it may be rational to view the desirability of information disclosure in this way, but in terms of patient autonomy it can only be denounced as paternalism. But the reasons often given for not disclosing risks can be defeated when the professional standard is given less than optimum weight and consideration.[30] If patient autonomy is crucial, then even information that prevents acceptance of therapy must be disclosed. In other words, for patient autonomy to be adequately protected, there must be a standard set not by medicine but by a legal system concerned about patients' rights to make choices in therapeutic encounters.

On the strict autonomy model then, all risks – and not merely some of them – must be disclosed if the patient is to be free to make personalized and meaningful decisions. That this is not common practice will be seen in more detail below, but for the moment there is one further consideration which follows from this claim. It is routine for courts and doctors to adopt a form of assessment of medical behaviour that equates to the kind of paternalism described, for example, by Buchanan.[31] Even where it is accepted in principle that risks should be disclosed, a further refinement is often used which delineates the nature of the relevant risks. Thus, it may be said that 'real' or 'material' or 'substantial' risks should be disclosed, but that by implication, those risks which do not fit into these categories need not be disclosed. Of course, if this is to be an acceptable modification of patient autonomy, it is necessary to formulate a test for 'realness' and so on. The materiality of a risk, it seems to be assumed, depends on the medically definable and determinable characteristics of the risk. If this were not so, then the patient would have to be informed of each risk in order that he or she could decide on whether or not it actually *was* real or material. Thus, the choice of risks to be disclosed remains very much the province of the doctor. But what implications does this have?

Clearly, since the physician in most cases will not also be the patient, it is necessary for the doctor to make calculations about the materiality of the risk, and this can only be done in a limited number of ways, none of which are satisfactory for the vindication of patient autonomy. On the one hand, the doctor may decide that his or her knowledge of the patient is sufficient for a decision to be made that only certain risks really matter. This is open to objection on the very obvious ground that the doctor can never know the full facts of the patient's life, nor what values the patient places on certain aspects of that life. This kind of assessment, therefore, amounts to little more than guesswork, and is unacceptable to those who have knowledgeable decision making as a goal.

Equally problematic, but less open to allegations of the casual importation of uninformed value judgement, is the use of scientifically known or knowable fact. A given therapy, for example, may be known to have a 5 per cent risk of causing a skin rash, a 1 per cent risk of causing severe headache and a 0.2 per cent risk of causing paralysis or death. There are two possible 'scientific' ways of approaching this range of possible effects. One, and the most obvious, is to use statistical method and to consider as substantial only that which is statistically significant. On this form of calculation, the patient would be informed of the two greatest risks, but not of the smallest statistical one. In terms of patient autonomy, this is obviously unsatisfactory since it omits to provide patients with some information, and, in particular, information which might seem to them to be most significant – that is the small, but potentially real, chance of paralysis or death. Using this approach then, the patient is denied access to information which may be vital in the decision whether or not to accept therapy. Of course, the standard arguments about unnecessarily frightening patients, or possibly deterring patients from accepting therapy, could be, and are, used to explain the making of such a choice, but it is contended that they scarcely justify it. It is not irrational for people to attempt to avoid even a very small risk of possible death, and indeed in wearing seat belts or minimizing flying time, many people do this routinely.

The alternative use of the statistical probability equation is equally open to objection. This approach could suggest that only the gravest of possible risks should be disclosed. In this calculation, the patient would be told of the small risk of paralysis or death, but not necessarily of the possibility of headache or skin rash. While this is equally autonomy-reducing, it has one further possible side effect which can adversely affect patient care. That is, patients who are unaware that these are possibilities may suffer considerable distress, and require further medical time, if they are not aware that what is happening is a result of the current therapy and not a manifestation of a new and unpleasant illness. Patient care is, it has been claimed, enhanced by respect for the patient, and this simple example serves to show one situation in which that conclusion is validated.

## Conclusions

Thus, it can be concluded that patient autonomy is only protected where there is a meaningful choice made by the patient, on the basis of adequate information, about which of the available therapies is acceptable and as to whether or not to participate in any therapy at all. Disclosure of risks and benefits protects not only the patient but also the doctor. No subsequent allegation of a lack of real consent can succeed where the doctor has respected his or her patient sufficiently to make such a disclosure, and to discuss the implications of accepting or rejecting therapy with the patient. This latter point is also highly significant, since it must be remembered that advocates of full disclosure do not simply advocate disclosure of *risk*. It is equally essential that the patient is given access to information about potential *benefits*, in order to permit the making of a choice which takes account of these competing factors. When this is borne in mind, fears that patients will routinely reject therapy become not merely insulting to the common sense of patients, but minimized considerably.

## Notes

1.  McKeown, T., *The Role of Medicine*, London, Nuffield Provincial Hospitals Trust, 1976; Illich, I., *Limits to Medicine. Medical Nemesis: The Expropriation of Health*, Harmondsworth, Penguin, 1985 edition; Kennedy, I., *The Unmasking of*

   *Medicine*, London, Allen and Unwin, 1981; Szasz, T., *The Theology of Medicine*, Oxford, OUP, 1979.

2.  For discussion of the contemporary role of doctors, see Brazier, M. M., *Medicine, Patients and the Law*, Harmondsworth, Penguin, 1987, particularly at p. 5, where she notes 'Few professions stand so high in general public esteem as that of medicine . . . Yet few individuals attract greater public odium than the doctor or nurse who falls from the pedestal.'

3.  Kass, L. R., *Towards a More Natural Science*, New York, Free Press, 1985; Currer, C. and Stacey, M. (eds), *Concepts of Health, Illness and Disease*, New York, Berg, 1986; Klass, A., *There's Gold in Them Thar Pills*, Harmondsworth, Penguin, 1975; Melville, A. and Johnson, C., *Cured to Death*, London, Secker & Warburg, 1982.

4.  Mohr, J. C., *Abortion in America*, New York, OUP, 1978.

5.  For discussion of the role and standing of 'alternative' medicines, see, for example, Inglis, B., *Natural Medicine*, London, Fontana/Collins, 1979; Stanway, A., *Alternative Medicine, A Guide to Natural Therapies*, Harmondsworth, Penguin, 1982.

6.  For a critique of the role of pharmaceuticals in medicine, see Klass, op. cit.; Melville & Johnstone, op. cit.

7.  Wood, C. (ed.), *The Influence of Litigation on Medical Practice*, London, Academic Press, 1977.

8.  For further discussion of a 'good' or 'right' or 'proper' medical act, see Pellegrino, E. and Thomasma, D., *A Philosophical Basis of Medical Practice*, Oxford, OUP, 1981.

9.  Op. cit.

10. C.f. Downie, R. S. and Calman, K. C., *Healthy Respect*, London, Faber and Faber, 1987; Downie, R. S. and Telfer, E., *Respect for Persons*, London, Allen & Unwin, 1969; Downie, R. S. and Telfer, E., *Caring and Curing*, London, Methuen, 1980.

11. C.f. Declaration of Helsinki (1964), as amended by the 29th World Medical Assembly, Helsinki (1975) and the 35th World Medical Assembly, Venice (1983); see also, the Statement on the Rights of the Patient, adopted by the World Medical Association, Lisbon, 1981, clause c) of which reads 'The patient has the right to accept or refuse treatment after receiving adequate information'. For a full description of the various ethical codes governing the practice of medicine, see *The Handbook of Medical Ethics*, London, BMA (1984) pp. 69–89.

12. For further discussion, see chapter 6, infra.

13. As Brazier, op. cit., says at p. 6, 'The medical marvels with which the public are bombarded reinforce the image of the doctor as superman. And so when a member of the public becomes a patient and 'superman' lets him down he is unsurprisingly aggrieved. Nor can doctors entirely blame the media for their image. Doctors decide on who get merit awards. Doctors vote with their feet as to which branch of medicine they enter. Many continue to vote for the glamorous world of 'high tech' medicine.'

14. Shultz, M. M., 'From informed consent to patient choice: a new protected interest', 95 *Yale Law J.* 219 (1985), at p. 221.

15. C.f. Brewin, T., 'What to tell the cancer patient', *Pulse* July 12 1980; Brewin, T., 'The cancer patient: communication and morale', 2 *Br. Med. J.* (vol. 2) 1619 (1977).

16. Katz, J., *The Silent World of Doctor and Patient*, New York, Free Press, 1984.

17. For discussion, see Brazier, op. cit.; see also Dyer, C., 'In pain? Sue the doctor!' *Law Magazine* 10 July, 1987.

18. McLean, S. A. M. and Maher, G., *Medicine, Morals and the Law*, Aldershot, Gower, 1983, reprinted 1985; Brazier, op. cit.

19. *Muir* v. *Glasgow Corporation* 1943 SC (HL) 3; the standard to be applied was discussed in *R.* v. *Bateman* (1925) 41 T.L.R. 557; for further discussion, see Gamble, A. J., 'Professional Liability' in McLean, S. A. M., (ed.), *Legal Issues in Medicine*, Aldershot, Gower, 1981; Mason, J. K. and McCall Smith, R. A., *Law and Medical Ethics*, (2nd edn), London, Butterworths, 1987.

20. For discussion, see Brazier, op. cit.; McLean and Maher, op. cit.; Mason and McCall Smith, op. cit.

21. For further discussion, see Currer and Stacey, op. cit., Illich, op. cit., see also, chapter 2 infra.

22. One of the most noted protagonists of this view is Szasz – for further discussion, see Szasz, op. cit.; see also, Hallek, S. L., *Psychiatry and the Dilemmas of Crime*, Berkeley, University of California Press, 1971.

23. Harris, P., *An Introduction to Law*, (2nd edn), London, Weidenfeld and Nicolson, 1984, at p. 379.

24. Hollander, R. D., 'Changes in the concept of informed consent in medical encounters' 59 *J. Med. Educ.* 783 (1984) at p. 784.

25. Per Cardozo, J. in *Schloendorff* v. *Society of New York Hospitals* (1914) 105 NE 92, at p. 93.

26. Hollander, loc. cit., at p. 784.

27. *Hunter* v. *Hanley* 1955 SC 200, at p. 217.

28. Schultz, M. M., loc. cit p. 223.

29. C.f. *Hatcher* v. *Black, The Times* 2 July 1954: see also *Palmer & Anor* v. *Eadie* (unreported, May 1987, CA).

30. C.f. Buchanan, A., 'Medical Paternalism' 7 *Philosophy and Public Affairs* 49 (1979).

31. For discussion, see Buchanan, loc. cit.; McLean, S. A. M. and McKay, A. J., 'Consent in medical practice' in McLean, S. A. M. (ed.) *Legal Issues in Medicine*, Aldershot, Gower, 1981; Shultz, loc. cit.; Hollander, loc. cit.

# 2 The role of law

In its traditional role as balancer of interests in disputes, the civil law plays a fundamental part in setting the standards to which practitioners of medicine (and of course all citizens) are expected to aspire. In the medical context this generally means by use of the law of negligence. Failure to achieve the standards set by law, coupled with consequential damage, will result in an award of damages designed to place the injured party in the position he or she would have been in but for the negligence involved.[1]

As noted above, the majority of challenges to doctors arise from a perceived shortfall in the nature and quality of technical skills. Judgements are concerned with the doctor's professional competence – routinely narrowly conceived as relating to the manner in which technical matters are effected. The fundamental duty of the doctor can, then, be described as being to exercise his or her technical expertise reasonably in line with the expected performance of other doctors of similar standing. However, despite assertions that doctors are judged by the law as we all are, there are additional difficulties in reaching judgement in these cases. The increasingly specialized nature of medicine makes it more difficult for courts to assess what the reasonable doctor knows or should have been able to achieve. Thus, a number of eminent lawyers have remarked on the difficulties of assessing technical skills, and even of understanding technical (and apparently inevitably jargonized) evidence.[2]

The difficulties of assessing professional behaviour without possession of the relevant skills render accountability of all professional groups problematic, yet accountability is of vital importance if one professional group is not to dominate. Accountability to the community is obtained substantially by the use of the law and through the mechanism of the courts. The law sets appropriate standards, however vague, and it is against these that behaviour will be measured. For the 'ordinary' citizen, the test will be that of the 'reasonable' man[3] and for the professional, the test will generally equate to the reasonable professional at that level of skill.[4] However, while courts are deemed to understand in what way a reasonable man would or should behave, and also how to assess the behaviour of lawyers,[5] doctors amongst others pose more difficulties. A court inevitably has problems in assessing the technical aspects of their behaviour, and must therefore depend heavily on the evidence of fellow professionals. Whereas no individual is permitted to testify as to what a reasonable man (or woman) would or would not have done in a given set of circumstances,[6] the sophistication of the medical act is such that others skilled in the same profession are seen as necessary to assist in making an assessment of what level of skill it is reasonable to expect, and whether or not the person whose behaviour is currently under scrutiny can be deemed to have deviated from that level, or to have fallen below the standard which is reasonably expected of him or her. This problem is, of course, not confined to medical practice, but for the purposes of this discussion, it remains the central area.

Nor is this the only factor that is apparent in court decision making in medical cases and that has an impact on the law's capacity to perform its role of interest balancing. Although it has been suggested that the role of the doctor in the community may have altered with the changing face of medicine itself, none the less the credibility of medicine and its practitioners remains at a high level. The perception of medicine as a specially protected social good is, if anything, enhanced by its high technology image. The capacity of medicine to achieve what – in the public eye – amounts to nothing short of miracles, for example in heart transplantation, ensures that it is held in the highest esteem, and that medical practitioners are viewed with the mixture of awe and deference due to the contemporary witch doctor. Nor are courts immune from this apparently unquestioning belief in the value of medicine. In many court decisions, society is reminded of the value of medicine, of its contribution to the world and of its responsibility for the common good in the shape of health.[7]

This is not an insignificant point, nor is it unrelated to the context of this discussion. Decision making in the courts has a profound effect both on the standards set by medicine and, of course, on the rights of patients. The attitude of the law to doctors and their discipline may profoundly affect the capacity of the patient to succeed in obtaining redress for a grievance. Equally, the standards required by these same courts in decision making provide some guidelines for the professionals themselves as to the behaviour which is acceptable to society. What is clear from analysis of judicial statements is that often, in the United Kingdom at least, a number of extra-legal criteria are influential in assessing medical behaviour.[8]

The use of these factors may relate to the perceived social good of medicine – by and large unreservedly accepted, although some commentators, notably McKeown,[9] Illich[10] and Szasz[11] would dispute this. However, other factors have also influenced decisions in respect of patients' claims – for example the status of the doctor,[12] the possibility of awards encouraging defensive medicine,[13] and so on. The burden of proof, it has been said, is higher when a challenge is made to the doctor than it is in other allegations of negligence.[14] The rationale for the significance of these factors is linked, therefore, to the status accorded to orthodox medicine and its practitioners.

Moreover, yet another rule of law may be affected. The normal rule is that the greater the risk of the enterprise, the higher the standard of care against which the practitioner will be judged.[15] However, in medical cases, the existence of this high risk is sometimes used to restrict rather than to expand liability. Of course, where the unavoidable risks of therapy occur, there must be no necessary implication that negligence was involved. If courts confined themselves to this view few would quibble with it. However, the use of the risk factor often surpasses this relatively unexceptionable one, and results in acceptance of behaviour which might seem to be questionable. That 'we cannot accept the benefits of medical treatment without also accepting its risks'[16] need not expose the public to a high risk unless the assumptions of beneficence, benign motivation and high profile credibility are taken too far. Certainly, risks are inherent in medicine, and – if agreed to – can be accepted. However, the individual patient is neither obliged to accept them merely because medicine is thought to help many people, nor to run unspecific risks in the interests of medical practice or advancement.

For example, the doctor who experiments in the hope of improving standards might well elicit approval, and sympathy, even if something goes wrong, but to relieve him or her of liability because he or she did not know there could be a risk is to omit to consider one other crucial factor, namely the harm done to the patient as a result of non-standard treatment, administered without approval and without the benefit of proven safety requirements. Although some patient must be the first, simply to deny responsibility because medicine is a risky business, even although the particular risk was self-generated, seems legally unusual to say the least, and yet this is precisely what happened in the case of *Roe* v. *Ministry of Health*.[17] Indeed, it is plausible to argue that the risk factor in medicine is precisely *why* accountability is so important, and accountability is ultimately achieved through the civil courts.

So in summary it can be seen that there are a number of factors which influence legal decisions on the technical practice of medicine. Whatever their credibility, they have informed the approach of the courts to challenges to medicine, and to the assessment of the behaviour of physicians in carrying out the operational aspects of their profession. In brief, these factors seem to be the status of orthodox medicine and its contribution to the general social good and the temptation to rely heavily, if not definitively, on the evidence of fellow practitioners – a reliance that stems at least in part from the increasing complexity of the practice of medicine. The reluctance of any professional group to criticize its members in any but the most overtly negligent situation is a further contributor to the difficulties facing the litigant who seeks to challenge medical behaviour. Yet, as has been said in one leading American case, fairness to the patient demands a standard set by law and not by doctors themselves.[18]

Of course, where operational matters are concerned, the law cannot set rigid standards. Professional competence will vary on a personal basis, but a general standard will none the less be required as a yardstick. Just as people are all tested against the mythical reasonable man, whatever the characteristics of the individual, so too the doctor is judged on a common denominator approach. Information as to what the average or standard or reasonable doctor is, or what he or she would do in a given situation, will primarily come from those who share the expertise - that is, those in equal possession of the knowledge and skills of the person whose behaviour is challenged. Little wonder that courts are loath to interfere in the assessment of medical behaviour when it is made by an eminent representative of the profession itself. In view of this, that the law sets the standards is in some situations not obvious, and it seems to many to be objectionable that medicine is often apparently self-regulating even in the courts.

But it may, of course, be said to be misleading to talk of dependence on professional evidence as a problem. Indeed, could it not be argued that only through this kind of informed decision making can the courts reasonably be expected to reach an accurate and appropriate conclusion? In any event, the courts reserve to themselves the right to make the ultimate decision, disregarding if they so choose the evidence of professionals. In this context this right could take on considerable significance as a way of controlling what otherwise may be seen as merely a system in which professionals themselves assess the legal standing of their colleagues' behaviour. Indeed, were the courts not to make a stand of this sort, then their role would be reduced to that solely of calculating damages, and not of actual decision making on liability. If the evidence of fellow professionals were to be all important, then there would be little justification for expensive, protracted hearings of the sort that often arise in difficult cases such as allegations of medical negligence, and the opportunity for public accountability of professional groups would be significantly reduced.

However, the paradox also is that where courts decide about medical behaviour relating to the exercise of technical skills, they do perceive a genuine difficulty – a shortfall of expertise which, when combined with other factors, can result in a heavy dependence on medical evidence, and render the role of the law symbolic rather than truly decisive.

The rule of law is that the value of competing evidence is a matter for the courts.[19] Whereas it has been suggested in at least one case that uncontested psychiatric evidence must be accepted by the court,[20] at least in the criminal law it is clear from the recent trial of Peter Sutcliffe that even eminent and uncontested medical (in this case, psychiatric) evidence need not be taken as definitive of legal matters.[21] However, it is also worth noting that in other situations, also involving the criminal law, for example the trial of Dr Arthur,[22] medical evidence as to standard practice *was* deemed to be decisive even although it was of no technical relevance to the charge of murder (subsequently reduced to attempted murder). Courts, therefore, may be said to have shown a certain confusion, in the criminal law at least, as to the emphasis to be placed on medical evidence - an ambivalence that seems to relate to the nature of the desired outcome as much as it does to the value of evidence in any strict sense.

Thus, one cannot underestimate the importance of expert testimony on the determination of whether or not the behaviour in question falls below the level of skill which can be reasonably expected of the person in question. While there are practical reasons for this, it may also seem that some highly technical or sophisticated professions, such as medicine, may find themselves, however unwittingly, in the position of effectively usurping the role of the court. Moreover, these are the very groups whose professional etiquette most strongly demands that a colleague should not be publicly criticized. Thus, for one doctor to speak against another requires the most serious consideration. Professional and defence organizations alike will caution silence and the group – not unusually – prefers to keep its problems internal. In fact, at least one eminent commentator has indicated that the ultimate condemnation for a doctor is the criticism of his fellow professionals, and not censure by a court.[23]

This attitude has also been accepted by some members of the judiciary, notably Lord Denning, who has been highly influential in forming the body of knowledge which makes for case law. In a number of cases, Lord Denning made it clear that the court should hesitate to condemn medical behaviour if other doctors would not condemn it.[25] In other words, the doctor's behaviour is most accurately and appropriately assessed by his or her own colleagues and not by the courts or by a standard generated by law. That is, the standard may be set by the law – in the technical sense that the law may insist that the standard to be achieved is not necessarily that thought suitable or sufficient by doctors – but the nature, extent and shape of medical responsibility may actually be formed by the profession itself.

Doctors, as expert witnesses, are, however, no more competent to speak to the ultimate issue than are other experts. Their business is to inform the court as to their opinion of the behaviour under challenge – that is, their opinion as to whether the behaviour meets the standard of the reasonably competent practitioner. This capacity to give opinions is what distinguishes the expert witness from the ordinary one.[26] However, the opinion which the expert is entitled to give is not in fact, or as a matter of law, an opinion as to whether or not the legal test is met. In other words, negligence is a legal and not a professional matter – in this case not a medical matter. If courts rely too heavily on expert evidence then the legal rule is in danger. Blanket acceptance of professional assessment does no good for the theory of law nor for its practice.

However, there is a certain logic – indeed it might be argued a necessity – in the importance given to medical evidence in cases of operational negligence. The fact that other doctors would not criticize their colleague is informative, as will be descriptions of what the profession regards as good or competent medical practice. Inevitably, although reluctant to criticize their colleagues, doctors will also not wish to offer a description of competent medicine which seems to set so low a standard as to render it not worthy of esteem. For this reason, it is likely that a balance of interests can be achieved. However, it remains the case that the law must decide not merely whether doctors *think* the behaviour in question was acceptable, but rather whether or not it *was* negligent.

Negligence is described and delineated by rules of law and is not commensurate with accepted professional conduct. While the latter will be informative, there are issues involved in the decision making of the courts which are wider in their implications than the preservation or reinforcement of narrowly professional standards.[27] The courts, in considering whether or not to redress grievances, are also capable of taking into account issues of justice, need and so on. Moreover, and perhaps more fundamentally, the courts must satisfy themselves that the legal requirements of a successful action are met.

Thus, judicial decision making is central to the ultimate assessment of the validity of a claim. Of particular significance will be the extent to which decision makers emphasize the rule of law, and the rights of patients, or the interests and evidence of the group under challenge.

*Summary*

Even ignoring the extra legal factors which can – and it has been claimed, do – affect decision making in medical cases, there remains a plausible distinction between medical and legal interpretation of a given piece of behaviour. At least, there remains this potential difference, since in theory each of the parties involved is seeking to make different calculations and to answer different questions – however subtle that difference may be. The medical expert seeks to assess his or her colleague's behaviour in terms of its clinical validity, within certain boundaries, and in the light of certain allowances. The expert will, of course, inevitably also have an eye on the impact which his or her conclusion may have on the ultimate assessment of the court. However, it has been claimed that expert assessment need not point to the ultimate decision of the court.

In matters of technical or operational competence, it may – as has been seen – at first sight seem most plausible to argue that the best people to assess whether or not the doctor is negligent would in fact be his or her fellow professionals. After all, they are the experts in a highly specialized and technical discipline. Who better than a fellow specialist to judge such behaviour? However, it has also been indicated that the description of the doctor's behaviour as negligent or not is for the courts and not for other professionals. Nor is this a narrow academic point, since the significance of a finding that the legal test has been met goes beyond professional censure or approval. Thus, even in those aspects of the doctor's business which are intimately linked to technical skills – that is, in matters often referred to as operational – the legal assessment of his or her behaviour cannot appropriately or competently be made merely by reference to what others in the profession might think of as good, or alternatively substandard, behaviour – however valuable this information may be.

## An introduction to patients' rights in medicine

The most important implication of accepting the right to receive information is that it represents some underlying value which is protected by information disclosure and which is independent of medicine itself. It has already been said that there is a value in using rights discourse in teasing out the complex relationship of doctor and patient, medicine and illness. This value lies in the fact that, if a right to receive information can be plausibly established, then the courts and the medical profession will be required to respect it. From the point of view of the patient, this can only enhance his or her moral standing in the medical enterprise.

But in order to achieve this, it must be established that such a right does exist – merely to claim that it does, does not make it so. And, consequentially, it must be conceded that the nature of the right – if established – will affect the behaviour which we can legitimately expect to follow on its recognition. There are many and varied ways to talk about and describe human rights, but they would be out of place here. What is argued here is that we can identify something sufficiently important about personal autonomy – on whatever view of rights – which makes it an essential component of the respect which we should show to others. Not perhaps the most tightly argued point, but one which, nevertheless, suffices for our purposes. Few philosophers, whatever school of thought they belong to, would argue with the values to be attached to autonomy although they may choose to place limitations or exceptions at different points on the scale.

Accepting, therefore, that human beings are inherently entitled to respect – to physical and mental integrity – the only question that remains is whether or not it is a legitimate expectation that such respect extends to them even when they are or may be sick, or otherwise separable from the 'normal' community. If not, then of course the argument need go no further. If so, however, then the implications are many and far-reaching.

Clearly there is a level to the medical act which goes beyond the purely technical. Indeed, the moral aspect of medicine – as with all human interactions – cannot properly be described solely in terms of the narrow discipline. The responsibilities of the lawyer to his or her client, the psychologist, the architect, as well as the doctor, share characteristics which make it impossible to describe the factors under consideration as only 'medical' or 'legal', and so on. The extent to which professional groups deal with their clients as self-determining human beings is not a question specific to any one discipline, but relates to the characteristics of the client as much as, if not more than, it does to the profession or the professional involved. So, while the technical skills which clients seek may differ, the essential characteristic of a good transaction need not change. A good act remains one which respects the client's moral autonomy (as well as being one which demonstrates the level of technical competence which can reasonably be anticipated) and facilitates his or her capacity (and right) to make free and uncoerced decisions based on the honest provision of information.

Although the courts have placed heavy emphasis on medical evidence in describing the doctor's technical duty to his or her patient, can or should this equally apply to the moral aspect? If it is questionable when technical professional skills are under scrutiny, is it not even more questionable when what is at issue is not technical at all, but rather is concerned with reinforcing and respecting a view of the individual which is treasured by national and international law and morality.[28] This is not to say that acknowledgement of the status of the patient is not intimately tied into the provision of the technical skill being sought, but it is an aspect of the professional relationship which also transcends it. It is the right of the individual that generates the duty of the professional not to overstep authority in the name or the interests of professional or technical superiority. Thus, although the technical gap can seldom if ever be bridged, respect for the individual demands that relevant information is disclosed and an opportunity presented for either individual or consensual decision making.

In the case of medicine, this provision of information permits the patient to make choices about whether to run certain risks, and what risks to run. While information disclosure can easily been seen as an aspect of the doctor's professionalism, it is scarcely *only* an aspect of the exercise of technical skills. Assessment of the doctor's behaviour in this aspect of medical intervention is less obviously susceptible of clinical assessment or judgement. If the aim of disclosure is the protection of individual autonomy, then it represents a wider issue than the clinical, and is not a matter appropriately defined by standard medical practice, but rather one which is to be determined by reference to considerations which go far beyond the gap in technical skills and expertise between doctor and patient. Respect for persons demands that the opportunity for free decision making is made available, and that the choice – albeit coupled with professional recommendation – is that of the individual who holds the right. The invitation to exercise technical skills, for example in a request for diagnosis, cannot and does not impose on the person making the request a duty to accept even clinically optimal recommendations.

If medicine *is* to be a good, it must do more than merely show a high level of technical expertise. It must also contain and foster the moral element which protects the integrity of the individual. But this moral element goes beyond professional definition, and demands external considerations of a type which doctors, in common with other professionals, are not inevitably the best or most appropriate persons to judge. Moreover, it is here also that the significance of the medical enterprise can be seen to impose even greater responsibility. When communities delegate vital decisions about health and illness to orthodox medicine then it is even more important that participation in the enterprise is both free and knowing. In this way, autonomy is respected.

Viewing medical intervention in this way makes analysis of the relationship between doctor and patient in the terms of human rights intelligible. Admittedly some claims which patients may argue for may not be capable of practical resolution, even if they can be couched in the language of rights. For example, difficulties may arise because the medical enterprise is itself circumscribed by resource problems. The fact that health care resources are unlikely ever to meet potential or actual demand may result in the denial of appropriate care in some cases. The shortage, for example, of dialysis equipment, means that decisions must be made as to how limited resources are allocated.[29] However these decisions are made, they represent a lack of universality in health care, which renders the use of the language of rights rhetorical rather than real.

Equally, while the patient may reasonably feel him or herself to be entitled to the best possible care, or even to cure, it would be an unreasonable and intolerable burden to place on any discipline a demand that this was universally the actual result. However, the patient can legitimately demand a reasonable standard of care, and a perceived failure to supply care at this reasonable standard can, and sometimes does, form the basis of a grievance redressable at law.

Although the language of rights may not always point a clear way for resolution of perceived problems, it none the less plays a part in the determination of the relevant interests at stake. In any event, the sane adult who enters into a relationship with medical practice will have two distinct sets of conscious or unconscious expectations. On the one hand, he or she may reasonably anticipate receiving a level of care which is acceptable – not primarily as an aspect of human rights but rather as an aspect of what can be expected from a group setting itself up as having special skills which are the basis of the patient's decision to seek them out. On the other hand, however, the patient can expect that mere admission or suspicion of illness does not affect his or her standing as a moral agent. In other words, just as involvement with a lawyer does not diminish the moral standing of the client neither does involvement with a doctor inevitably imply or justify any reduced standing in a human being.

At a national level, protection of autonomy is generally offered by the law recognizing its significance and vindicating its existence as a legal and a moral right. Whether by formal or informal rules about due process, or the careful determination of rights and duties, it is the law which can deter the unwarranted assumption of authority, and provide the capacity to redress grievances. The responsibility for such protection is one which is, in theory at least, taken seriously by the law. But, as Shultz[30] notes:

> Judges and legal scholars have long asserted the importance of patient autonomy in medical decision-making. Yet autonomy has never been recognized as a legally protectable interest. It has been vindicated only as a by-product of protection for two other interests – bodily security as protected by rules against unconsented contact, and bodily well-being as protected by rules governing professional competence. Neither bodily security nor bodily well-being, however, is an adequate surrogate; they do not coincide with autonomy. Nor is autonomy merely a formal issue. Decision-making by competent professionals does not provide an adequate substitute for patient choice. Injuries that arise from invasion of patients' interest in medical choice are both substantial and distinct.[31]

Moral autonomy is, albeit often without direct reference, protected by most advanced legal systems. In situations where individuals are denied autonomy through, for example, the removal or refusal of valued political rights, or unwarranted denial of liberty, it is not merely the instant symptoms which are the source of outrage. Rather the fundamental concern is the denial of autonomous and self-determining status to the individual, of which the action under consideration is symptomatic, striking as it does at common morality. Although seldom put into words in courts of law, at least in the United Kingdom, the concept of respect for autonomy is as much a matter of concern as the concept, for example, of due process – again not technically a part of Scots or English Law, but nevertheless one whose characteristics are generally respected.

However, law is not merely concerned with narrow technicalities. Not only do laws develop to protect the individual, but the determination of breach of these laws takes into account more than the mere assessment of technicalities. Whether it is the rights and duties of a civil servant or the rights of the newborn, law and its decision makers are creative. Constant concern is demonstrated for the rights of individuals both as an aspect of what a developed legal system regards as good, fair and proper, and in due deference to international commitments to respect for the individual. Thus, it makes real sense to emphasize basic human rights, in all aspects of daily life. Indeed, as has been suggested above in some aspects of that life consideration of the rights involved is more than just desirable - it can become absolutely essential to the matter in hand. The significance of the political enterprise for example makes the use of rights terminology routine. 'The right to work', 'the right to take industrial action' are now common-place terminology, as are demands for industrial and political autonomy and equality of bargaining power. Whether or not these 'rights' show all of the characteristics of what are called fundamental human rights, there is a perceived value in the symbolism of rights discourse, which serves to emphasize not merely the power of language, but also the conceptual importance of the individual worth.

The potential invasiveness of medicine, and its social and political potential, make it an area ripe for rights discourse. More importantly, the inevitable personal – in physical and mental terms – impact of any therapy or diagnosis places medical care in the forefront of concern for the individual. But rights are not merely protected by payment of lip service to the conceptual framework within which they play a part. Translation of rights into reality is also vital to their personal, national and international significance. For this translation, we generally turn to the law to provide both a statement of what rights are, and the machinery whereby infringement of rights can be remedied.

So it is not enough merely to say that, for example, patients have rights in their interaction with medicine, nor that doctors' duties flow from these rights. The willingness of the law to redress legitimate grievances, and the mechanisms available for such redress, are of equal, if not even greater, ultimate significance to their description and realization.

## Conclusions

It is evident, therefore, that the practice of medicine and the application of its techniques – preventive, diagnostic and therapeutic – are not value-free. At one level, the content of the interaction between medicine and the individual is a technical one. But the application of clinical skills, although important, is but one aspect of what is actually going on. Beyond this, and subsuming it, is the moral quality of the act which transforms a mere clinical act into a 'good' medical act. Even taking into account the doubts which some commentators have expressed about the real benefits of orthodox medicine, and in particular doubts about its actual impact on health[33] the medical act has a significance of its own. This significance is more than the capacity to cure or to alleviate suffering – it is also a recognition of the fact that the individual must not be subordinated to the acquired skills of any single group in the community. Just as consensual politics is deemed to represent the best form of government, so consensual medicine is the best form of that discipline. Indeed, most doctors (and patients) would find little to argue with in such a statement. However, breaches of faith do occur, and it is here that the law has a major role to play. Whatever the motivation, however benign the exercise of professional paternalism, the important issue remains the rights of the patient not to be the subject of involuntary or unauthorized intervention in his or her life.

This discussion therefore will concern itself with consideration of the rights of patients to receive information about risks, benefits and alternatives in medicine. The provision or withholding of a real consent is the act of an informed and autonomous individual. But only full knowledge of the implications of accepting or rejecting therapy will place the patient in a position to make the (personally) appropriate choice about his or her future. This contention becomes less apparently extreme when it is accepted that information sharing is not solely a clinical matter, but is something which offers, or has the capacity to offer, freedom of choice and respect for autonomy. Autonomy is defined as 'the power or right of self-government',[34] and a patient has no less right to this than does the person who is not sick. Equally as medicine changes and becomes inherently more risky, as well as potentially more therapeutically valid, the patient's voluntary involvement is even more desirable.

It will be argued here, therefore, that information disclosure plays a central and fundamental role, both in the autonomy of the individual and in the morality of the medical enterprise. Moreover, it will be contended that only legal decision-making which distinguishes between the technical and the moral aspects of the medical act can adequately safeguard either of these important considerations; although ideally the two should be inseparable in the practice of the physician.

The provision or withholding of consent on the basis of adequate information is the right of the patient, and on this depends the morality of the medical act. But acceptance of the 'good' of medicine, may obfuscate the need for a 'good' medical act. The value of orthodox medicine, it will be contended, is, however, the sum of its individual acts, rather than being some abstract, generalized good. The significance of consent provisions, which require information disclosure, lies in their capacity to reflect and enhance the moral standing of the individual, and therefore they have a collective impact on communities. The law has a major role to play in guiding professionals (including doctors) as to what is acceptable behaviour and what is not (whatever other professionals may believe) a necessary commitment to disinterested decision making, and an interest in the provision of a viable method of redressing grievances.

Moreover, there are further implications which flow from a reluctance to see information disclosure as separable from professional tests. If matters which are actually about human rights are technologized or professionalized with the backing of the law, then paternalistic arguments about patient understanding, rationality and capacity (in a legal sense) which are apparently defeasible, come back into the picture with more chance of carrying the day. If the sufficiency of information disclosure *is* assessible primarily by reference to good medical practice then justifications for non-disclosure can include the (potential) avoidance of patient distress, the (probable) technical validity of the doctor's choice between therapeutic options, and the (possible) inability of the patient to understand the information and use it properly.

It is therefore contended that it is plausible to separate issues of information disclosure from matters that relate to the exercise of professional/technical skills. Simply, it is the provision of adequate information which pre-dates any invitation to *use* technical skills. Each time a patient consults a doctor this invitation must be re-extended. The doctor has a continuing *duty* to act in a manner consistent with the level of skill which can reasonably be expected, but has no *right* to do so unless the patient voluntarily agrees to it.

The patient, therefore, is entitled to respect in the medical enterprise as much as in, for example, consultation with an accountant. Only the availability of information satisfies a legitimate demand for autonomy. At this point, however, it must be conceded that hanging the entire argument on autonomy might seem to be self-defeating. What of people, such as children and the mentally handicapped who are generally seen as lacking legal capacity? If they have insufficient capacity at law, then surely they could not claim the rights talked about here? Would this not, therefore, minimize the importance of the whole argument, by making the discussion one which is not about rights in a fundamental sense but really only about interests which the sane adult may have but which needn't necessarily be respected?

There are two things which flow from these questions. First it must be asked whether legal capacity is the essential prerequisite to making decisions in this area. In other words is a person who is legally *incapax* inevitably also not to be treated in any circumstances as autonomous? Second, does the law never concede decision-making powers to those whom it classifies as *incapax*? If it can be shown that the law does respect some decisions made by those who are otherwise deemed *incapax* and if that respect is based on the implied or explicit autonomy or rights of these groups, then challenging the significance of the rights of patients is less likely to succeed. And if, where decisions are only validated when taken by others, they none the less are tested against respect for the *incapax* rather than solely on legal or medical criteria then that respect is enhanced.

Accordingly, at this stage, account must be taken of those groups whose legal capacity is in doubt, since if it *is* legitimate to exclude them from the rights which it has been argued are due to the sane, adult, human being, then the case for information disclosure is considerably weakened. It is also, of course, necessary to consider what significance is attached to patient understanding of information, a factor which – if one were wedded to the language of 'informed' consent [35] – might seem to take on a particular importance.

## Notes

1. For discussion of the negligence action, see Walker, D. M., *The Law of Delict in Scotland*, (2nd edn), Edinburgh, W. Green & Son Ltd., 1981; Weir, T., *A Casebook on Tort*, (5th edn), London, Sweet and Maxwell, 1983.
2. C.F., Lord Denning, 'The freedom of the individual today' 45 *Medico-Legal J.* 49 (1977), at p. 59 where he said 'The medical people, the engineers, the chemists – all have their jargon which none of the rest of us understands.'
3. For description, see, e.g. *Hall* v. *Brooklands Auto-Racing Club* [1933] 1 KB 205, 224. As Lord Macmillan said in *Muir* v. *Glasgow Corporation* 1943 SC (HL) 3, at p. 10 'The standard of foresight of the reasonable man . . . eliminates the personal equation and is independent of the idiosyncracies of the particular person whose conduct is in question.' For further discussion of 'reasonableness' see Walker, D. M., op. cit.; Rogers, W. V. H., *Winfield and Jolowicz on Tort*, (12th edn), London, Sweet & Maxwell, 1984.
4. *Lanphier* v. *Phipos* (1838) 8 C & P 475; *Hunter* v. *Hanley* 1955 SC 200, per Lord President Clyde at p. 205 ' "Reasonable care and skill" is . . . what is reasonable for a qualified member of that trade or profession . . .' see also *Wilsher* v. *Essex* AHA (1988) 1 All ER 871 (HL).
5. This being a decision for the court, see Walker, op. cit., p. 201, 'The standard of reasonable care is not subjective . . . but objective, namely *the standard of care which the court thinks a hypothetical standard individual, the reasonable man, would display.*' (emphasis added).
6. C.f., Gordon, G. H., 'The expert witness', in McLean, S. A. M., (ed.) *Legal Issues in Medicine*, Aldershot, Gower, 1981.
7. C.f. *Roe* v. *Ministry of Health; Woolley* v. *Same* [1954] 2 QB 66.
8. For further discussion, see McLean, S. A. M., 'Negligence – A dagger at the Doctor's Back?' in Robson, P. and Watchman, P. (eds), *Justice, Lord Denning and the Constitution*, Aldershot, Gower, 1981.
9. McKeown, T., *The Role of Medicine*, London, Nuffield Provincial Hospitals Trust, 1976.
10. Illich, I., *Limits to Medicine. Medical Nemesis: The Expropriation of Health*, Harmondsworth, Penguin, 1985 edition.
11. C.f. Szasz, T., *The Theology of Medicine*, Oxford, OUP, 1979.
12 C.f. *Hucks* v. *Cole The Times* 9 May 1968, where Lord Denning said that: 'A charge of professional negligence against a medical man was serious. It stood on a different footing to a charge of negligence against a driver of a motor

car. The consequences were far more serious. It affected his professional status and reputation.'

13. C.f. *Hatcher* v. *Black The Times* 2 July 1954; *Roe* v. *Ministry of Health*, supra cit.

14. *Hucks* v. *Cole*, supra cit.; but see also Kilner Brown, J., in *Ashcroft* v. *Mersey Regional Health Authority* [1983] 2 All ER 245, particularly at p. 247.

15. *Muir* v. *Glasgow Corporation*, supra cit., per Lord Macmillan at p. 10 'Those who engage in operations inherently dangerous must take precautions which are not required or persons engaged in the ordinary routine of daily life.'

16. Per Lord Denning, in *Roe* v. *Ministry of Health*, supra cit., at p. 83.

17. Supra cit.

18. For example, in the case of *Canterbury* v. *Spence* 464 F 2d. 772 (1972).

19. C.f. Gordon, loc. cit., at p. 209 'Where experts disagree, the court must choose between them.'

20. C.f. *R.* v. *Matheson* [1958] 1 WLR 474; see also, *R.* v. *Bailey* [1961] Crim LR 828; *Walton* v. *R.* [1978] AC 788.

21. For discussion of this case and the nature of the treatment of psychiatric evidence, see Silverman, G., 'Psychiatry after Sutcliffe' (1981) 125 *Sol. J.* 518; Prins, H. A., 'Diminished responsibility and the Sutcliffe case: legal, psychiatric and social aspects (a "layman's" view)', 23 *Med. Sci. Law* 17 (1983); see also, Mason and McCall Smith, op. cit., ch. 19.

22. *R.* v. *Arthur The Times*, 6 November 1981.

23. Leahy Taylor, J., *The Doctor and Negligence*, London, Pitman Medical, 1971 (at p. 1) 'It is no disrespect to Her Majesty's judges to consider that their condemnation should disturb a doctor less than condemnation by his professional brethren.'

24. For discussion, see McLean, loc. cit.

25. C.f. *Hatcher* v. *Black*, supra cit.; see also, Lord Denning's discussion of appropriate decision making in medical cases in *The Discipline of Law*, London, Butterworths, 1987, esp. at p. 237.

26. For discussion, see Gordon, loc. cit.; The role of the expert is described by Lord President Cooper in *Davie* v. *Magistrates of Edinburgh* 1953 SC 34, at p. 40 'Their duty is to furnish the judge or jury with the necessary scientific criteria for testing the accuracy of their conclusions, so as to enable the judge or jury to form their own independent judgement by the application of these criteria to the facts proved in evidence.'; see also, *Evidence of Opinion and Expert Evidence*, Cmnd 4489/1970; Criminal Law Revision Committee, 11th. Report, Cmnd 4991/1972; Scottish Law Commission Memorandum No. 46: *The Law of Evidence* (1980).

27. For discussion, see, Harris, P., *An Introduction to Law*, (2nd edn), London, Weidenfeld & Nicolson, 1984. Harris says (at p. 49) 'A prime concern of any legal system is the protection of certain things (tangible or not) which are of value to human beings. Not all these things can have the same value; nor can they always be given efficient protection against all invasions. A hierarchy is thus dictated by moral, economic and other considerations with the result that the law affords better protection to the better things in life.'

28. Universal Declaration of Human Rights; European Convention on Human Rights.

29. For discussion of resource allocation, see Rescher, N., 'The allocation of exotic medical lifesaving therapy', 79 *Ethics* 173 (1969); Note 'Patient selection for artificial and transplanted organs', 82 *Harvard Law Rev.* 1322 (1969); Leenan, H J. J., 'Selection of patients', 8 *J. Med. Ethics* 33 (1982); Doyal, L., *The Political Economy of Health*, London, Pluto Press, 1979; see also, McLean, S. A. M. and Maher, G., *Medicine, Morals and the Law*, Aldershot, Gower, 1983 (reprinted 1985) chapter 10.

30. Shultz, M. M., 'From informed consent to patient choice: a new protected interest', 95 *Yale Law J.* 219 (1985).
31. Ibid. at p. 219.
32. For further discussion of these types of claim, see Attwooll, E., 'The right to be a member of a trade union', in Campbell, et al. (eds), *Human Rights: From Rhetoric to Reality*, Oxford, Basil Blackwell, 1986.
33. C. F. McKeown, op. cit.; Illich, op. cit.; Kennedy, I., *The Unmasking of Medicine*, London, Allen & Unwin, 1981.
34. Chambers Twentieth Century Dictionary.
35. In any event, 'informed' consent has not shown itself to have been an entirely successful legal mechanism. For further discussion, see infra.

# 3   Special groups: children

It has been claimed that the right to receive sufficient information on which to make therapeutic decisions is of considerable importance for the would-be autonomous human being.[1] That the law at present seems, in most if not all jurisdictions, to be ill-equipped to handle this right effectively or sensitively is a subject for concern. This is so, not merely because there is something inherently valuable in the abstract about the claim to self-determination in medicine, but also because only direct access to this right minimizes people's vulnerability to the power of medicine, and stimulates their capacity to challenge professional paternalism which, however well intentioned, can be, and often is, a face-on threat to autonomy.

However, there are some groups of individuals for whom this significance may be either downgraded or denied. It has, for example, been a most important aspect of rights as formulated here, that their primary value lies in their capacity to facilitate self-determination, or perhaps to express self-determination in a clear and uncompromising way. Thus, it seems clear, the capacity to act in a self-determining manner is central to the right as described. In so far as this goes, however, it is obvious that describing the right in this way leaves one open to the charge that it will therefore have a limited application. Those groups whose capacity for autonomy is in doubt could, on this basis, find themselves clearly outside the scope of the right and denied the protection which it is claimed it can offer.

If this were, therefore, an inevitable conclusion, then clearly, both practically and theoretically, it could have serious implications for demands for information disclosure. At a practical level it would, unless legal or social change were instituted, automatically exclude groups such as children, the mentally ill and the mentally handicapped, and deny to them the respect and protection that being within the ambit of the right can provide. At a theoretical level, it could challenge the very claim that there is a fundamental right to participation in therapeutic choice, firmly based in information

31

disclosure, and demanding that disclosure whether or not it is actively sought in individual circumstances. At best, therefore, the right becomes merely something which is of interest to certain privileged groups, and at worst it loses the universality which is said to characterize a human right and distinguish it from a mere interest. If this position is adopted, then one might well question the importance of information disclosure, since it appears to be relevant only to certain groups in the community. Moreover, it might be further noted that these groups probably equate fairly closely to those with whom the doctor would most likely share information in any event, since they are the rational, sensible and intelligent members of the community who could be trusted, even perhaps by paternalists, to take the 'right' decision and not over-react to distressing information.

So, it could be concluded, detailed discussion of the right to information disclosure and the value of the resulting therapeutic partnership, whilst perhaps of academic interest, is, in reality, a redundant and unnecessary exercise, since ultimately all that it amounts to is a reaffirmation of the way in which a 'good' doctor would in any event treat a 'good' patient. For the rest, paternalism is essential – a necessary evil, perhaps, but necessary none the less. To draw such a conclusion, however, would be seriously to misunderstand the value of the application of the right, and further to make seriously erroneous deductions from the state of current legal and social thinking. Moreover, to adhere to this position is to place an intimidating amount of power in the hands of one professional group. Even a right based on capacity for, or interest in, making autonomous choices need not be so limited as to make blanket exclusions of such a sweeping nature as this.

In considering the special position of two of these groups, there-fore, it will be argued that it is not the case that their legal status *in se* denies them access to rights in general. Rather, it will be claimed, it is clear that current laws do countenance and validate autonomy-enhancing behaviour by them, and it will further be shown that recognition of the importance of the right may lead to expansion rather than contraction of the numbers of these currently privileged individuals.[2]

The blanket assumption that a right firmly based on autonomy has no relevance for these groups is based on a number of miscon-ceptions. The first of these is that the setting of a legal barrier, or the classification of mental condition, necessarily always justifies differential treatment, and the second is the assumption that the law invests its admittedly artificial barriers with an almost mystical force which demands that they are always applied without analysis.

In any event the law is somewhat complex in regard to those who are regarded as *incapax*.[3] As Walker[4] notes:

> The whole private law is stated by reference to the individual who is bodily and mentally *capax*, and every person is presumed *capax* . . . If not under curatory an *incapax* may sue and be sued himself, his capacity and responsibility in relation to the matter in issue being a question of fact. It is always a question of fact whether the alleged *incapax* did or did not, at the material time, have the mental capacity to appreciate the legal force of the transaction he was entering into . . . [5]

Boundaries therefore may be created which practically describe groups, but it need not be assumed that their force is overwhelming when deciding whether or not the decision of an individual can or should be binding.

The law routinely sets barriers, often acknowledging their essential arbitrariness, and certainly noting that their applicability may change with changing circumstances and social mores.[6] However, where guidelines do seem to be required (for example the legal statement of the age at which a child may be criminally responsible[7]) their purpose may or may not be to raise an irrebuttable presumption. In the case of the above example, the presumption *is* irrebuttable, because of the potentially unacceptable consequences of individual and subjective judicial or prosecutorial decision making about the imponderable, and because of the consequences of a finding of responsibility. Other legal barriers however, are designed to establish what *should* be the case. For example, the presumption that a child under the age of 16 years cannot legally consent to intercourse is more a device to avoid exploitation and to express what society thinks behaviour should be, than a presumption of the same sort as that made in respect of criminal responsibility. Absolute certainty in the application of the law is achieved by the former, and relative certainty by the latter.

However, whether the magical age of majority (the age at which a person becomes fully responsible for all of his or her behaviour and is therefore also accorded the full panoply of civil rights), is fixed at 16 or at 18 or even 21, there is little doubt that contemporary law seems reluctant to make a blanket assumption that below this age no rights (and equally no responsibilities) can be attributed.[8] However, it is clear that the very existence of different legal classifications presents difficulties for those who would wish to argue for a universally applicable right to receive, and use freely, information about risks, benefits and alternatives in therapy. If narrowly interpreted, the implication logically seems to be that those who do not satisfy the legal criteria always lack the *legal* capacity to enter into certain agreements. They are thus effectively denied the status of autonomy, and by definition could not therefore be *legally* able to make autonomous choices about health care. If this interpretation were applied, all children, and possibly all of the mentally handicapped, would be denied the protection offered by the right because they are not legally autonomous. Decisions would always have to be taken by other authorized people on their behalf and their own decision or preference would be given no weight.

However, the right to receive this information is not necessarily dependent on a legal definition of capacity, nor is there any imperative that artificially created barriers must be applied in a rigid and inflexible manner. Indeed, it has been claimed *supra* that the right is not routinely applied by courts even in respect of those whose legal capacity is *not* in any doubt. In other words, the right itself cannot simply be defeated by the fact that the law fails to acknowledge it in all circumstances where it has value and merit. The mere existence of legal hurdles (in the form, for example, of temporary legal disability or current decision-making practices) does not defeat the right if it has an intrinsic worth.

Even those most closely wedded to medical paternalism would scarcely adopt such a position, for to do so would render *all* of us vulnerable to disinformation, misinformation or to receiving no information at all. It can safely be argued, therefore, that there is a significance to be attached to a therapeutic alliance, even where legal systems are reluctant to give outright support to it, and even where they limit its applicability.

Before considering these groups in more detail, therefore, at least one conclusion can be drawn. The law is *already* prepared to look beyond the apparent certainties of age or mental condition, and that it does so points convincingly to the conclusion that there is seen to be a value or set of values which require careful protection even where legal capacity is in doubt. As Lord Scarman made clear in the *Gillick* case[9] the law must be prepared to take account of changing attitudes even when faced with apparent legal truisms.[10] Given the extent to which the law (through judicial discretion and decision-making) has altered the face of rights and their applicability,[11] it would be difficult to argue that they cannot, or should not, take account both of changing circumstances and of forceful theoretical arguments which accord with a satisfactory moral position. It can legitimately be argued, therefore, that the mere appearance of blanket denial of autonomy in certain groups neither reflects *in fact* the current legal position nor need it affect the claim that these groups should have access to the same information as the 'sane adult'. Consideration of those groups will, rather than denying the value and applicability of the right to participation in medicine, highlight even more clearly the inherent importance of its vindication.


## Children and medical treatment

The position of children in law can perhaps best be described as confused. This confusion arises substantially from the tradition of parental control and custody over children.[12] Where a parent and child conflict, it is tempting to assume value in the adult perspective, and in any event, since adults are charged with the responsibility for ensuring the well-being of children, and for managing their affairs,[13] it seems logical to attribute decision-making powers to them. Only in the most extreme cases, for example in cases of child abuse, will parents lose their control over children. As Walker puts it:

> Parental rights and powers are of two kinds, that of guiding and directing the persons of children under full age, and that of legal administration, of managing their property and legal business or advising thereon.[14]

In Scots law, therefore, the parental role is either, in effect, one of control or one of guidance. Walker further notes that the extent to which the parental role is either all-powerful or merely advisory depends on the age of the child.

> So long as the child is a pupil, the father had at common law, and now each parent has, the right of custody, and the power and authority to regulate the child's upbringing and discipline and govern its person; this power is diminished but not ended when the pupil child becomes minor, and terminates when the minor child becomes major.[15]

English law too, although based in a different tradition and not recognizing concepts of minority in precisely the same way as Scots law, none the less has long acknowledged the limitations on parental authority. As Lord Denning, for example, noted:

> . . . the legal right of a parent to the custody of a child ends at the eighteenth birthday and even up till then, it is a dwindling right which the courts will hesitate to enforce against the wishes of the child, the older he is. It starts with a right of control and ends with little more than advice.[16]

Since it is the custody right which gives parents the authority to make decisions on behalf of, or in the best interests of, the child, then there is considerable significance in the view that this right is not only not absolute, but is also diminishing. That it is not absolute is shown by the way in which courts can and will step in where parents are thought to be abusing their position.[17] That it is dwindling may be evident when courts place weight on the views of a child, in matters, for example, of custody after divorce.[18]

However, the fact of parental authority, however much it dwindles even when someone is under age, does mean that the weight to be given to the views of children is often preliminarily subject to scrutiny, not in terms of children's rights but rather in terms of parents' rights.[19] In other words, the current legal assumption may be expressed in such a way as to imply that the choice of the parent, so long as it is not overtly against the best interests of the child, is the choice which has force. It is necessary, therefore, to consider at this stage the extent to which parents *do* have rights over their children with particular reference to medical matters. Although it may be morality which attributes theoretical status to individuals, the response of the law to demands for, e.g. autonomy, has a primary significance in the practical extent to which rights can be vindicated.

It has already been noted that the fundamental problem in the attribution of rights to children is the fact that autonomy based rights are presumed to require actual, as opposed to potential, capacity for autonomy. The attribution of many fundamental rights to adults is based on their capacity for autonomy – hence the purported justification for the exclusion of the mentally handicapped or children, for example. The restrictions placed on children reflect a recognition of the fact that they may not yet have achieved that level of maturity and understanding of consequences which would enable them to make decisions which would be upheld whether or not they seem to the outsider to be the best decisions. It is this dubiety which routinely invokes the use of parental authority as a proxy decision-making tool (this applies equally to those who stand *in loco parentis* to the child).

However, the law is no longer – if, indeed, it ever was – prepared to draw such a clear-cut line as this. This is not to deny the role of the parent or guardian, but rather to define it more clearly, and to recognize the immense variety of attributes which both children and their legal guardians may have. Moreover, it also serves to recognize that children may have certain rights which can be vindicated even where parental views conflict with them. As Lord Scarman said in *Gillick*[20]:

Parental rights clearly do exist, and they do not wholly disappear until the age of majority. Parental rights relate to both the person and the property of the child: custody, care and control of the person and guardianship of the property of the child. But the common law has never treated such rights as sovereign or beyond review and control. *Nor has our law ever treated the child as other than a person with capacities and rights recognized by law.*[21] (emphasis added)

Much of the case law in this respect has grown up around the issue of custody after divorce. In this most important matter of where the child should live and with which parent, courts have been increasingly prepared to give weight to the view of the under-age child. Respect is given to the wishes of the child particularly where the child is older and is thought to be capable of understanding the implications both of the situation and of the choice. It is self-evident that in disputed custody cases the views of the child will not equate with the view of one of its parents, but they nevertheless will be given priority or at least considerable weight. For example, in the case of *Gover* v. *Gover*,[22] the court indicated that it would be unrealistic – even wrong – not to give 'very great and usually decisive'[23] weight to the views of the child. There is no reason why a similar view could not be taken in respect of medical treatment, even despite a somewhat unhappy ambivalence on the general question of children's rights and parental rights.

Different approaches to rights may be taken by states and their legal systems, and to some extent these variations stem from differing legal, social and political traditions. Countries with a written Bill of Rights have a relatively clear framework within which to operate, whilst those – like the United Kingdom – without such a formal statement of rights may tend to a more *ad hoc* type of decision-making, based on factors which relate as much to entrenched social attitudes, or even matters of current concern, as they do to human rights *per se*. Thus, it is relatively unusual for British courts to debate issues in the clear language of human rights, whereas in the United States such language is relatively commonplace.

The position in the United States does not, of course, inevitably guarantee consistency of approach either between or among states, since interpretation of constitutionally guaranteed rights may vary.[24] However, the existence of a rights-dominated constitution can be said to provide a backcloth against which disputes can be tested. Equally, litigation is relatively more common in the United States so that courts have had the opportunity of testing and refining their approach to certain questions, for example the question of children's rights in general, and rights in health care in particular. Thus, it has been held that children need not be subject to a parental refusal of treatment,[25] and that, over parental objection, cosmetic surgery can proceed even where known to be risky (because the child's right to a normal development would be enhanced if the surgery were successful).[26] Moreover, despite theoretical prohibitions on the use of young children as organ donors or in experimental situations, a young child's wish to donate bone marrow to a sibling has been upheld because of the possible distress to the child should the sibling die.[27]

In the United States, courts, in deciding on health care matters, have tended to make certain assumptions which predispose them to view the issues under consideration from a particular perspective. Most states, therefore, have tended to view the problems arising in disputes over health care not from the perspective of children's rights pure and simple, but also by taking into consideration other – and sometimes competing – rights, such as the right to family intergrity.[28] What is at stake, then, is primarily the power of the parent over the child – in other words, parental rights – and the extent to which the state may interfere in this classical privacy right.[29] That the resulting decision may be couched in terms of children's rights can be misleading. None the less, the American child can, at least, appeal to the language of rights in seeking to vindicate and obtain authority for his or her own views.

Identification of the extent to which their British counterparts may validly claim to have rights in health care matters is perhaps more subtle, and is certainly confused by a number of court decisions. Bearing in mind the fundamental question as to whether or not courts *do* give rights to children in health care decisions, there are two main scenarios which can be postulated to elucidate the response of the courts. These are as follows: first, where parental choice conflicts either with the views of the child and/or with the state's interest in health care provision, and second, where the child's view cannot be ascertained but there remains a potential conflict between parental decisions and the interests of the state (as represented by the judiciary). Both of these encompass situations already considered by British courts.

## Parents and children

Despite earlier doubts as to whether or not the provision of contraceptive advice and treatment is indeed an aspect of health care, the court in the *Gillick*[30] case were confident that it was. The question to be answered, therefore, was – at least in part – the extent to which the child was entitled to make personal, and authoritative, decisions about using contraception without parents necessarily being notified or involved in the decision-making process.

At the first hearing of the case,[31] Mr Justice Woolf was in no doubt that there was here no conflict of rights. Parents, in his view, had responsibilities rather than rights, and the resolution of the problem depended on the legal status accorded to the individual child.[32]

Scots law adopts a number of distinctions which *prima facie* predict the extent to which the behaviour of a child will be given authority. Although a lengthy discussion of them is not necessary here, there are facets of them which are relevant to the current discussion. The most critical difference between Scots and English law is the division, drawn by Scots law, of the status of childhood into pupillarity and minority. Its effect is to offer some assistance in the assessment of capacity to make certain decisions, even although the question of children's rights in health care has not been directly confronted by a Scottish Court.

It can safely be assumed, however, that – where the child is a pupil – it will be presumed that decisions should be taken on behalf of, and in the best interests of, that child by another. The position of the pupil child is as follows:

> Pupils, that is boys aged under fourteen and girls aged under twelve, the traditional age of presumed puberty, have, for reasons of their natural incapacity, strictly limited legal personality . . . [33]

Given this, '[a] pupil must . . . have a parent or other person to act as his tutor and administrator-in-law.'[34] It can, therefore, safely be deduced that decisions about therapy will probably, in the case of pupils, be taken by authorized others. This is, of course, subject to the overriding authority of the court to scrutinize, modify or overrule decisions which seem to conflict with the 'best interests' of the child.

The minor child, however, is in a different situation and has:

> . . . legal personality and considerable though limited legal capacity and powers . . . He is capable of entering into legal transactions, though requiring the protection of the laws by reason of his inferior judgement or discretion.[35]

The minor child in Scots law, therefore, will be given some authority to make decisions which have significance – a limited capacity to exercise autonomy is thereby recognized.

From the status traditionally accorded to children in Scots law can be inferred the likely approach of the courts to disputes concerning therapeutic choice. Where the child is a pupil, the decision of an authorized adult would probably be validated subject to that decision being in the best interests of the child.[36] In the case of a minor child, subject to certain limitations designed to afford a degree of protection, the child will have decisions respected in recognition of developing capacity and maturity. As has been said.[37]:

> Whereas much of the law on the legal capacity of minors is concerned with the question whether they can make themselves liable, the law on consent by minors to medical treatment is concerned with the question whether they can absolve other people from liability.[38]

At present, SHHD Circular DS (79)2 seems to adopt the view that the age of consent to medical treatment is sixteen, but there are serious reasons, already expressed, for doubting the validity of this view in the case of the mature child. In addition, as the Scottish Law Commission's Consultative Memorandum[39] further notes:

> Medical practice does not make law. If 16 is the age of consent to medical treatment in Scots law then this must rest on the common law or on statute. It cannot rest on the common law because the age of 16 has no special significance at common law. It does not rest on statute because there is no statutory provision on this subject in Scotland. There appears, in short, to be no legal foundation for the widespread view that 16 is the age of consent to medical treatment in Scotland. The question is governed by the common law and at common law the only relevant age is the age of minority – 12 for a girl and 14 for a boy.[40]

Since in contemporary society the perceived distinctions between males and females are less routinely succesful in justifying differential treatment it seems likely that all children, whatever their sex, would be treated in a similar manner over the age of twelve. In addition, the Memorandum continues:

> . . . it is by no means certain that a child below the ages of 12 and 14 could not give consent, at least to certain types of medical treatment, which would provide an effective defence to a prosecution for assault or a civil claim for damages for assault. Much would depend on the age and understanding of the child and on the nature of the treatment.[41]

Before *Gillick* the capacity of a child to consent to medical treatment was governed somewhat ambivalently in English law by the provisions of the Family Law Reform Act 1969, s. 8 of which states that 'the consent of a minor who has attained the age of sixteen years to any surgical, medical or dental treatment, which, in the absence of consent, would constitute a trespass to his person, shall be as effective as it would be if he were of full age.' However, s. 8(3) of the same Act makes it clear that the Act does not affect the validity of any consent which would have been effective had the legislation not been passed. The court in *Gillick* was therefore at liberty to interpret the legislation, as it in fact did, as implying that the consent of someone *under* sixteen could also be effective.[42] The decision as to the validity of any purported consent would, the House of Lords declared, rest on the maturity of the child and her capacity to understand the implications of her choice.[43] The child who is thought to be sufficiently mature is therefore given the status of autonomy, even although the rules may at first suggest that capacity depends on age and not maturity. In the United States it has been held to be unconstitutional to make a blanket requirement of parental consent based solely on the fact that the child is under age.[44]

The position therefore would seem to be that the 'mature' child has the right to make free choices in health care matters – choices which will be upheld by the courts. However, the right to make these choices would seem to rest also on the nature of what is being consented to, and so cannot be taken necessarily to be generally applicable even to the 'mature' child. In the United States, on the other hand, although '. . . recognition of independent rights for children is a recent development . . .'[45] none the less:

> . . . the scope and character of those rights has been a focus of scholarly attention. Children's rights have been found to include due process, privacy, and first amendment rights. Additionally, the child has an interest in family integrity and in protection of personal autonomy and individual choice.[46]

British courts seem to be slightly less theoretically developed in this area. In the *Gillick* case the ultimate value was apparently given to the rights of children to privacy (of a sort), and the decision seems to lend some credibility to the assertion that children do have rights in health care matters which are distinguishable from the parents' views (or potential views) as to what is in the best interests of the child. The nature and extent of these rights remains relatively unclear, although Lord Fraser at least was in no doubt as to their purpose. In his view:

> . . . parental rights to control a child do not exist for the benefit of the parent. They exist for the benefit of the child and they are justified only in so far as they enable the parent to perform his duties towards the child, and towards other children in the family.[47]

This statement seems to provide some flexibility in the assessment of the extent to which competing, or apparently competing, parental views can affect the choice of a given child. However, merely to conclude that parental rights diminish with the child's age, or that they exist for the benefit of the child, indicates something about parental rights, but very little about the rights of children. If the effect of judgements of this sort is to be to give children certain autonomy rights, then the child's statement of preference (assuming any other criteria have been met) would be sufficient to validate the action to which they have consented, or to support their refusal. This, however is not necessarily the case, since the validity of the decision may also have to run the gamut of a different set of criteria – namely, the views of the court.

On the one hand, courts have been prepared to countenance certain levels of independence for children or at least for the older child. As Lord Fraser said in *Gillick*:

> It is, in my view, contrary to the ordinary experience of mankind, at least in Western Europe in the present century, to say that a child or young person remains in fact under the complete control of his parents until he attains the definite age of majority . . . and that on attaining that age he suddenly acquires independence.[48]

On the other hand, courts will not in fact merely accept the view of a child even where parental views are deemed to have no value or relevance. On the contrary, it can be said that courts will uphold the views of the child most commonly where, although they conflict with parental views, they concur with the views of the court as to what is 'in the best interests of the child'. What, therefore, even the *Gillick* judgement may amount to is not so much a statement of rights for children in health care, but rather evidence that the judiciary were of the view that the interests of the child can sometimes be best served by permitting her access to contraception, and by encouraging or facilitating that access, even without reference to parental views, in circumstances where it is clear that the alternative is the risk of unwanted pregnancy. Courts, therefore, are somewhat loath to commit themselves to an outright championing of children's rights in health care. This ambivalence reflects both confusion as to the applicability of the concept of rights, and the competition between on the one hand the value of allowing a child free rein, and on the other the responsibility of the court to have the welfare of the child as its paramount consideration. Often, therefore, subjective judicial values are imported to replace those of the parent or the child, and these values, as with adults, may be dependent on medical criteria. It has been argued already that medical considerations are secondary to the interest in protecting free choice, but by recognizing on the one hand that children can make free choices whilst on the other testing the status of that choice against its medical 'rationality', courts give with one hand and take away with the other.

Whether couched in terms of family integrity or in terms of the responsibilities of custody, developed jurisprudence traditionally pays respect to parental powers. Although these powers may be removed, there is generally a presumption that parents do and will act in their child's best interests – not merely physical but also moral, and some might say, spiritual. Careful protection is given, for example, to the rights of parents to choose their children's religious upbringing[49] – a choice which may not be value free in medical matters. Thus, parental rights in this area will be upheld *unless* their decision, and its implications, conflict with the views of others (notably the judiciary) as to what is in the child's best interests.[50] Parental refusal, on behalf of their children, of life-preserving medical treatment on religious grounds is now routinely overridden,[51] but the question remains, if parents have the right to make religious choices, on what grounds do they become defeasible (even, it should be noted where the child agrees with the parent)?

On the one hand, it could be said that the child has a right to life which in this situation implies a right to treatment, and it must always be 'in the best interests of the child' that this right is upheld. Whether or not this right is always upheld by the law will be considered later. It could also be argued that, in the case of the 'mature' child, while an affirmative choice would probably be respected by the court, a negative choice defeats the presumption of maturity and therefore places the onus back on the court to safeguard the potential autonomy of the child in the face of parental or individual irresponsibility. Whichever is the correct interpretation, and it seems in the light of recent decisions more likely to be the latter than the former, it represents in no way a recognition of children's rights as such, but merely indicates that where the child behaves in accordance either with the views of its parents, or the views of the court, that choice will be upheld. The attitude of British courts, therefore seems to be at best ambivalent to the question of children's rights.

Of course, it is possible to argue that children *do* have rights, but that decisions are taken for them in order that they may ultimately be able to do so for themselves. In line with this view, children should have their fundamental rights protected so that they can reach maturity and then make their own choices. If this is the case, then the age of the child is irrelevant – what matters is that the child should be permitted to reach the age at which people are free to take their own decisions, however irrational these may appear to others. Thus, respect for the most important of all rights – the right to life - would become a prerequisite of this approach. Although children (particularly the very young) have no way of expressing a preference for life over death, the law is entitled to assume it, either because it enhances the child's opportunity of choosing for him or herself in the future, or because it must always be 'in the best interests of the child' to be alive rather than dead. Indeed, in actions for 'wrongful life',[52] which are rejected by British courts,[53] the courts have made it clear that it can never be worse to be alive than dead.[54] Thus, apparently uncontentiously, the law must at least in this situation attribute rights to children, whatever the views of their parents. But is this the reality?

## Parents and courts

British courts have recently taken two decisions which, although at first sight in conflict with each other, in fact display similar characteristics and can serve as illustrations of the second postulated scenario. In the case of R v. Arthur,[55] a doctor – with parental consent and authority – failed to operate to remove an intestinal blockage in a Down's syndrome child. Without the surgery, the child would inevitably die and all parties were in agreement that this was the appropriate outcome (except, of course, the child). The doctor instructed that the child should receive nursing care only, and in due course, he died. At the subsequent trial of the doctor for murder (subsequently reduced to attempted murder) the court was apparently impressed by a number of arguments, not least of which was that the parents had co-operated in the taking of the decision, and agreed with it. In view of the earlier discussion of the courts' attitude to parental refusal of life-saving therapy this decision seems somewhat strange, not to say paradoxical. If rights are attributed to children, then this case seems to suggest that they are not attributed without differentiation. In fact, of course, both judge and jury were reluctant to hold the doctor criminally responsible for his behaviour in the exercise of his profession,[56] and in any event they sympathized with the views of the parents – quite a different situation from that where they disagree, but none the less very little to do with children's rights.

The second case referred to above seems at first sight to contradict the Arthur decision. In Re B (a minor)[57] the court, in the face of medical and parental objections, did authorize the removal of a similar intestinal blockage in a Down's syndrome child, and apparently vindicated the child's right to life. However, on closer examination, the court was considerably more ambivalent than this. This child was saved because her 'quality of life' after surgery would not be unsupportable – not because she had a right to life.

A further example of the overriding of parental wishes can be found in the case of *Re D (a minor)*[58] in which case, having asserted the fundamental right of the citizen to reproduce,[59] the court refused to permit the sterilization of an 11-year-old child, even given medical and parental consent. Again, however, the court did not in fact make a general statement of rights for children, but rather felt that in this particular case the girl would eventually reach a condition in which she would be legally capable of consenting to marriage, and that therefore she would be entitled to recognition of her right under the European Convention on Human Rights[60] and the Universal Declaration of Human Rights,[61] to marry and found a family.

In terms of the kind of right described here, therefore, it can be seen that current attitudes do not facilitate its routine application to children unless (a) the child is 'mature' and understands the information and (b) the child's decision accords either with that of the parents or that of the court. Yet, the position overtly adopted by courts seems to differ from this somewhat bleak analysis. Lord Brandon, for example, in the case of *R v. D*[62] said:

> In the case of the very young child, it would not have the under-standing or the intelligence to give its consent, so that the absence of consent would be a necessary inference from its age. In the case of an older child, however, it must, I think, be a question of fact for the jury whether the child concerned has sufficient understanding and intelligence to give its consent . . . While the matter will always be for the jury alone to decide, I should not expect a jury to find at all frequently that a child under 14 had sufficient understanding and intelligence to give its consent.[63]

Or, as Lord Scarman put it in the *Gillick* case:

> . . . I would hold as a matter of law that the parental right to deter-mine whether or not their minor child below the age of 16 will have medical treatment terminates if and when the child achieves a sufficient understanding and intelligence to enable him or her to understand fully what is proposed.[64]

As has been seen, therefore, courts are apparently reluctant to commit themselves to an outright recognition of children's rights *per se*. However, they are prepared, in certain circumstances, and provided that certain criteria are satisfied, to acknowledge the validity of a given child's viewpoint. To intervene in family life is admittedly not something to be undertaken lightly, but neither is the denial of a basic right – that is the right to be given and be permitted to use information in relation to matters affecting the individual's health. Moreover, a reluctance to weigh the child's over the parent's view may simply reflect a failure to understand the significance of individuality. It has been said, for example, that:

> Courts tend to view the family as a unit and to assume that the parents' interests are the same as the child's. It is possible, however, to separate the interests of parents and child: a parental decision regarding a child's medical care is, in effect, 'other-regarding' and not 'self-regarding'. Even if the decision purports to be in the child's best interests, it is still made by someone external to the child.[65]

## Do children have rights?

At the moment however, it is not overstating matters to say that the courts (if somewhat grudgingly) are prepared to concede a certain amount of autonomy to certain individual children. The child's position at law is evidently rather complex. On the one hand the law seems prepared to agree that the mature child can make autonomous choices about a number of matters, including health care, while on the other, this concession apparently rests not on a clear attribution of rights to children but rather on the court's assessment of a number of other factors. Thus, rather than assuming the capacity to exercise a given right, as the law would theoretically do with adults, a number of other criteria have to be satisfied before a child will be given the benefit of the protection afforded by the right. Most notably, the court has to be satisfied that the child is sufficiently 'mature' (however that is defined) and that the child's choice is in his or her 'best interests', as decided either by the parents or by the court.

Thus, there are evident difficiulties for those who would wish to ascribe the right here described to those under the age of 16. This right is dependent on autonomy – indeed, it may even be said that it is *justified* by autonomy. However, it is clear that there is a move away from a blanket assumption that children are not autonomous, towards acceptance that some of them may be. Admittedly, such autonomy as is granted seems likely, at present, to be limited – most especially by the apparent fact that children will be given decision-making credentials only where their choice is thought to be rational.

If, therefore, we were forced to conclude that so substantial a group as children were excluded from the right, then one might wish to argue that it becomes less of a right, and more of a courtesy. If the conclusion is to be different then the problems of attribution of rights to children must be tackled, and in particular, two questions require to be answered. First, are current problems insurmountable, and second, if some concessions do require to be made to paternalism, do they sabotage the right?

By accepting, in some cases, that children can consent, or withhold consent, to medical treatment, the courts may be said to be accepting that, at least in certain circumstances, children may validly make choices about health care. In this respect, at least, they recognize a limited applicability of the right to receive information. However, information disclosure *per se* is insufficient since it is the authority to act on that information which permits the making of autonomous decisions. Merely to say that children have the right to information, therefore, would not be sufficient for those who would argue for children's rights in health care. If the child's choice is only given credibility when it accords with what others regard as rational or appropriate, then the child is severely disadvantaged. The addition of qualifications about maturity and intelligence, when coupled with this apparent requirement of rationality, both restricts access to information and limits freedom of choice. It is, in fact, almost double jeopardy for the child. On the one hand, he or she needs to convince that he or she is intelligent and mature, and thereby merits information disclosure, while on the other hand if that information is used 'unsatisfactorily' or 'irrationally' by the child then they may be redefined as insufficiently mature to make a valid choice. The welfare model which dominates child law serves to restrict freedom of choice unless that choice satisfies the opinions of others. Thus, an affirmative decision by a child to opt for therapy would likely receive support in the way that a negative decision may not and yet, as Hoggett says:

> . . . the capacity to consent must logically include the capacity to dissent: if, then, parental control is diminished to the extent that the child herself has acquired capacity, the parents should have no power to insist . . . a duty to provide adequate medical aid does not necessarily import a power to force it upon a competent child who has rejected it.[66]

Courts themselves have been ambivalent about the standing of parental decision-making in respect of treatment for their children. In the *Arthur*[67] case, the court was impressed with the fact that the parents opposed therapy, while in *Re D (a minor) (wardship proceedings)*[68] and *Re B (a minor)*[69] the courts were prepared to go against parental views. Moreover, in the case of *Re B (a minor) (wardship proceedings) (sterilization)*[70] the court made it clear that parents alone could not make decisions about the sterilization of their children, and that the authority of the court was needed for such a major step, particularly where a human right was involved.

If it is, therefore, accepted that parents do not have absolute rights over their children (even, it would appear over a very young child), then it can also be accepted that courts have neither a supervisory monopoly on what is in the best interests of the child, nor do they require to deny the application of rights, at least to the child who is capable of expressing a view. To accept this would be to alter the basis of decision-making in respect of children and to permit and authorize the child to make supported treatment decisions more often than is currently the case – particularly where the child's choice is to reject therapy. It is submitted that the real barrier is the confusion engendered by the apparent rigidity of the law's adoption of an age at which maturity and discretion are attributed.

Although courts themselves are reluctant to assume any finality associated with mere age, there seems, none the less, to be a knock-on effect which makes them suspicious of at least some of the decisions which children may wish to make. Cases concerning children under this age require the courts to consider two issues which may well conflict: first, the child's claims to have the right to make decisions which he or she regards as appropriate, and second, the court's own responsibility to act in the best interests of the child. Clearly, there is as much scope for disagreement between courts and children as there is between parents and children.

However, de-emphasizing the artificial age barrier could pave the way for more children to be accorded the authority to make autonomous choices, and need not threaten either the family unit, or the protective role of the courts. It is conventional wisdom that children mature at different rates, and some would claim that they mature younger in contemporary society. For courts to begin by making the assumption of maturity (where the child can express a view), rather than the assumption of immaturity, would be to recognize this and would adequately reflect the position of children in contemporary society. Lord Fraser, indeed, would seem to have acknowledged the need for the law to take account of this position, when he said '[s]ocial customs change, and the law ought to, and does in fact, have regard to such changes where they are of major importance.'[71]

Further support for the suggestion that the law does in fact acknowledge the autonomy of the child can be gleaned from the fact that the age of criminal responsibility is considerably lower than the apparent age of consent to medical treatment, and yet the attribution of criminal responsibility implies that the child is capable both of making choices to behave in a given way and of bearing the consequences (however harsh) of that behaviour. In other words, children already are credited with the capacity to make self-determining choices at a very early age. A Scottish court, for example, has held a child of 5 to be capable of behaviour which amounts to contributory negligence.[72]

Further, it is not apparent that the age at which a child is presumed capable of making choices in the important area of health care need be set at the age at which *most* children would be capable of so doing (e.g. 16). To make a preliminary presumption of authority below that age would not defeat the role of the court in having the welfare of the child as its paramount consideration. Merely, it would require justification for *not* accepting the child's views, rather than as at present almost requiring justification *for* accepting them. In doing this, the courts or parents would be required to show a good or compelling reason why the child's view should not be authoritative, and this could be done in a consistent and logical manner and within a clear framework.

## Conclusions

Since it is conceded even by the law that children can and do make decisions for which they are accountable, then we can assume that they are the holders of certain duties and of certain rights. Since it is widely regarded as vital that people are not unknowingly or unwillingly subjected to medical intervention then it is not unreasonable to argue in defence of the recognition of rights for children in health care choices. Indeed, courts already seem prepared to acknowledge this, but there is one major flaw in their approach.

Just as it has been said that the medicalizing or professionalizing of health care choices has adversely affected the value of information disclosure for adults, so too this has happened in respect of children. Where the court rejects an under-age decision it seems to do so often on the basis that the opposite decision would accord with the child's 'best interests'. What this really means, of course, is that 'best interests' is often taken to equate with medical choice or recommendation. This pattern is particularly prevalent when dealing with children, but it is not unusual when dealing with adults 'Best interests', however, might equally reasonably be taken to mean vindication of free choices – perhaps particularly where these choices cause no harm to others.

The advantages of this view are many, not least that the protection of the rights attributed to and important for adults would be available to a greater number of young people. Moreover, were the question to be approached from this perspective, more certainty may be introduced into the law, since it would be necessary to elaborate the reasons for invalidation of the child's position, thereby providing guidelines for future resolution of disputes.

It is admitted, however, that this approach also expressly countenances that there are some children whose views would be overridden, and this leads to the second question posed *supra*, namely, does the acceptance of limitations defeat the right itself? It is conceded that it may, in the case of children – or at least some children – be necessary to consider whether or not their choice is in fact based on both adequate disclosure of information and on an understanding of that information and the implications of the choice. It would, for example, be evident nonsense to suggest that a baby should have the *practical* right to make choices about therapy. However, it may also be thought that:

> If a consent is real provided that the patient understands in broad terms what is proposed and agrees to it, then logically the capacity required of the patient to give that consent should not be great. A child who is capable of understanding the proposed treatment in such terms should be able to give her own consent.[73]

Moreover, making the fundamental assumption *for* rather than *against* the applicability of rights, both extends their ambit and removes the essential discrimination which is inherent in current attitudes. It further defeats some of the paternalism which is evident in judicial or parental decision-making, and permits children access to information about their health care and the freedom to make decisions which *they* regard as being in their best interests. To place some limitations on a given child's legal capacity to make such decisions does not, therefore, sabotage the right. Rather it may be said to enhance it, since the assumption that there is value in free decision-making re-emphasizes the importance which is attached to the right itself. For the moment, however, the question is approached from an erroneous perspective, which both diminishes the value of rights and fails to reflect the differential capacities of children.

Limitations may, therefore, be placed on the exercise of the right without radically affecting its value. Indeed, these limitations may well be invoked as a recognition of the value of autonomy. For example, courts may only choose to intervene where the decision made by the child would deny him or her the capacity to become autonomous. As Hoggett puts it:

> The destinction between knowing what is involved and having the capacity to make a wise decision is an important one. In the case of an adult, it is axiomatic that understanding, not wisdom, is all that is required for a man may go to the devil if he chooses. Perhaps in the case of a child, it is permissable to ask for more, on the ground that the first and paramount consideration throughout the law is the welfare of the child herself, so that the only treatment which anyone may permit is that which will promote her welfare.[74]

Respect for the autonomy of children would, therefore, imply in one case that parents could not authorize medical behaviour which causes the death of their child. But the converse could equally be said to be true – that is, that the only situation in which someone may interfere with the decision of a child is where the child's decision is a threat to others or to his or her welfare. Moreover, this threat must be grave, since the overriding of the child's choice represents the denial of a right.

In conclusion, therefore, the fact that some limitations may have to be placed on a child's capacity to exercise the right to receive and use information about medical treatment need not be seen as fatal. Nor is it inimical to the claim that rights should be extended to children, and that they should be the cornerstone of decision-making. It is not unusual for rights, even those which are said to be fundamental, to be none the less subject to some limitation,[75] but conflict is resolved from the perspective that the right is in operation and that it does have value. Thus, good reasons have to be shown for interference with its exercise. There is no reason why such an approach should not equally be applied to children's rights in health care.

So what can be concluded from this – admittedly brief – consideration of the position of children in respect of therapy? It is clear firstly that the mere fact of being a child does not in practice mean that decisions must always, and only, be taken on a proxy basis. The law's concession of capacity is very significant, then, since it seems to suggest that it is prepared to acknowledge that there are important interests at stake and significant values to protect.

Children are, therefore, accorded in some cases the equivalent to autonomy in a variety of situations, including health care. This means that rights to receive information in order to facilitate autonomy-enhancing decisions can reasonably also be said to be due to them. This has two important implications. First, it enhances the claim that there is value in viewing free decision-making based on adequate information as something which transcends the professional or technical aspect of health care. And perhaps even more importantly, it challenges the view that information disclosure is, and should be, a matter of medical judgement alone, described or delineated by evidence of standard medical practice. In an admittedly extreme way, the case, for example, of Dr Arthur is evidence that – even in good faith – practices may come to be accepted by doctors which seem to be fundamentally at odds with the moral consensus or the law. Accepting that this is a difficult and dramatic example, if the right to make self-determining choices is seen as having value, infringements of this – based on accepted medical practice – are no less worrying, even if they are less emotive or striking. If anything, the complexities of the legal position reinforce concern that rights should be both attributable and attributed. Children are generally conceded to be vulnerable to exploitation and the unwarranted assumption of authority. In some ways, their position is not dissimilar to that of the uninformed or ill-informed adult. Just as we are concerned to act in the best interests of children, or to ensure that their best interests are served, so we should be with adults, but it need not simplistically be presumed that 'best interests' can be defined solely, even primarily, by reference to what others (lay or professional) *think* are best interests. It is also in all of our 'best interests' to respect knowledgeable judgements of others and to value their autonomy sufficiently to admit it to be an independent moral right and not therefore susceptible of definition by the interest of others – even beneficent professionals. While intrusion into the behaviour of the individual is not uncommon, nor always objectionable (for example, by prohibiting murder or rendering the negligent liable) it is also the case that such intrusions should be kept to the minimum if individual liberty is to be protected. There is no overwhelming good in being unwittingly subjected to the judgement of someone else, merely because he or she possesses certain skills. Nor should the possessor of skills be permitted to avoid or deny the human (not technical) consequences of applying them. The example of the law's response to conflict concerning children demonstrates on the one hand recognition of the value of rights and on the other the consequences of their subjugation to professional judgement.

## Notes

1. See chapters 1 & 2, supra.
2. The mentally ill are another relevant group, but space does not permit serious consideration of them.

3. That is, legally incapable.
4. Walker, D. M., *Principles of Scottish Private Law*. (3rd edn). Oxford, Clarendon Press, 1982. Vol. 1.
5. op cit., at pp. 211–212.
6. Cf. the comments of Lord Fraser in *Gillick* v. *West Norfolk and Wisbech Area Health Authority & Anor.* [1985] 3 All ER 402, [1985] 3 All ER 830.
7. In Scotland the age of criminal responsibility is set at 8. In England the common law age was 10, but this was theoretically raised to 14: for discussion, see McLean, S. A. M. and Grant, J. P., 'Police contact with children under eight: the under age "offender" ', (1981) *J. Soc. Welf. Law* 140.
8. For discussion, see e.g. Walker, op cit., particularly at 3:1 and 3:2.
9. Supra cit.
10. At p. 419.
11. For discussion, see e.g. Harris, P., *An Introduction to Law*, (2nd edn), London, Weidenfeld and Nicolson, 1984.
12. For discussion, see Walker, op cit; Hoggett, B., and Pearl, D. S., *The Family, Law and Society*, London, Butterworths, 1983, (2nd edn 1987).
13. Cf. Walker op cit; Hoggett and Pearl, op cit.
14. Op cit. at p. 278.
15. Op cit. at pp. 278–279.
16. Per Lord Denning in *Hewer* v. *Bryant* [1969] 3 All ER 578, at p. 582.
17. *Hannah* v. *Hannah* 1971 SLT (Notes) 42: 'It is not nature but the welfare of the child which is the material matter.'; see also Children and Young Persons Act 1933; Children and Young Persons (Scotland) Act 1937; Criminal Procedure (Scotland) Act 1975; Social Work (Scotland) Act 1968; *R* v. *Senior* [1899] 1 QB 283: *R* v. *Spencer and Spencer* (unreported 1958); *Oakey* v. *Jackson* [1914] 1 KB 216; *R* v. *Hayes* [1969] 1 QB 364; *Andrews* v. *D. P. P.* [1937] AC 576; *R* v. *Lowe* [1973] QB 702.
18. E. g. *Gover* v. *Gover* 1969 SLT (Notes) 78.
19. For discussion, see Sher, E. J., 'Choosing for children: adjudicating medical care disputes between parents and the state' 58 *N. Y. Univ. Law Rev.* 157 (1983).
20. Supra cit.
21. At p. 420.
22. Supra cit.
23. At p. 78.
24. For discussion, see Sher, loc. cit.
25. Id.
26. Sher, loc. cit.; see also *In re Karwath* 199 NW 2d 147 (1972); *In Re May* 95 Misc. 2d 1026 (1978); *Custody of a Minor* 378 Mass. 732 (1979); *In re Hofbauer* 47 NY 22d 648 (1979).
27. For discussion, see Dickens, B., 'The use of children in medical experimentation' 43 *Medico-Legal J.* 166 (1975).
28. *H. L.* v. *Matheson, Governor of Utah et al* 450 US 398 (1981); for further discussion see Sher, loc. cit.; see also *City of Akron* v. *Akron Centre for Reproductive Health Inc. et al.* 103 S Ct 2481 (1983).
29. Although privacy is not *in se* a right guaranteed by the Constitution, it has become customary to refer to it in a number of cases, e.g. *Roe* v. *Wade* 410 US 113 (1973).
30. Supra cit.
31. [1984] 1 All ER 365.
32. At pp. 373–375.
33. Walker, op. cit., at p. 202.
34. Id.

35. Walker, op. cit., at p. 203.
36. For discussion of the 'best interests' approach, see Goldstein, J., Freud, A. and Solnit, A. J., *Beyond the Best Interests of the Child*, London, Collier Macmillan, 1973; Goldstein, G., Freud, A and Solnit, A. J., *Before the Best Interests of the Child*, London, Burnett Books, 1980.
37. Scottish Law Commission, Consultative Memorandum No. 65. *Legal Capacity and Responsibility of Minors and Pupils*.
38. At p. 44.
39. Supra cit.
40. At pp. 47–48.
41. At p. 51.
42. *Gillick*, supra cit. (HL).
43. At pp. 407–408.
44. Matheson, supra cit.
45. Sher, loc. cit., at p. 164.
46. Id.
47. At p. 410.
48. At pp. 410–411.
49. *Agar-Ellis* v. *Lascelles* (1883) 24 Ch D 317.
50. See Freeman, M. D. A., 'Freedom and the welfare state: child rearing, parental autonomy and state intervention' [1983] *J. Soc. Welf. Law* 70.
51. Cf. Skegg, P. D. G., 'Capacity to consent to medical procedures on minors' (1973) 36 MLR 370; Cusine, D. J., 'To sterilize or not to sterilize' 18 *Med. Sci. Law* 120 (1978); McLellan, M. F., 'Jehovah's Witnesses and child protection legislation: the right to refuse medical consent' 1 *Leg-Med. Q.* 37 (1977); Dickens, B. M., 'The modern function and limits of parental rights' (1981) 97 LQR 462.
52. For discussion, see Liu, A. N. C., 'Wrongful life: some of the problems' 14 *J. Med. Ethics* 69 (1987); Symmons, C. R., 'Policy factors in actions for wrongful birth' (1987) 50 MLR 269.
53. *McKay* v. *Essex Area Health Authority* [1982] QB 1166, [1982] 2 All ER 771; *Eyre* v. *Measday* [1986] 1 All ER 488; *Udale* v. *Bloomsbury Area Health Authority* [1983] 2 All ER 522; *Emeh* v. *Kensington & Chelsea & Westminster A. H. A.* [1984] 3 All ER 1044.
54. See note 53, supra; but see also *Gleitman* v. *Cosgrove* 296 NYS 2d 689 (1967).
55. *The Times* 6 November 1981.
56. Id., See also discussion of the professional standard in *R* v. *Bateman* (1925) Cr. App. Rep. 8; see also McLean, S. A. M. and Maher, G. *Medicine, Morals and the Law*, Aldershot, Gower, 1983 (reprinted 1985). chapter 4.
57. [1981] 1 WLR 1421.
58. [1976] 1 All ER 326, per Mrs J. Heilbron, at p. 332: 'The type of operation proposed is one which involves the deprivation of a basic human right, namely the right of a woman to reproduce, and therefore it would, if performed on a woman for non-therapeutic reasons and without her consent, be a violation of such a right.'
59. For discussion of the right to reproduce, see McLean, S. A. M. 'The Right to Reproduce' in Campbell, et al. (eds), *Human Rights: From Rhetoric to Reality*, Oxford, Basil Blackwell, 1986.
60. Article 12.
61. Article 16(3).
62. [1984] 2 All ER 449.
63. At p. 457.
64. At p. 423.
65. Sher, loc.cit., at p. 164.

66. Hoggett, B., 'Parents, Children and Medical Treatment: The Legal Issues', in Byrne, P. (ed.) *Rights and Wrongs in Medicine*, London, King's Fund (OUP) 1986, at p. 158.
67. Supra cit.
68. Supra cit.
69. Supra cit.
70. *The Times* 17 March 1987; see also *T. v. T. & Anor*, *The Times* 11 July 1987.
71. At p. 411.
72. *Shillinglaw v. Turner* 1925 SC 807; for further discussion, see Walker, *The Law of Delict in Scotland*, (2nd edn, revised), Edinburgh, W. Green & Son Ltd., 1981, pp. 86–88, and pp. 368–370; Rogers, W. V. H., *Winfield and Jolowicz on Tort*, (12th edn), London, Sweet & Maxwell, 1984, pp. 155–156.
73. Hoggett, loc. cit.
74. Id.
75. For example, the schema of the European Convention on Human Rights is to state the right and immediately follow with the exceptions.

# 4 Special groups: the mentally handicapped

The mentally handicapped are another group which can be discussed to illustrate the value of analysing legal capacity as an acceptable basis for attributing or withholding rights. Our conclusions about their position can equally point to the importance of the two main themes of this discussion. First, it will be argued that, although disadvantaged in law in a general sense, this need not be and is not always necessary. Second, it will be shown that – perhaps even more acutely than in the case of children – it is the professionalization of *all* aspects of the medical act which permits the denigration, disvaluation or denial of human rights. While in the case of children, it is generally therapeutic intervention that is countenanced, the mentally handicapped may find themselves the victims of medical intervention that is at best tenuously 'therapeutic' and at worst, blatantly non-therapeutic. In fact in their respect, the professionalization of decisions which affect human rights is nowhere more potentially invasive.

In many ways it is true to say that a separate body of law has not been created for the mentally handicapped. As Ward says:

> . . . an understanding of the law of children helps with the less well developed law of the mentally handicapped, and indeed there has been a tendency for aspects of the law of the mentally handicapped to be stated by referring to equivalent concepts in the law of children.[1]

It is also clear that, both in common law and in statute, the mentally handicapped are sometimes dealt with as if they were indistinguishable from the mentally ill.[2] This confusion, or lack of distinction, can have unfortunate consequences, particularly in the latter case, since the crucial distinction remains that the mentally ill may be treated with some hope of success, whereas mental handicap would seem more likely to be a life-long condition for which no therapy is available.

Perhaps through a lack of understanding of the nature of mental handicap, the law – as with children and the mentally ill – could find it tempting to assume general disability, an assumption which denies legal standing to the whole group. Yet:

> When it comes to mental incapacity, we have at one extreme the normal adult of full capacity, and at the other extreme the person completely lacking legal capacity. In between these extremes is an area of partial legal capacity, which, broadly speaking, is an area in which people have capacity for some legal purposes and not for others. This area of partial incapacity is not sub-divided in the law, and it therefore covers the whole spectrum from mild mental incapability until one crosses the threshold of complete legal incapacity . . .[3]

However, it is clear that, as with children and the mentally ill, the law tends not to make entirely blanket assumptions about capacity, considering each individual case very much on its merits. This *ad hoc* type of decision making may indeed by necessary given the range and variety of degrees and types of handicap. Indeed:

> . . . the law has never sought to draw clearcut boundaries across the chart, so as to create categories similar to the age-groups of children. There are no generalized 'packages' of law which apply to any particular range of disability. The law does not generalise to any great extent. It will define whether a particular individual has legal capacity for one particular purpose, at one particular time, and in one particular set of circumstances. It will define whether one particular form of legal intervention is or is not appropriate.[4]

However, it will be argued here that even *ad hoc* decision making is, and should be, undertaken against a background of respect for human rights.

## Do the mentally handicapped have rights?

In December 1971, the General Assembly of the United Nations adopted a charter of *Rights for the Mentally Handicapped Person*.[5] The first and fundamental right contained in this agreement is as follows: 'The mentally retarded person has the same basic rights as other citizens of the same country and same age.'[6] Naturally, the charter does acknowledge that there may also be need for a right to proper medical care and 'physical restoration',[7] but its general tenor requires acceptance of the moral equivalence of the mentally handicapped. This assertion of rights is important on two counts. On the one hand, the law – as has been said – seems somewhat confused, perhaps even ambivalent, about the status to be accorded to the mentally handicapped, and on the other this group has been historically vulnerable to exploitation which in some cases has been condoned by the law.[8]

In terms of therapeutic medical intervention, there seems little doubt that the handicapped person would be treated in the same way as a child. In terms of detention or reception into guardianship, their position is similar to that of the mentally ill.[9] In other words, they are always vulnerable to the assumptions of others as to their best interests, or to legal presumptions that categorize their decision-making in such a way as to validate it only in a situation where it seems rational - 'rationality' being closely linked with the view of the parent or guardian on the one hand, and the law on the other.

The handicapped are also vulnerable to non-therapeutic intervention, and in respect of basic human rights their position can, despite the United Nations agreement, be described as uncertain. The earlier discussion of the cases of *R v. Arthur*[10] and *Re B (a minor)*[11] shows clearly that the fact of handicap can be sufficient to encourage juries and courts to make assumptions about the value of lives. If, it might be asked, the attribution of the basic right to life is not always made to the handicapped, then on what grounds could it make sense to insist on the attribution of admittedly less fundamental rights? This question can, of course, be answered relatively simply by noting that just because something happens currently need not imply that it should continue to happen or that it is right. The chapter dealing with the rights of children may be called on in support of the argument that to adopt a different, rights dominated, approach may well relieve these problems.

The handicapped (in this case including the physically handicapped) are, of course at risk from the moment of conception. The Abortion Act 1967, bearing in mind the tragedy of thalidomide, was at pains to permit the termination of any seriously handicapped pregnancy and even David Alton's Abortion (Amendment) Bill 1987 would have conceded this.[12] Genetic screening is now highly sophisticated and makes the detection of handicap in the womb easier, and genetic counselling may either facilitate the decision to avoid a pregnancy where handicap is likely, or provide the opportunity to choose abortion when the foetus is known to be suffering from severe handicap.[13] It is worthy of note that the section, which permits termination where severe handicap is shown, is the only section in the Act which authorizes termination solely on the basis of the attributes of the embryo or foetus. Other terminations can only be authorized where the risk to the mother of carrying the child to term is greater than the risk of termination, or where the health of other children in the family would also suffer.[14] However, the fact that a child may be born with severe handicap is sufficient to legalize termination of the pregnancy. Some of the handicapped, therefore, will not even be permitted to be born.

After birth, their rights are equally suspect. Although the utilitarian, such as Glover,[15] might argue that babies, having no interest in life, can have no right to it, this scarcely reflects common morality or general law.[16] In any event it is interesting that this argument is only used in regard to those who are not 'normal'. Any legal system which condoned or countenanced the routine killing (whether by act or omission) of healthy and 'normal' babies would be regarded as an international scandal. Not even the consequential utilitarian argument that to terminate the life of a damaged baby may maximize the general good by encouraging the parents to have a subsequent (healthy) one,[17] can be taken seriously, unless the first argument is accepted.

The comments made in respect of children can equally be taken to apply to the handicapped, although it may be true to say that, at least in some situations, the needs of the handicapped for the law to take a clear position on human rights are, if anything, even more acute. Perhaps more than any other vulnerable group, the handicapped are at risk, not merely of therapeutic decisions being made without reference to, or despite, their wishes, but also of the imposition of a non-therapeutic measure. Thus, they are used here as an example of the potential for non-therapeutic intrusion since they remain the group most strongly represented in this area. Analysis of their position can be conducted by reference to a number of jurisdictions and highlights some revealing attitudes which, it is submitted, serve to reinforce the need to maintain at all times an awareness of, and respect for, human rights.

It is important at this stage to remember the distinction between therapeutic and non-therapeutic medical intervention, and to bear in mind also that, outside of clear experimental situations, it can be blurred – indeed, can be manipulated. Although 'therapeutic' is generally taken to imply something which is of benefit to the patient, and 'non-therapeutic' as something which may benefit knowledge and/or future patients, there is a very real sense in which the former could be, and is, interpreted in a somewhat different way. The assumption behind the use of the term 'therapeutic' is that it represents treatment of a medical condition and offers hope of benefit. Thus, chemotherapy, however unpleasant, may offer a hope of cure and is therefore therapeutic.

However, therapy which is designed to avoid social difficulties may also be forced into the framework of 'therapeutic' treatment, unless courts are very careful, and it is here that the vulnerability of the mentally handicapped is at its most acute. The courts of a number of jurisdictions have, in recent years, been asked to consider precisely this issue in respect, most often, of a request to sterilize a mentally handicapped woman, in order, not to cure a pre-existing physical condition, but on the social grounds that she may be unable to cope with a pregnancy, cannot be trusted to take contraception, and would be unable to look after any child born, the alternative being the trauma of an abortion.[18]

One thing at least is clear, however. Unlike the apparent, albeit limited, power of parents to make therapeutic choices in respect of at least some of their children, courts are loath to permit the making of such a major decision as sterilization without the proper legal formalities being undertaken. This attitude reflects the United Nations view, which in Article VII[19] makes the following comment:

> Some mentally retarded persons may be unable, due to the severity of their handicap to exercise for themselves all of their rights in a meaningful way. For others, modification of some or all of these rights is appropriate. *The procedure used for modification or denial of rights must contain proper legal safeguards against every form of abuse, must be based on an evaluation of the social capability of the mentally retarded person by qualified experts and must be subject to periodic reviews and to the right of appeal to higher authorities.* (emphasis added)

So legal systems which demand court approval of proposed steriliz-ation of the mentally handicapped provide at least some of the safeguards demanded by the United Nations. However, against a philosophy which is prepared to stretch the concept of 'therapeutic' treatment, and which places less than sufficient weight on the value of certain human rights, the mere fact of court authorization – while complying with the letter of the commitment – may not, in fact, meet its philosophy. Whether or not the handicapped person is an adult or a child will, in some jurisdictions, make an apparent differ-ence to the capacity of courts to intervene. In England, for example, the use of wardship proceedings is thought to be competent only up to the age of majority, but not beyond, although recently a court has been prepared to authorize sterilization and pregnancy termination on a young mentally handicapped woman.[20] In Scot-land, the authority to make major decisions ceases at the age of majority.[21] In Canada, those over the age of 18 will be dealt with under the power of *parens patriae*.[22] In the United States, appeal may be made on behalf of the handicapped person by reference to Constitutional rights which it is held apply equally to all citizens.[23] The clearest example of the ambivalent attitude of the law to the mentally handicapped is where reproductive choice is at stake. For this reason, the next section will concern itself with this area in an attempt to elucidate the attitudes which underlie decision making.

## Reproduction and mental handicap

The history of involuntary sterilization of the handicapped is a long one.[24] In the early part of this century (and in some states until comparatively recently) some United States courts were prepared to authorize sterilization, and to deny the unconstitutionality of laws permitting its enforcement.[25] These decisions must be seen against the background of the rapid rise of the eugenics movement in that country and its adoption by a large, and interestingly disparate, number of groups and individuals. For a time, therefore '[b]irth control became an issue primarily in as much as it related to forcing those who could or would not voluntarily control their reproductive capacities, not to breed.'[26]

Nor was compulsory sterilization randomly used. There was a very definite bias towards sterilizing those who, it was said, would either weaken the genetic stock of the country or who would, in any event, scarcely miss the capacity to breed or note the denial of a human right.[27] Thus, involuntary sterilization:

> . . . by 1950 had accounted for the sterilisation of over 50,000 persons in America, 20,000 in California alone. By 1964 the accumulative total had reached 63, 678. Of these persons, 27,917 were sterilised on grounds of mental illness, 32,374 on grounds of mental deficiency and some 2,387 on other grounds.[28]

The attitude towards the handicapped, therefore, however genetically unsophisticated, was that there was a real probability that their offspring would be as much of a drain on the state as they themselves were seen to be and that, in any event, they probably did not have rights in this area and wouldn't notice their removal even assuming they had them.[29] In *Buck* v. *Bell*,[30] for example, a case which involved the compulsory sterilization of a mentally defective young woman, the court had this to say:

> We have seen more than once that the public welfare may call upon the best citizens for their lives. It would be strange if it could not call on those who already sap the strength of the State for these lesser sacrifices, *often not felt to be such by those concerned*, in order to avoid our being swamped with incompetence. It is better for all the world, if instead of waiting to execute degenerate offspring for crime, or to let them starve for their imbecility, society can prevent those who are manifestly unfit from continuing their kind.[31] (emphasis added)

Again in *State* v. *Troutman*,[32] the court doubted even the existence of rights in the mentally defective, saying: '[i]f there be any natural right for natively mental defectives to beget children, that right gives way to the police power of the State in protecting the common welfare . . .'[33]

With the exposure of the eugenics movement as scientifically and morally dubious, and the well-documented atrocities of the Nazi regime, the United States began, however, to move away from overt and involuntary intrusion into the procreative practices of the mentally unsound. Cases such as *Carey* v. *Population Services International*,[34] and *Skinner* v. *Oklahoma*,[35] asserted the existence of a human right to procreate whose restriction demanded considerable and compelling justification. This was not, however, an entirely wholehearted move, although in the case of *Katie Relf et al.* v. *Caspar Weinberger et al.* in 1974 the court sounded a note of caution:

> We should not drift into a policy which has unfathomed implications and which permanently deprives unwilling or immature citizens of their ability to procreate without adequate safeguards and a legislative determination of the appropriate standards in light of the general welfare and individual rights.[36]

A mere two years later, however, a North Carolina court concluded that mental retardation was an identifiable category, and given that 'such persons are in fact different from the general population' they 'may rationally be accorded different treatment for their benefit and for the benefit of the public.'[37] It is clear from these more recent decisions that the grounds on which courts are prepared to authorize sterilization of the mentally handicapped are not in fact always therapeutic although they may partially be so. In effect, they were concerned with the 'general welfare' as much as with the individual. In some cases, they may also have been concerned for the specific welfare of, for example, parents who may feel that a sexually active handicapped dependent who becomes pregnant, or runs the risk of so doing, places a great strain on them, and may mean that they have to bring up any subsequent child.

Courts in the United States have further blurred the distinction between therapeutic and non-therapeutic medical intervention by, in some cases, apparently assuming that the risk of pregnancy alone is sufficient to merit the sterilization being considered as therapeutic and not merely contraceptive. For example, no clear distinction between the two was made in the 1976 case of *In Matter of Sallmaier*,[38] where the court said:

> The decision to exercise *parens patriae* must reflect the welfare of society as a whole, but mainly it must balance the individual's right to be free from interference *against the individuals' need to be treated*, if treatment would in fact be in his best interest.[39] (emphasis added)

Canadian courts too have considered these questions, most recently in the case of 'Eve'.[40] In this case, the court was unprepared to adopt a disingenuous approach to the distinction between therapeutic and non-therapeutic treatment of the mentally handicapped. 'Eve' is an adult who suffers from mental handicap, and who, it was thought, ran the risk of pregnancy. Her own capacity was such that she could not legally give her consent to the operation herself, and the court was asked to exercise its *parens patriae* jurisdiction to authorize the surgery (in this case, sterilization by means of hysterectomy).

The court noted that the proposed surgery was 'admittedly non-therapeutic',[41] that is, it was not needed to deal with a medical condition, but merely to provide effective contraception. The purpose of the surgery was explained by the court as follows:

> One such [non-therapeutic] purpose is to deprive Eve of the capacity to become pregnant so as to save her from the possible trauma of giving birth and from the resultant obligations of becoming a parent, a task the evidence indicates she is not capable of fulfilling . . . it should be noted that there is no evidence that giving birth would be more difficult for Eve than for any other woman. A second purpose of the sterilization is to relieve Mrs E. [Eve's elderly mother] of anxiety about the possibility of Eve's becoming pregnant and of having to care for any child Eve might bear.[42]

In reaching its decision, the court undertook a thorough review of English, American and Canadian cases and the case provides an excellent analysis of the law and the points of principle which are central to the debate. LaForest J, who delivered the judgement of the court, restated firmly the extreme caution which courts must use in exercising their *parens patriae* powers, particularly where the exercise of that power would affect fundamental rights.[43] Noting that the scope of the power was historically unlimited, he was unprepared to concede that this entailed authority to make *any* decision. Rather:

> . . . it by no means follows that the discretion to exercise it is unlimited. It must be exercised in accordance with its underlying principle . . . It is a discretion, too, that must at all times be exercised with great caution, a caution that must be redoubled as the serious-ness of the matter increases.[44]

In particular, the court considered the earlier decision in *Re K*,[45] where the Court of Appeal in British Columbia ordered that a hysterectomy be performed on a seriously retarded child on the basis that the operation *was* therapeutic given the child's alleged phobic reaction to blood which, it was thought, might cause serious emotional problems at the onset of menstruation. In taking this decision, the court was at pains to point out that their conclusion hinged on the individual circumstances of the case, Anderson J A saying 'I say now, as forcefully as I can, this case cannot and must not be regarded as a precedent to be followed in cases involving sterilization of mentally disabled persons for contraceptive purposes.'[46]

Faced with a considerable weight of evidence in respect of the impact of sterilization, the fact of its irreversibility and with their concern for basic human rights, the court in 'Eve' concluded that the operation could not be authorized by them. As the court said:

> . . . the decision involves values in an area where our social history clouds our vision and encourages many to perceive the mentally handicapped as somewhat less than human . . . Moreover, the implications of sterilization are always serious.[47]

The court had the advantage of consulting a report of the Law Commission of Canada,[48] which reviewed the available evidence in respect of sterilization, and felt able to reach certain conclusions on its use in a non-therapeutic context in the case of the mentally handicapped. In particular they emphasized that the mentally handicapped have different reactions to sterilization, just as do the rest of the community. It was their conclusion that sterilization could have a major psychological impact on the handicapped particularly when they had had no previous children.[49]

In other words, their conclusion was that the handicapped do not differ so dramatically from others in this sensitive issue that we can legitimately make presumptions that, for example, they don't care about reproduction or wouldn't notice if they couldn't reproduce. In the 'Eve' case the court were also impressed by the sheer scale of the intervention proposed. Removing the freedom to reproduce without consent, and by sterilization, they regarded as a 'grave intrusion on a person's rights'[50] and were unprepared to see it as being in a person's best interests.

It is significant that this thoroughly reasoned and rights dominated judgement referred with considerable favour to the judgement of Mrs Justice Heilbron in the (English) case of Re D (a minor) (wardship proceedings).[51] This case concerned the proposed sterilization of an 11-year-old girl who suffered from a syndrome which, amongst other disabilities, resulted in mental handicap. Both the girls' mother and her doctors had agreed that sterilization was appropriate in order to avoid the risk of pregnancy and the problems of the girl being unable to care for any child which she might have. The decision to sterilize was challenged and wardship proceedings were raised in order to place the child under the protection of the court.

The wardship jurisdiction is designed to protect those who are thought to be incapable of protecting themselves, and its scope is wide. As Latey J said in *Re X (a minor)*:[52]

> . . . the powers of the court in this particular jurisdiction have been described as being of the widest nature. That the courts are available to protect children from injury whenever they properly can is no modern development.[53]

Protection of the interests of a child can be given a relatively wide interpretation, as in the case of *Re S* v. *McC; W. v. W.*, [54] where the court authorized, in exercise of its protective jurisdiction over an infant, the taking of blood tests from a husband, his wife and child in an attempt to ascertain paternity.

As the court noted in '*Eve*', however, the fact that the jurisdiction is wide does not mean that the court can authorize activities which are outside the underlying principles, and to this extent they were in agreement with Mrs Justice Heilbron's decision in *Re D*.[55] Both judgements relied heavily on a rights dominated approach in order to deny the validity of non-consensual, non-therapeutic sterilization of a mentally handicapped person. Mrs Justice Heilbron presented the matter thus:

> It is apparent . . . that the jurisdiction to do what is considered necessary for the protection of an infant is to be exercised carefully and within limits . . . The type of operation proposed is one which involves the deprivation of a basic human right, namely the right of a woman to reproduce, and therefore it would, if performed on a woman for non-therapeutic reasons and without her consent, be a violation of such a right.[56]

However, unlike the Canadian decision, this decision left loopholes available, of which advantage has now been taken. The court in the case of *Re B (a minor) (sterilization)*, [57] while also noting the decision in *Re D* with approval, none the less felt able to distinguish it from the case under their consideration. The apparent reason for this distinction was the court's claim that the operation was therapeutic in nature. But it is questionable whether such a claim can in fact be justified, and in any event it reflects the position which the court in '*Eve*' was at pains to criticize – namely, the blurring of distinctions in the interests of social or other considerations.

This English case concerned the proposed sterilization of a 17-year-old mentally handicapped girl, who, it was said, would at best achieve the intellectual and motor skills of a 5 or 6 year old. It was thought that she was beginning to show signs of sexual awareness and interest, and her mother felt that the best method of avoiding unwanted pregnancy would be to arrange for her to be sterilized. The evidence was that she would be unable to take the contraceptive pill for medical reasons, but also because she might not remember to do so, and the court presented the alternative to this as being the permanent removal of her capacity to procreate. They concluded that:

> The court had jurisdiction to authorize a sterilization operation on a ward of court in wardship proceedings but it was a jurisdiction which should be exercised only as a last resort when all other forms of contraception had been considered. Moreover, there was no question of a natural parent or local authority having parental rights giving consent to a sterilization operation without first obtaining the leave of the court in wardship proceedings.[58]

The latter aspect of their judgement seems to reflect the commitment to legal control which was advocated by the United Nations, although it may again reflect its letter rather than its spirit.[59] Moreover, the former leaves room for some argument. Some dubiety, for example, has already been expressed as to whether or not the options as presented by the court were in fact the only ones available.[60] Further, the judgement seems not to be disposed to consider the situation in all its gravity from the perspective of human rights, dismissing the rights argument on the basis that '[a]s far as she was concerned the right to reproduce would mean nothing to her.'[61] The dangers of making access to rights dependent on awareness of them, or an interest in them, are clear and do not require restatement here.

The court was also able to take advantage of one major loophole in the *Re D* judgement. Despite the apparent vindication of the rights of the young child in that case, the decision was in fact considerably less rights dominated than at first appears. In *Re D*, it was confidently anticipated that the girl would have the legal capacity to marry, and she was therefore protected by the right to marry and found a family as propounded in the European Declaration of Human Rights.[62] The fact that she *would* be able to consent to marry was a cornerstone of the court's decision not to authorize the sterilization.

In *Re B*, however, the young woman will clearly never be in that position and, unless the right to reproduce were considered absolute, or a real value were placed on the need for consent from the individual based on information disclosure, the court felt free to make the decision it did in authorizing the operation. As a leading article in *The Observer* noted in the aftermath of this case:

> English law on this is in a mess. Every year, some dozens of handicapped girls are discreetly sterilised by specialists at the request of their parents, but nobody knows whether it is legal or not . . . Britain urgently needs better law and regulation for such cases.[63]

One could scarcely agree more.


## Summary

This discussion of the position of the mentally handicapped has been undertaken to reinforce the vulnerability of certain groups, not only in their involvement in therapeutic medical acts, but also in regard to those acts that either are non-therapeutic, or are therapautic only by sleight of hand. As Laforest J says: '. . . sterilization may, on occasion, be necessary as an adjunct to treatment of a serious malady, *but I would underline that this, of course, does not allow for subterfuge or for treatment of some marginal medical problem*'[64] (emphasis added). What, it is suggested, has emerged from this discussion is that there are two main schools of thought currently adopted in decision making in these cases. Leaving aside the now largely discredited manipulation of children, the mentally ill and the mentally handicapped for social or eugenic reasons, the picture can be presented thus.

Most of the decisions reviewed have started from the presumption of incapacity – the persons so defined are then left with the task of establishing that they *are* capable of making decisions for themselves, a task seriously hampered by the initial presumption. Moreover, where capacity is in doubt and disputes arise, the courts have generally been tempted to adopt one of two approaches, sometimes seeking to justify the outcome in terms of both. These approaches are referred to as the 'best interests approach' and the 'substituted judgement approach'.

In the former, particularly prevalent in cases relating to mentally sound children, the presumption is that parents or courts can decide – indeed have a responsibility to decide – what is in the best interests of a given child. That their conclusion in some cases may result in the child's death seems not to have been a matter of grave concern. Nor does it seem to be regarded as significant that the decision to impose or withhold therapy may conflict with the views or the rights of the child him or herself. In these cases, the preference for therapy over non-therapy dominates the attitude of society and the courts, rendering the opinion of the reluctant child apparently less weighty than would be that of a child who sought treatment in the face of parental objection.

Societal concern for the best interests of those whose legal and moral standing is in doubt, is equally appropriate in the case of the mentally handicapped, although in their case it can be said that the pendulum has swung even further away from respect for the rights of the individual, at least in the case of compulsory intervention in reproductive freedom. For both of these groups, competition with those in authority (either parents or courts) is a truly unequal struggle.

The second approach adopted would justify treatment without consent on the grounds that, had the person been in a position to give or withhold consent, they would have opted for therapy. This is often taken as self-evident. Surely people prefer the hope of cure or alleviation of symptoms to the prolongation of ill-health? Yet, if the right described in this discussion is to have any real meaning it must inevitably include the right to prefer no treatment – in other words, to prefer illness to the possibility of cure. This 'substituted judgement' approach has gained a certain credibility in decision making in difficult areas such as these, because, it is claimed, it seems to give more credence to the individual's standing as a human being than does the overtly paternalistic 'best interests' test. The logical flaw, however, is that the fact that the decision is *not* made by the individual denies the very basis of the justification for using it.

To return to the *'Eve'* case briefly, the judge, in response to advocation for the substituted judgement test, made the following statement:

> I do not doubt that a person has a right to decide to be sterilized. That is his or her free choice. But choice presupposes that a person has the mental competence to make it. It may be a matter of debate whether a court should have the power to make the decision if that person lacks the mental capacity to do so. *But it is obviously fiction to suggest that a decision so made is that of the mental incompetent. What the incompetent would do if he or she could make the choice is simply a matter of speculation.*[65] (emphasis added)

Although sterilization may seem to be a particularly intrusive action, these views can equally be translated into the more routine medical intervention. There may be additional significance attached to the final denial of the capacity to procreate, but there remains significance in *all* medical intervention undertaken without the consent of the individual. That significance is vested in the value of the right to make independent decisions, free from duress, based on information and in the light of the personal implications of the outcome. *All* therapy undertaken without consent is intrusive of the individual's integrity and invasive of the right to make knowing choices about therapy.

## Conclusions

What, then, can be concluded from an examination of special groups? It was suggested at the beginning of this chapter that, if these groups were to be routinely excluded from the ambit of the right, then its significance and value would be considerably diminished. What this discussion has, however, shown is that blanket assumptions need not be, and in fact are not, made by the law as to the capacity of children and the mentally handicapped. However limited the ascription of rights, it none the less is there. Yet, there are restrictions imposed on access to information and on freedom to choose or reject therapy which may still pose problems. In particular, the tests adopted in the event of conflict present a serious threat to the number and range of persons who could claim the protection of the right. The question remains, therefore, whether or not this threat is inevitable and insurmountable.

There is no doubt that there are some members of the community who are incapable, whether by reason of age or mental incapacity, of taking decisions. The choice to consent or not to medical treatment is for them not a reality and information disclosure would represent a mere time-consuming farce. On the other hand, as was noted earlier, although they do not appreciate the value of choice or cannot freely choose to exercise it, the right itself still exists. The fact that the comatose have no known interest in life, and certainly cannot express a preference for it, does not entitle those in authority to kill them, nor does it diminish the overwhelming value placed on life – indeed, it is precisely this value which precludes proxy decision making *for* death in these circumstances. This is also true of the right to consent to or refuse treatment based on adequate disclosure of information.

Accepting, therefore, that rights remain important, the fact that they may be denied to some need not be fatal to their place on the list of rights to which humanity can aspire. Indeed, the examples of children and the mentally handicapped serve rather to reinforce the need to take the right seriously. Neither of the currently favoured approaches to decision making is satisfactory, substantially because both begin from the wrong premise. Certainly, restrictions may have to be imposed, but the presumption should be that the right has priority. If this were the approach adopted then fewer individuals would be precluded from its protection. It is admitted that such an approach may in some rare cases preclude therapy altogether, but it is argued that the morality of the proposed therapy in these cases would in any event be somewhat dubious – for example, the sterilization for non-therapeutic purposes of those whose consent cannot be obtained. The responsibility, were the right taken seriously, would pass from those who are vulnerable to those in authority who would have to demonstrate a manifest and acceptable justification for proceeding without consent, and would reinforce the rights of all individuals to have access to the full range of civil and moral rights.

These conclusions have importance for the sane adult also. If the courts' present lack of respect for the rights of special groups to involvement in a therapeutic alliance were to be considered fatal to the right itself, then as the right is also badly defined, and sometimes ignored, in the case of the sane adult the same conclusion would necessarily be implied. This is a position that even the most rampantly paternalistic would surely find unacceptable. The solution, therefore, lies not in the continual erosion, redefinition or categorization of those to whom the right is applicable, but in a radical re-thinking of the right itself – its scope, its nature, its value, and most crucially of all, its legal status and the corresponding mechanisms for its vindication.

Discussion of these two groups has also shown the danger associated with the presumption – common in respect of the sane adult also – that there is something technical or professional about decisions to accept or reject therapy. If so, then of course best medical choice or even a reasonable medical choice, would be an adequate and appropriate basis on which to proceed, and recognition of this would help to decide what information should be given to patients and the amount of weight to be given to any choice made by them.

So, it could be said, doctors would be justified in giving patients no information, or in giving them information only to the extent that it would encourage them to agree to the physician's own preferred course of action. If the whole event is technical, then why not? The answer, of course, takes us back to the initial claim that there is very much more at stake than mere technical competence. It is understandable that doctors wish to press ahead with therapy where they believe that it may alleviate or cure, but it is equally intelligible that some patients – if they knew the risks and benefits – would prefer no therapy. Of course, patients may choose to undergo discomfort in the interests of palliation or cure, but they cannot *prefer* this option if they are never told of the possibility of the discomfort happening.

It is important, therefore, to bear in mind the thinness of the line between the unwilling patient and the unknowing patient. Few would argue for treatment which goes expressly against the wishes of the patient. Enforced therapy is not a course generally acceptable to physicians, society or the law.

However, it should be remembered that unknowing patients – those who have not been informed of risks, benefits and alternatives – are not truly willing either. In fact, they have been denied the opportunity, by lack of information, to be either willing or unwilling. It is, however, no less unacceptable to inflict therapy on them, even when it is thought by physicians to be 'in their best interests'. To permit this is to fall squarely into the trap of assuming that both the nature and the outcome of the medical act depend primarily or even solely on the technicalities of what is going on, and to ignore the moral and human rights constituents.

But, it might be said, the patient is no more 'knowing' even after information is given, if they can't understand it. What, it is asked, is the point of telling them, then? This question – admittedly one which needs to be tackled – is asked, of course, about children and the mentally handicapped whose presumed incapacity to understand forms a substantial part of the denial of full autonomy to them. But it is also presented as a rationale for limiting or denying information to those who would otherwise be seen as autonomous. Undoubtedly, it remains a difficult question for those who are opposed to the paternalistic model, and it needs to be dealt with.

## Notes

1. Ward, A.D., *Scots Law and the Mentally Handicapped*, Edinburgh, Scottish Society for the Mentally Handicapped, 1984 at p. 2.
2. Both the Scottish and the English legislation apply equally to both groups despite distinctions in the nature of their conditions – distinctions which may in fact be of considerable importance; for discussion, see Ward, op, cit., at p. 108 et seq.
3. Ward, op. cit., at p. 6.
4. Ward, op. cit., at p. 76.
5. For the full text, see Ward, op. cit.
6. Article I.
7. Article II.
8. E.g. *Buck* v. *Bell* (1927) 274 US 200, per Holmes, J, at p. 207: 'We have seen more than once that the public welfare may call upon the best citizens for their lives. It would be strange if it could not call upon those who already sap the strength of the State for these lesser sacrifices, often not felt to be such by those concerned, in order to prevent our being swamped with incompetence'; for further discussion, see McLean, S.A.M., 'The right to

reproduce', in Campbell, et al., (Eds) *Human Rights: From Rhetoric to Reality*, Oxford, Basil Blackwell, 1986.

9. See Ward, op. cit., chapters V and VI.
10 Supra cit., chapter 3.
11. Supra cit., chapter 3.
12. Abortion Amendment Bill (1987). For discussion of this possible concession see, for example, *Guardian* 23 January 1988.
13. In Britain, in terms of the Abortion Act 1967 s 1(2); in the USA this would form part of the 'privacy' right described in *Roe* v. *Wade*, 410 US 113 (1973) and *Thornburgh* v. *American College of Obstetricians and Gynecologists* 476 US 747 (1986).
14. Abortion Act 1967 s. 1(1).
15. Glover, J., *Causing Death and Saving Lives*, Harmondsworth, Penguin, 1977.
16. Cf. Glover, op, cit., chapter 12.
17. Id.
18. Cf. *Re K* (1985) 19 DLR (4th) 255; *In the Matter of Sallmaier* (1976) 378 NYS 2d 989; *In Re Grady* (1981) 426 A 2d 467; but see, *Re D (A Minor)*, supra cit.; *Application of A. D.* (1977) 394 NYS 139; *"Eve"* v. *Mrs. "E"* 115 DLR (3d) 283 (1986) – references to this case will be taken from a transcript.
19. Rights for the Mentally Handicapped Person (1971).
20. *Re B (Wardship Proceedings) (Sterilization)*, [1987] 2 All ER 206 (CA); *The Times* 17 March 1987 (HL); but see, *T* v. *T & Anor, The Times* 11 July 1987: 'His Lordship was convinced that it was in the best interests of the girl that the proposed procedures should be performed . . . [He] was content to rely on the principle that in exceptional circumstances where there was no provision in law for consent and no one who could give consent and where the patient was suffering from such mental abnormality as to be unable ever to give consent then a medical adviser was justified in taking such steps as good medical practice demanded.'
21. Cf. Walker, D.M., *Principles of Scottish Private Law*, (3rd edn), Oxford, Clarendon press, 1982, at p. 208.
22. For a description of wardship powers see *Re X (A Minor)* [1975] 1 All ER 697, per Latey, J, at p. 699: '. . . the powers of the court in this particular jurisdiction have always been described as being of the widest nature. That the courts are available to protect children from injury whenever they properly can is no modern development.'; *Re S* v. *McC: W* v. *W* [1972] AC 24; Heilbron, J in *Re D (a minor)*, supra cit., at p. 332: 'It is apparent . . . that the jurisdiction to do what is considered necessary for the protection of an infant is to be exercised carefully and within limits.'; *Re P (a minor)* [1982] CLY 2077.
23. Cf. *Skinner* v. *Oklahoma* 316 US 535; *Planned Parenthood of Central Missouri* v. *Danforth* 428 US 52 (1976).
24. For discussion, see Meyers, D., *The Human Body and the Law*, Edinburgh, EUP 1971, chapter 2.
25. Cf. *Buck* v. *Bell*, supra cit.; *North Carolina Association for Retarded Children et al.* v. *State of North Carolina et al.* 420 F. Supp. 451 (1976); *State* v. *Troutman* 50 Idaho 763 (1931).
26. McLean, loc, cit. at p. 105.
27. *State* v. *Troutman*, supra cit.; more recently in the United Kingdom, see *In Re B (sterilization)*, supra cit., per Dillon, LJ, 'As far as she was concerned the right to reproduce would mean nothing to her.'
28. Meyers, op, cit., at p. 29.
29. *Re B (sterilization)*, supra cit.
30. Supra cit.
31. At p. 207.

32. Supra cit.
33. At p. 767.
34. 431 US 678.
35. Supra cit.
36. 372 F Supp. 1196 (1974).
37. *North Carolina Association for Retarded Children*, supra cit.
38. Supra cit.
39. At p. 991.
40. Supra cit.
41. At p. 13.
42. At pp. 13–14.
43. At p. 59.
44. At p. 53.
45. Supra cit.
46. At p. 275.
47. At pp. 53–54.
48. Law Commission of Canada, *Sterilization*, Working Paper 24 (1979).
49. For discussion, see, for example, p. 50.
50. For discussion, see, for example, p. 59.
51. Supra cit.
52. Supra cit.
53. At p. 699.
54. Supra cit.
55. Supra cit.
56. *Re D*, supra cit., at p. 332.
57. Supra cit.; see also *T* v. *T.*, supra cit.
58. *Re B ( a minor) (sterilization)*, supra cit.
59. Rights for the Mentally Handicapped Person (1971) Article VII.
60. Cf. Amiel, B., 'The Rules of a Sterile Society' *The Times* 30 July 1987: '. . . it was difficult not to conclude that this court was using the phrase "last resort" in a rather hypocritical fashion, enabling them to agree to sterilization without really facing what they were doing.'
61. Per Dillon, L. J., loc. cit.
62. Article 12; for discussion of the possible implications of this, see McLean, S.A.M. and Campbell, T.D., 'Sterilisation', in McLean, S.A.M. (Ed.), *Legal Issues in Medicine*, Aldershot, Gower, 1981.
63. *Observer* 22 March 1987.
64. At p. 63.
65. At p. 64.

# 5 Patient understanding and 'rational' choices

It may be said that, since patients cannot understand highly technical information, then its provision is a meaningless and time-consuming farce. If the rationale for information disclosure is to enable the patient to make a knowing (albeit not necessarily a 'rational') choice, then what, it might be asked, is the value of disclosure without understanding? And in any event if the patient lacks the technical skills to undertake the medical enterprise, then how could he or she ever understand information which is known by virtue of having these skills? If such understanding is impossible, then what is the point in making the disclosure? And, could it ever be reasonable to make the doctor subject to a duty to ensure patient understanding, because, if not, then surely information could be disclosed in highly technical terms which would render the patient no more capable of making a knowing choice, and therefore in no better a position to protect his or her autonomy?

These questions were formally, and it is submitted appropriately, answered in *Canterbury* v. *Spence*, [1] and the answers given there serve to explain why it is that the emphasis in this discussion has been on the duty to disclose, rather than on 'informed consent'. As the court said:

> In duty to disclose cases, the focus of attention is more properly on the nature and content of the physician's divulgence than the patient's understanding and consent. Adequate disclosure and informed consent are, of course, two sides of the same coin. The former is a *sine qua non* of the latter. But the vital enquiry on duty to disclose relates to the physician's performance of an obligation, while one of the difficulties with analysis in terms of 'informed consent' is its tendency to imply that what is decisive is the degree of the patient's comprehension.[2]

Thus the duty to disclose, when based on the patient's right to receive information, can be tested independently of patient understanding, however desirable that understanding may be. The doctor fulfils his or her obligation by making the disclosure in a reasonable way, so as to facilitate patient understanding, even given that it cannot be guaranteed. As the court further said, '. . . the physician discharges the duty when he makes a reasonable effort to convey sufficient information, although the patient, without fault of the physician, may not fully grasp it.'[3] In any event, problems of patient understanding may be overstated since it is not the technicalities of drug action or surgical technique which alone constitute information which is autonomy-enhancing, although some patients may be sufficiently interested to want to know about these also. It is the risk of hair loss, or voice loss, or other disability which concerns the patient, and not the mechanics of the therapy, except where these are inseparable from the likely risks or benefits.

A moment's reflection on the previous two chapters – perhaps particularly the one dealing with children – will reinforce this claim. If courts are prepared to support children's decisions in some cases, they do so on the basis that the child is sufficiently mature to understand. But understand what? Surely the courts are not suggesting that children understand technical information?

Of course they are not. By admitting that children *can* make decisions the courts are actually conceding that what is to be understood is the human and not the technical. In other words, they are conceding that the relevant information on which decisions are made is the likely personal impact of that choice. It might be thought to be somewhat paradoxical that these same courts will often support or uphold limited disclosure to adults on the basis of the complexity of the information which was withheld.

This is not to say, however, that the question of patient understanding is totally irrelevant. Some writers while insisting on the necessity of information disclosure, equally maintain that disclosure without understanding is useless and merely a parody of patient involvement. For example, Robertson[4] has said that:

> The doctrine of informed consent can only become meaningful in terms of the patient's right to self-determination if he actually comprehends the information which is disclosed to him – without such comprehension the patient is not given the opportunity which he requires, in order to make a rational decision. Even accepting that the patient's right to self-determination dictates only that he be given a reasonable opportunity of making a rational decision as to proposed medical treatment, the extent of the patient's comprehension of the disclosed information should still be a vital issue. The opportunity given may be 'reasonable' if viewed from the standpoint of the doctor, in terms of the information which he has disclosed, but that opportunity becomes wholly unreasonable for the purpose for which it

is given and completely meaningless, if viewed from the patient's standpoint, if he fails to understand the information given to him.[5]

This emphasis on patient understanding is not, however, shared by all commentators. The act of disclosure is itself seen by some as going a long way towards protection of patient autonomy, particularly where the disclosure is couched in terms that the average patient could understand. Indeed, with due respect to Robertson, it might be said that he falls into two of the same traps as medical paternalism. First, he makes the assumption that information which should be disclosed is difficult information – almost certainly because it is technical. It is not clear, however, that this is in fact the case. Certainly, the patient consults the doctor because the doctor possesses technical skills, but the impact of the exercise of these skills is not solely to bring about a technical result. Rather, it effects a cure, brings relief or, in unfortunate cases, causes harm. None of these are technical matters, as experienced by the patient, although they may be brought about by the exercise of technical skills.

If this is accepted, then the second fallacy in this type of argument becomes clear – namely, that the average patient cannot understand the information which is in fact relevant to him or her – for example, that he may or will recover, that the best that will be done is to relieve discomfort, or that there may be some harmful side effects of treatment. In other words, what renders the patient competent to make decisions is the fact that he or she can understand (given the information) the likely *personal* impact of his or her choice. If Robertson really means that information is difficult to understand because it is technical and this argument were to be pursued to its logical conclusion, then only those who could understand the technical impact of therapy are able to give *real* consent. No one, therefore, bar a doctor in the same specialism and at an equal or superior level of skill, could legally offer a meaningful consent. This is a *reductio ad absurdum* of the whole context in which information disclosure and consent are considered.

Robertson's view is that in the American courts '. . . the doctrine of informed consent is a legal mechanism whose function has simply been to expand the liability of the medical profession, in order to compensate a greater number of victims of medical accident'.[6] This, of course, does not detract from the symbolic, the practical or the moral position which demands that such consent is in fact provided. Even if the desire to expand liability has become a highly significant rationale for the use of the doctrine in the United States, or indeed in other jurisdictions, it cannot be totally separate from issues of patient autonomy. The desire to expand liability, therefore, is not mutually exclusive to legal recognition of the value of the interests at stake.

This is not, of course, to minimize Robertson's excellent consideration of the consent question, and in particular it is not to underestimate the problems that patient comprehension can pose for the autonomy theorist. The technical gap between doctor and patient is great and even non-technical information may be misunderstood by patients. Finding a way of evaluating patient understanding is, however, unlikely. In any event, not even the autonomy theorist would want to place a duty on the doctor to *ensure* understanding, since, logically, failure in this duty (for reasons which could relate to the patient and not the doctor) would result in the possibility of a law suit against the doctor solely because of the patient's incapacity. Clearly this is not to be taken seriously.

## The sub-plot

There remains, however, one further problem concerning patient autonomy and information disclosure and that is the significance given by some writers (and judges) to the need to make a rational choice. Dependence on rationality may open the door to yet further tests of the efficacy and desirability of information disclosure, which resemble to some extent the reasons sometimes presented for non-disclosure by the medical profession itself.[7] While it is true that the patient requires information which *permits* him or her to make a rational decision, it is not clear that the *making* of a rational decision is the delimitation of his or her rights to autonomy or self-determination, nor that the rationality or otherwise of the decision should be used as a yardstick against which the merit of disclosure can be tested. The risks of so doing have been shown in the discussion of children.

Except in situations where there is a clear risk to others involved in patient decision making, it is not, in the first place, clear that self-determination is intimately connected with making rational choices. Indeed it is plausible to argue that the right to self-determination necessarily includes the right to act irrationally. Moreover, the concept of rationality is in itself problematic, and may be particularly so in the case of decisions about therapy.

The decision as to what is a rational choice in this situation, as in others, is seldom value-free. In the abstract, it may be thought to be rational to choose possible or probable cure over continued ill health. But where this choice involves the acceptance of therapy, its rationality may be challengeable. To take a simple example, it has been claimed by some that a substantial proportion of all illness is self-limiting.[8] In other words, a large percentage of complaints for which people consult doctors would go away if left alone. Many of the most common reasons for consultation are believed to be susceptible to environmental or other change (that is to be capable of political, social, economic or non-scientific resolution).[9] In these cases, it may be rational not merely to reject therapy, but, given the inevitable risks of many diagnostic techniques and therapies, to avoid treatment altogether. Of course, this is a rather extreme position and not one that most people would recommend, but it serves to highlight one potential variation on 'rationality' which should command some consideration. Recent concern over the involuntary addiction of millions of people to prescribed tranquillizers is a case in point.

More serious consideration may, however, be merited in respect of demanding rationality where the choice taken is to prefer illness to therapy when the therapy is known to have a reasonable or certain chance of success. In this situation, rationality could be viewed in two distinct ways. Where cure is possible, probable or certain, it might be said to be rational to accept the therapy. Thus, it could be argued, there is no purpose served, and indeed harm may be caused to the patient, by disclosing the inevitable risks of that therapy. It is not, in this view, in the interests of patient care to distress the patient so that therapy is rejected or to emphasize the risk factor with the same possible outcome. This view has received considerable judicial backing notably in the case of *Bolam* v. *Friern Hospital Management Committee*.[10] where McNair J made the following remarks to the jury:

> Members of the jury, although it is a matter entirely for you, you may well think that when dealing with a mentally sick man and having a strong belief that his only hope of cure is ECT treatment, a doctor cannot be criticized if he does not stress the dangers which he believes to be minimal involved in that treatment.[11]

Although this case involved a patient whose mental health was unstable, there was no suggestion that he did not have the legal capacity to consent. What was in dispute was whether or not a warning as to the existence of specific risks (which were known, albeit unusual) should have been given. Here, the judge chose to believe (as did the jury) that the statistical improbability of the risk occurring minimized any duty to make disclosure, but the decision also shows the extent to which the therapeutic imperative (and the rationality of accepting treatment) was given credence. The fact that the therapy was seen *medically* as a viable and good option, invested it with a level of credibility which apparently overrode the patient's right to know. The second possible interpretation can be seen here also – that is, that it is rational to accept medical decisions about the appropriateness of therapy.

The view that accepting medically recommended treatment is the rational decision, often sits uneasily with the desire to maximize patient autonomy. What is medically rational may be personally irrational. The only person in the doctor/patient relationship who can, in fact, determine what is rational is the person in possession of the totality of personal details – that is the patient. As Shultz[12] says:

> Medical choice increasingly depends on factors that transcend professional training and knowledge. As medicine has become able to extend life, delay and redefine death, harvest and transplant organs, correct abnormality within the womb, enable artificial reproduction and trace genetic defect, questions about values have come to the fore in medical decision-making. Health care choices involve profound questions that are not finally referable to professional expertise.[13]

This leads to the fundamental question as to what it is that truly characterizes that aspect of the doctor/patient relationship which relates to disclosure of information and the provision or with-holding of consent. Few would doubt that much of what is characteristic of the doctor/patient relationship is the use of professional (technical) skills, or that the proper exercise of these skills should seldom, if ever, be circumscribed by non-professionals. The decision as to whether this or that antibiotic is specific to this or that particular condition is scarcely one which courts or patients are qualified to make or to judge. Equally, the mere fact that one doctor may legitimately prefer one to the other on technical grounds is not in dispute. These matters relate to professional competence and the level of technical information possessed by the skilled practitioner. As Giesen[14] puts it:

> The determination of the standards of medical science may . . . be difficult. Medical science is (as any science) characterised by some scientific controversies. It must be emphasised in this context that the lawyer (and especially the judge) cannot and must not presume to decide controversies of medical science. In such cases, especially, the courts can do nothing other than act in accordance with the practical experiences of the medical profession, rather than with the theoretical and dogmatic arguments put forward by this or another school.[15]

Thus non-experts cannot presume to know, where different opinions on technical matters are competently held, or scientifically justified, which school of medical thought is the appropriate or correct one.[16] However, it does not follow that a court cannot decide that this or that particular practice has failed to meet the legally required duty of care.

More important, however, for the purposes of this discussion, is the question whether – even accepting the above statement of the law's role – what is being dealt with in controversies over information disclosure and consent is in fact a technical question at all. On the answer to this question hinges both the relevant legal machinery and the very form of decision making itself.

From the outset, it has been claimed here that the rules about consent which exist in developed legal systems are rules designed to perform a specific purpose. That purpose is to permit the patient the continued exercise of self-determination or autonomy. Whereas illness may be autonomy reducing – and this is particularly the case in certain types of ill health[17] – autonomous choices can also be made within the context of the patient's interaction with medicine. It has also been suggested that the doctor's duty to obtain the consent of his or her patient is a duty which derives from the patient's right. The delineation of that duty therefore is dependent on recognition of, and respect for, such a right.

To this extent, therefore, the duty to obtain a real consent is one which transcends the doctor's professional (technical) expertise. Its boundaries cannot be drawn solely by reference to this expertise, although it is its possession which puts doctors in the situation whereby they are under the duty in question. But the duty is not dependent exclusively on technical skills, although it may have some link with them. Rather, the duty – its nature and content – is specifically correlated to the right from which it derives. To put it another way, there is a very real question as to whether or not the duty can be defined without first establishing the corresponding right. As Skegg, for example, has said:

> There is nothing especially 'medical' about the requirement that a doctor must obtain a patient's consent . . . These requirements are imposed not in the interests of the patient's health, but in the interests of individual liberty.[18]

## Conclusions

It is important, therefore, that this crucial distinction between the types of duties that doctors owe to their patients is borne in mind. On the one hand, there is the set of technical duties, described above, and on the other there is the moral or ethical (but also legal) duty which demands information disclosure. The latter duty is defined not by the amount of information that the doctor thinks the patient should know, could handle or might want to know, but by the amount of information that the patient needs so that they are able to make an autonomous choice. The role of law in our society makes the legal process the commonest and most effective mechanism for providing such definition – for filling out the qualities of the duty owed and protecting the patient whose rights are breached. As has been said in a number of cases this requires a standard for disclosure that is set by law and not by professionals.[19] This implicit recognition of the significance of the right under consideration lends weight to the claim that in considering questions of consent, what is at issue is something more valuable, and certainly more difficult to define, than a professionally given assessment of the technical manner in which acquired skills should have been, or were actually, used.

In this respect, the physician is in no different a position from that of the financial adviser who is required to make full and frank disclosure of a variety of – often incredibly complex – matters to a client. Understanding them is just as likely as understanding the mechanics of surgery, but the client *can* understand the likely drawbacks or the benefits to be accrued from following the professional recommendation, because these are *personal* outcomes.

The duty to disclose information, therefore, can be said to be a professional duty in the sense that it is the duty of the doctor to carry it out in a professional manner – professional, that is, in the broadest sense. Most professionals are routinely faced with the problem of ensuring client understanding, and this can be, in many, if not most, situations, achieved by explanation which avoids technical jargon, and by providing the relevant information in a relatively stress-free setting. Of course, doctors will usually be dealing with a situation that does involve stress, but this does not excuse them from seeking to achieve the standard of professional behaviour that it is reasonable to expect from any group possessing special skills and dealing with basic human rights. The transmission of information is a vital aspect of much professional practice, and can and should be done sensitively and with due regard to the information gap between *any* professional and *any* client.

To sum up this discussion, so far, a number of claims have been made. First it has been suggested that medicine is much more than merely a technical event. Whatever its awe-inspiring capacities it should also acknowledge and foster the rights of patients – individually and collectively – by showing them respect. Second, it has been contended that a fundamental characteristic of showing that respect is the honest provision of information which permits the patient to make a self-determining decision about the personal benefits attached to therapy. And third, it has been claimed that it is incumbent on the law to validate these claims by decision making which prioritizes the rights in question and de-emphasizes the weight of professional opinion. The extent to which the law does this will be considered in the following two chapters.

## Notes

1. 464 F 2d. 772 (1972).
2. At p. 780.
3. Id.
4. Robertson, G., 'Informed Consent to Medical Treatment' (1981) LQR 102.
5. Ibid. at pp. 111–112.
6. At p. 112.
7. C.f. Buchanan, A., 'Medical Paternalism' 7 *Philosophy and Public Affairs* 340 (1978).
8. Cf. Stanway, A., *Alternative Medicine*, Harmondsworth, Penguin, 1983, particularly chapter 1.
9. Cf. Stanway, op. cit., at pp. 16–17, where he claims that only approximately 20 per cent of patients consulting doctors will actually benefit from orthodox medicine – at p. 17 'The other 80% . . . simply don't *need* Western medicine *per se*. Many of them would fare just as well if they didn't live in the sophisticated western world and from a sociological standpoint many would fare better in a society in which family ties were stronger and a sense of close community help more meaningful that it is in the West today.' He continues, at p. 18, 'We have to face up to the fact that modern medicine as we know it has done little to cure or prevent disease when compared with the advantages conferred upon society by good sanitation, improved housing, smaller families and other social improvements.'
10. [1957] 2 All ER 118.
11. At p. 124.
12. Shultz, M. M., 'From informed consent to patient choice: a new protected interest' 95 *Yale Law J.* 219 (1985).
13. At p. 222.
14. Giesen, D., *Medical Malpractice Law*, Gieseking-Verlag, Bielefeld, 1981.
15. At p. 163.
16. This was unequivocally stated in the case of *Maynard* v. *West Midlands R. H. A.* [1985] 1 All ER 635. For further discussion, see chapter 7, infra.
17. For example, severe mental illness.
18. Skegg, P. D. G., *Law, Ethics and Medicine*, Oxford, Clarendon Press, 1984, at p. 85.
19. e. g. *Canterbury* v. *Spence* 464 F 2d. 772 (1972).

# 6 Information disclosure and 'informed consent'

An examination of the way in which litigation is carried out and resolved is admittedly only one way of identifying the actual workings of legal process. In medicine, the law is often not directly involved, since defence organizations will screen out indefensible cases and those thought unlikely to be defensible, and settlements may be reached without resort to courts of law. Access to the information held by defence organizations is notoriously difficult, beyond that which is in the public domain as a result of publication in their annual reports.

However, although it is conceded that this shortfall in information is not unimportant there remain two good reasons for being able to draw conclusions from the actual process of law and reported decisions. In the first place, it is in courts of law that the attitudes of those who shape the law are most clearly expressed, and in the second, even out-of-court settlements will be offered only after the applicability of legal tests has been certified. In other words, defence organizations will – on legal advice – settle cases where that advice suggests that they would be compensable according to the rules laid down by the courts.[1]

From the point of view of this discussion, analysis of court decisions is even more instructive. If the contention that disclosure is a non-technical, non-professional matter is accepted, then one can legitimately expect courts to assess the quality of disclosure by direct reference to the interests at stake. Of course, this also assumes that the interest is one which is regarded as having legal, as well as moral and social, significance.

The law is not entirely value blind in making decisions about the relative weight of competing interests. Additional factors can be and are used to influence decisions. There is, and perhaps must be, a hierarchy of interests deemed worthy of protection.[2] This has particular significance for the practice of medicine and will be discussed in more depth below.

But the laws of tort or delict also have a symbolic purpose.

Although British courts do not routinely couch decisions in terms of human rights, essentially it is rights which are being protected when losses are distributed and claims recognized as meretricious. The symbolic significance of this should not be underestimated, particularly in countries without written constitutions where the language of rights must arise from social rather than constitutional consensus. Where reference can be made to constitutional principles it is more common to couch civil obligations in terms of the rights to which they relate. From the right to liberty, for example, enshrined in the United States Constitution stem other rights (such as the so-called right to privacy which forms the basis of a woman's absolute right to pregnancy termination in the first trimester of her pregnancy)[3] and also a number of duties to respect rights and not to intrude, for example by photographing private property or interfering in legitimate behaviour.[4] Equally, in the United Kingdom jurisdictions, '[i]n addition to its more obvious function of redressing harms the law of tort also indicates rights: it has a constitutional as well as a compensatory function.'[5]

In some sense, therefore, the decision makers – that is the judiciary – are also representing more than just disinterested law. But interests must also be legally recognized. As Walker says:

> It does not necessarily follow from the assertion of some right as a natural right or a human right, or as an individual or social interest, that the law will protect it and enforce legal rights and duties arising therefrom. Whether or not to recognise some interest is a policy decision for the law.[6]

The judiciary, therefore, also represent the state and give credence (or not) to the claims of individuals or groups that they have a particular right or interest which is worthy of protection, as well as making the consequential assessment of whether or not the right has been invaded. A creative judiciary can have an important impact on the social order, whereas a judiciary loath to conceptualize rights may equally have a deleterious effect on the range of rights accorded to citizens. Personal liberty can be defined, delimited or destroyed by conservative decision making or reinforced, expanded and vindicated by radical thinking.

It is conventional wisdom that US courts are considerably more wedded to rights discourse than are their British counterparts. For our purposes their most notable contribution has been in their development of the legal doctrine of informed consent and their tussles with the appropriate test to be used in assessing whether or not consent really was 'informed'. Although the terminology of 'informed consent' has been deliberately avoided here, because of potentially unwanted consequences which can flow from it, the development of the doctrine pointed the way towards the possibility of a recognition of the rights of patients to receive information before making decisions about therapy. For that reason, the doctrine and its implementation merit consideration. In particular it will be interesting to see if the doctrine has *in fact* led to a firm commitment to the rights of patients to receive and use information. Given the contention here that such recognition can be adequate only where the law will separate the technical and the moral aspects of medicine. The statements made by US courts will be examined primarily from this perspective.

It should also be said at this stage that the discussion will be conducted within the framework of negligence analysis, since it is clear in Anglo-American jurisprudence that, except in the rarest of cases, which might trigger the use of assault analysis,[7] the negligence action will be the appropriate source of redress. Although this has not been specifically tested in Scots law, it seems unlikely that the Scottish judiciary would adopt a different approach, although they are technically able to do so.

## Development of consent doctrines – USA

The rules governing the negligence action in both the USA and the United Kingdom are developed from broadly similar legal traditions and not surprisingly, therefore, tend to be roughly parallel. Yet, United States courts have occasionally shown a more aggressive stance in cases that they see as involving issues of fundamental values and rights. It is scarcely surprising, then, that American jurisprudence seems to have been more overtly concerned with patient choice – hence the development of what has come to be called 'informed consent'.[8] However, there are interpretational problems in the use of the word 'informed' which can make it a less than satisfactory qualification of consent. Thus, throughout this discussion, the writer will prefer to use 'real' or 'meaningful' consent based on information disclosure – disclosure of risks, therapeutic alternatives and potential benefits. The last of these is in any event uncontroversially a routine part of medical treatment and consultation. It is, therefore, with the first and second that this section is primarily concerned.

The classic statement in *Schloendorff*[9] as early as 1914 shows the American courts' interest in personal autonomy. At a theoretical level, it is the case that all developed jurisdictions share this concern, but it is also crucial that the rhetoric of rights-protection is translated into the reality of securing those rights. As Shultz notes:

Individuality and autonomy have long been central values in Anglo-American society and law. In general, the more intense and personal the consequences of the choice and the less direct or significant the impact of that choice upon others, the more compelling the claim to autonomy in the making of a given decision. Under this criterion, the case for respecting patient autonomy and decisions about health and bodily fate is very strong.[10]

In 1981, in the case of *Hunter* v. *Burroughs*,[11] the court made it clear that the doctor has a duty 'in the exercise of ordinary care to warn a patient of the danger of possible bad consequences of using a remedy.'[12] As concern about patient autonomy grew, and as doctors became more frequent subjects of challenge in the courts, these somewhat loosely drafted statements became more closely defined, and the shape of what was to become the doctrine of consent became more clear. Perhaps the most significant case at this early stage was the case of *Salgo* v. *Leland Stanford*[13] in which possibly the first real attempt was made to outline the scope of the doctrine. As the court said:

> A physician violates his duty to his patient and subjects himself to liability if he withholds any facts which are necessary to form the basis of an intelligent consent by the patient to the proposed treatment.[14]

From this innovative statement, however, are also apparent some of the difficulties of the use of 'informed' as legally accepted terminology in deciding on the validity of a given consent.

If 'informed' is to be used in constant conjunction with consent, then it must have a meaning relevant to the description of a legally acceptable consent. 'Informed', of course, could be said only to imply that information has been given and received. However, implicit in the above judgement is a further qualification which merits consideration as it is inherent, apparently, in the entire doctrine of 'informed consent', and renders this straightforward assumption less easily tenable.

The court, by phrasing the doctrine in this way, left the door wide open for the kind of interpretation which has, in fact, subsequently proved to be problematic for the aggrieved patient. 'Informed consent' depends on disclosure of information which enables a patient to make an 'intelligent' choice, not simply to make a choice. However, what *are* those facts which are necessary to make an 'intelligent' decision? What indeed, *is* an 'intelligent' decision? In effect, the court described what seemed to be a set of conditions for safeguarding patient autonomy, but additionally gave a hostage to fortune by countenancing, not full disclosure, but rather disclosure which facilitates an 'intelligent' choice. This could readily be taken to infer that the quality of the disclosure will, at least in part, be implied from the quality of the decision. Given what has already been said about the rationality of patient choice, it may, then, be arguable that an 'intelligent' choice is one approved by physicians. If this interpretation is adopted, then doctors would not be liable for failing to disclose information that would prevent acceptance of therapy. In other words, a decision on the questions posed above could be taken by reference to the views of the physician, subject only to the *caveat* that a duty to disclose does exist. However, it would be well to bear in mind that '[e]xperts may blind themselves by expertise. The courts should protect the citizen against risks which professional men and others may ignore.'[15]

This case is also atypical in that the court's view was that failure to obtain informed consent rendered the doctor liable in trespass rather than negligence. In *Natanson* v. *Kline*[16] (1960) the court reaffirmed the duty of the physician to make reasonable disclosure of risks, but regarded the decision as to whether or not disclosure was reasonable as one to be taken within negligence analysis. The shift to the negligence action has been described as one which de-emphasizes patient autonomy, since it concentrates on descriptions of duties rather than rights. This is blamed by some for an alleged over-dependence on professional descriptions of the behaviour in question, which could only be remedied by analysing the nature of the duty of care by direct and uncompromising reference to the right from which it is derivative.

Of course, if the issue *is* solely the execution of technical professional duties then it is logical for the court to accept a substantial, or at least important, medical input into the decision as to what and whether to disclose. The case is, therefore, decided by reference to medical duties, and only tangentially depends on the question of patients' rights. The shift to the negligence action, therefore, can be seen as having the almost inevitable (and legally logical) consequence of moving the focus of interest from patient autonomy to the standards accepted in medical practice.

These cases, whatever their shortcomings, were landmark decisions in the development of disclosure rules. Not only did they herald legal concern about information disclosure in medicine, but they also proffered both a definition (of a sort) of what consent rules should be, and a statement as to the appropriate form of action. This had wide reaching consequences, not only for the nature of the proof required for a successful action, but also for the types of evidence which could decide the case. That is, placing information disclosure firmly within the negligence framework emphasized that the crucial question is whether or not a doctor has failed in a duty (which his or her colleagues have a role in defining)

– thus shifting the ultimate responsibility for therapeutic decisions from the competent patient, and placing some (occasionally major) decision-making control firmly in the hands of the doctor.

Emerging from these cases also is what has come to be called the 'reasonable doctor' standard, or the professional test for negligence. In other words, the 'realness' or validity of apparent consent depends not on what the patient claims to have wanted to know, but rather on whether or not physicians regard the failure to disclose a given piece of information as having been professionally reasonable. Inevitably, therefore, this places the definition of 'reasonableness' for these purposes firmly within the competence of professionals and renders the court's ultimate function, of deciding on whether or not it actually was reasonable, vulnerable to medical pressure. Thus, unlike the common sense view which can be taken of the 'reasonable man', courts must weigh heavily medical evidence of current practice in deciding what the reasonable doctor would have done or for what he or she should be held liable. Policy considerations are therefore as likely to be imported into the area of information disclosure as they are into technical issues in medical behaviour. The courts in the United States were, at this stage, unwilling to make a distinction between the technical and the moral aspects of medical behaviour. Unwilling, therefore, to consider information disclosure as more than – perhaps even distinct from – the doctor's general professional duty of care to the patient.

The 'reasonable doctor' test received considerable support over the next few years and indeed continues to be the standard used in most American States.[17] However, the issue did not die there and other courts were prepared to reconsider this formulation of the appropriate values and interests involved in information disclosure. The most significant of these cases was the landmark decision in *Canterbury* v. *Spence*[18] in 1972. In this case, the court addressed itself to the rationale for disclosure rules and in so doing placed considerable emphasis on the right of the patient to receive information – a right which admittedly could only be satisfied by the doctor fulfilling a correlative duty to make that disclosure, but one, none the less, which generated, rather than was subordinate to, the duty. In so doing, the court distinguished neatly between those aspects of medical practice that are called technical and those that are not. As the court said:

> The context in which the duty of risk disclosure arises is invariably the occasion for the decision as to whether a particular treatment procedure is to be undertaken. To the physician, whose training enables a self-satisfying evaluation, the answer may seem clear, but it is the prerogative of the patient, not the physician, to determine

for himself the direction in which his interests seem to lie. To enable
the patient to chart his course understandably, some familiarity with
the therapeutic alternatives and their hazards becomes essential.[19]

At first sight, the decision in *Canterbury* seems to redress the balance
in favour of patient's rights. By making the distinction between
medical practice and the moral nature of the medical enterprise,
they moved towards the very basis of consent rules and requirements about information disclosure. Indeed, the court explicitly
acknowledged this distinction by indicating that interests other
than the purely medical are intimately connected with the ultimate
assessment of liability. As the court put it:

> We agree that the physician's non-compliance with the professional
> custom to reveal, like any other departure from prevailing medical
> practice, may give rise to liability to the patient. We do not agree that
> the patient's cause of action is dependent upon the existence and
> non-performance of a relevant professional tradition.[20]

Thus, although medical evidence as to standard practice was seen
as informative, it was not regarded as being definitive of good or
acceptable practice. In this case the court made clear its concern
that such should not be the case, seeing 'formidable obstacles to
acceptance of the notion that the physician's obligation to disclose
is either germinated or limited by medical practice'.[21]
But what are these obstacles, if they do not indicate that what is
being dealt with is an issue bigger than medical choice about the
need for, and type of, therapy? If the therapeutic imperative is not
to be dominant, on what grounds is this so? Quite simply, the
overriding value of therapy – while it may be agreed upon by
the medical world – is not, and cannot be, the most significant
characteristic in disputes about non-disclosure, if such disclosure is
required as a means of safeguarding the rights of patients – rights
which go beyond the fact of illness, alleviation of symptoms, or
even potential or probable cure. What is significant is the right of the
patient to autonomy and this right is one which is not minimized in
the standard medical interaction, nor is it one which can be
described by physicians themselves. As the court said, '[r]espect
for the patient's right of self-determination on particular therapy
demands a standard set by law rather than one which physicians
may or may not impose upon themselves.'[22] This was intended
neither to disvalue therapy nor to criticize medical practitioners but
rather to demonstrate the significance of the values to be protected
by information disclosure – values which the law reserves the right
to assess, and has the ultimate duty to secure.
Thus far, the court seemed to be unequivocally interested in

patients' rights, albeit within the context of negligence analysis. Reference to patient autonomy as the fundamental value in non-disclosure cases has been echoed in a number of subequent decisions, although it has not routinely formed the basis of decisions in many American States, nor in other countries throughout the world.[23] Indeed, despite a plea for acceptance of the *Canterbury* Test by Lord Scarman in *Sidaway*,[24] it remains by no means the standard test used. This is so despite the manifest philosophical problems in the 'prudent doctor' test.

In fact, however, the *Canterbury* case itself showed unfortunate equivocation, resembling that seen in the 'reasonable doctor' test. The court continued to emphasize the significance of choice-making by the patient but was forced to confirm the difficulties inherent in deciding how this could be protected. At first sight, it might seem logical that the emphasis on self-determination so evident in this case, would inevitably lead to the conclusion that all relevant information, which is within the knowledge of the doctor, should be disclosed to the patient. Theoretically it would seem that only in this way can the patient's autonomy actually be protected. Each possible risk, however slight – statistically or in terms of its consequences – might be valued by a patient in a way quite distinct from the weight accorded to it by a doctor or a court. This the court accepted.[25] However, there were further considerations taken to be significant, not least the role of the law itself. The court was faced with the task of formulating a definition of consent which was 'informed' or real but which permitted co-operation rather than confrontation between the doctor and the law. Indeed, the judgement *ab initio* shows marginal ambivalence on the issue of patients' rights to information disclosure – an ambivalence which is central to the standard ultimately formulated.

A number of factors seem to have contributed to this. Much concern, for example, has been expressed about the extent to which the liability of physicians would be expanded were the patient able to claim that the omission of any one piece of information resulted in legal liability. Patients, it has been suggested, could thereby give vent to their understandable disappointment, or even bitterness, when their contact with medicine goes wrong. Naturally, it is said, the patient will complain when something bad happens, but this cannot, it is contended, be given ultimate credence.[26] It was in this respect that the court ran up against its most significant difficulty in formulating an appropriate standard. On the one hand, in repudiating the professional test, the court placed considerable emphasis on the rights of the patient. On the other, however, too severe a standard was thought to place the entire practice of medicine at risk, by denying clinical freedom and generating excessive litigation.

Moreover, it was clear that problems could arise in settling appropriately and satisfactorily the question of causation. As has been said, where the basis of the action is negligence, it is necessary not only to decide what the duty owed actually was, and whether or not it was breached, but it must also be shown that the breach caused harm. In allegations that information disclosure was not adequate this may be problematic. Patients may be aggrieved if all information is not disclosed, on grounds which sit uncomfortably within the traditional negligence framework or which are not compensable in negligence analysis. They may feel that their right to self-determination was shown insufficient respect where a risk was concealed, even if that risk does not actually occur. Despite the fact that damages for invasion of personal integrity might be relatively small, none the less patients may feel that they should be entitled to register a complaint through the court process, and that they would be justified in obtaining some compensation for the unwarranted assumption of authority over their integrity.

However, there are limitations on the type of damage which is legally recognized, and this may pose considerable problems for the patient.[27] Further, there is a problem in squaring respect for human rights with the aims of the negligence action. Even where it is accepted that the basis of disclosure rules is the patient's right to self-determination, the very nature of the negligence action demands some form of rationalization. The action is ill-designed to cater for the immediate concerns of the individual, since the ultimate determination of whether or not there is negligence rests, not on theoretical considerations, but on an assessment of the extent or the manner in which *duties* were carried out.

Despite this court's concession that the provision of information about risks was something wider than the merely technical, other courts have long failed to make this distinction. Consider, for example, the views of Mr Justice Woodhouse in the case of *Smith* v. *Auckland Hospital Board*.[28]

> If the issue in the case was the maintenance of the individual's right of self-determination, the matter would quickly resolve itself. But it is not. This is a question within the duty of care concept in negligence . . . Negligence is not concerned with injury to dignity, but to the body or property. The philosophical consideration should not be allowed to submerge every other.[29]

If the source of the action is indeed not solely the protection of integrity, then inevitably patients whose case consists of an allegation that their integrity was invaded, will have little hope of success. In any event, it is vital that there is a causal relationship between the wrong complained of and the subsequent harm.[30] In a situation where the patient's claim is satisifed by demonstrating that risks were not disclosed (not that they actually occurred), the source of the harm complained of is relatively straightforward – essentially a matter of fact. However, policy considerations can and do influence decisions, and courts have continued to balk at the provision of redress, and the imputation of negligence, where no measureable harm has actually arisen. The patient will, in these circumstances, find the negligence action considerably less than sympathetic to their claims. As was said in the case of *Dessi* in 1980:

> Support for the subjective theory [of consent] derives from the broad principle underlying informed consent that a man is the master of his own body and may deal with it in whatever way he wishes, however irrational.[32]

In this case, as in *Canterbury* v. *Spence*,[32] this approach was, however, not ultimately held to be practical. Not only was there concern about the perceived likelihood of patients not telling precisely the truth, or at least being influenced by hindsight, but also the law's own need to have consistently applicable tests against which behaviour can be measured means that a subjective test sits ill with negligence analysis.

Some courts have been unprepared to give credibility to the professional test, but it was imperative that *a* test was available for use. This test, developed in *Canterbury* v. *Spence*, has come to be called the 'prudent patient' test – an objective test. However dificult it may seem to be to reconcile patient autonomy with anything other than a subjective test, such reconciliation was felt to be necessary, both to protect the general beneficence of medicine and the medical act, and to satisfy the rules of the law itself. Thus, the court made a brave attempt to marry two apparently conflicting aims. The formula was put thus:

> True consent to what happens to oneself is the informed exercise of a choice and that entails an opportunity to evaluate knowledgeably the options available and the risks attendant upon each. The average patient has little or no understanding of the medical arts and ordinarily has only his physician to whom he can look for enlightenment with which to reach an intelligent choice. From these almost axiomatic considerations springs the need, and in turn the requirement, of a reasonable divulgence by physician to patient to make such a decision possible.[33]

The crucial features of this last passage are the insertion of the words 'reasonable' before 'divulgence' and 'intelligent' before

'choice'. 'Intelligent' choices may take a number of forms, and
are open to considerable variations of interpretation. If 'intelligent'
choices are measured at the personal level then they may be defined
as 'intelligent' or rational even where the doctor or the judge might
have decided in a different way. Equally, what is 'reasonable'
disclosure will depend on the premise from which analysis begins.
To the patient, 'reasonable' disclosure might mean full disclosure,
whereas to the doctor 'reasonable' might merely mean disclosure
only of information which gives the patient a broad notion of the
possible risks, or some of them, but which equally does not deter
the patient from accepting recommended therapy. Provision of
further information, following this argument, might seem to be
folly – merely serving to increase the possibility that the patient
will make an unintelligent or medically irrational choice.

That the court was aware of these possibilities is not in doubt,
and if it was to maintain the appropriateness of these qualifications,
and of the use of negligence analysis, then some definition of what
was meant by these ambivalent words was necessary. It was in
undertaking this exercise that the movement away from strict
adherence to patient autonomy was most observable. As the court
in *Dessi* put it:

> To inject a reasonable man standard into this [subjective] determi-
> nation arguably undermines the patient's right to make his own
> decision. While this is a theoretically appealing rationale it ignores
> the practical problem with reliability of proof.[34]

In reality, this statement recognizes the very problems which the
*Canterbury* test sought to overcome. Dissatisfaction with merely
acting on the word of the patient, and the corresponding fear of
an unacceptable increase in litigation and expansion of liability,
were thought to vindicate both the use of the negligence action and
the setting of objective tests.

On the one hand, of course, this approach may protect the patient
by offering a standard which is separable – at least in theory – from
the professional test. That is, it is a standard set by law. On the
other hand, however, it generates the need for rationalized assessment of what the reasonable patient would have wanted in the way
of disclosure. Even if this standard is set by law, it will almost
inevitably be distanced to some extent from the views of the individual patient. Indeed, Mr Justice Woodhouse himself, whose
judgement in *Smith*[35] reinforced the professional test, and suggested
that the negligence action was appropriate, became, several years
later, one of the major critics of the negligence action, noting among
other things, its incapacity to make decisions in the instant case,

and its need to rationalize decision making to the extent that neither is the individual satisifed nor is there truly an assessment of the behaviour of the individual defender.[36]

The court in *Canterbury*, therefore, sought to offer a formulation which both satisfied the requirements of the negligence action itself, and represented a way of avoiding the over-expansion of liability which could result from a legal requirement to make full disclosure to patients. This is the 'prudent patient' test, formulated in this way:

> . . . the test for determining whether a particular peril must be divulged is its materiality to the patient's decision: all risks potentially affecting the decision must be unmasked. And to safeguard the patient's interest in achieving his own determination on treatment, the law must itself set the standard of adequate disclosure.[37]

However, this formulation evidently fails to answer the question as to how, without actually making the disclosure, it can be known whether or not any given piece of information would have a potential effect on the patient's decision. Who decides this? It is here that the move from the rhetoric of rights to the hard practicalities of 'realism' can be seen. Were commitment to patient autonomy truly regarded as the fundamental interest for protection, then – whatever the problems of proof – full disclosure would inevitably be required. The fact that patients might argue with hindsight in a subsequent court hearing, in essence poses no more difficulty than the assessment of witness credibility and conflicts of interest which are so often required of courts and juries.[38]

Inevitably, however, within negligence analysis, when patients have identified the particular risk of which they were not informed, and which they claim would have affected their decision, the question of reasonableness must be addressed. This, of course, is only true in actions where the mere fact of non-disclosure is not the crucial factor. Absolute commitment to the rights of the patient would obviate the need to decide whether or not the patient was reasonable in claiming that he or she would have refused therapy had a particular risk or cluster of risks been disclosed. The issue would then become one of fact and evidence of non-disclosure would be sufficient to etablish liability. Moreover, reasonableness also features in the assessment of whether or not the risk *should* have been disclosed.

The major breakthrough, however, in the *Canterbury* judgement was the court's insistence that the decision as to reasonableness is separable from professional (medical) assessment. As the court said:

The disclosure doctrine, like others marking lines between permissable and impermissable behaviour in medical practice is in essence a requirement of conduct prudent under the circumstances. Whenever non-disclosure of particular risk information is open to debate by reasonable minded men, the issue is for the finder of the facts.[39]

By this statement the court made it clear that, although the question did not hinge simply on whether or not disclosure had been made, the assessment of whether or not disclosure was appropriate in the circumstances was one which was properly made by the court. In other words, evidence that the doctor acted in good faith, and was not acting outside the bounds of professionalism, could be, but would not necessarily be sufficient to avoid liability.

However, by admitting the possibility that there may be circumstances in which non-disclosure is both prudent and justifiable, the court opened the door to the professional test. It was unprepared to import a subjective test, preferring an objective one, which although much more commonly used in judicial decision making, and fitting in much more easily with the format of the negligence action, none the less diminishes the right of the individual patient. The court regarded it as preferable that, although '. . . the very purpose of the disclosure rule is to protect the patient against consequences which, if known, he would have avoided by foregoing the treatment . . .',[40] the actual quality of disclosure should be tested on an objective standard.

Thus, the decision as to whether or not the patient *would* have avoided the therapy is undertaken by an objective analysis of what the reasonable or prudent patient would have regarded as significant, incorporating assessment of witness (i. e. patient) credibility. While effectively saying that the patient's evidence as to whether or not he or she would have regarded the risk as significant could not necessarily be trusted, the court was nevertheless prepared to give considerable credibility to its *own* view of what would be significant, even although it is inevitably distanced from the views and circumstances of the particular patient. Although this may diminish the input of the medical profession, it merely substitutes a further professional test – albeit the impressions of the judges rather than the doctors. As the court said:

Better it is we believe to resolve the causality issue on an objective basis: in terms of what a prudent person in the patient's position would have decided if suitably informed of all perils bearing significance.[41]

The court effectively, therefore, enunciated a two-fold doctrine. Although generally subsumed under the one heading – that of the 'prudent patient' test – in effect it includes two vital elements. In the first place, the question of which risks should be disclosed is tailored to what resembles a variation on the reasonable doctor standard – a standard which the court actually sought to defeat. That is, the court approved the proposition that disclosure should be of *material* risk, not of every risk.[42] The decision as to what is a material risk is to be made in accordance with the definition given by Waltz and Scheuneman[43] of which the court expressly approved. Thus, a risk is material when:

> . . . a reasonable person, in what the physician knows or should know to be the patient's position, would be likely to attach signifi-cance to the risk or cluster of risks in deciding whether or not to forego the proposed therapy.[44]

Materiality of risk is therefore dependent on medical knowledge – even medical speculation. The *actual* wishes of the patient are subsumed in a variation of 'doctor knows best'. The standard of disclosure under the 'prudent patient' test is, therefore, not so dramatically different from that demanded by the professional stan-dard, since in both cases medical judgement as to what needs to, or should, be disclosed is given legal credibility.

Moreover, in expressly accepting the concept of therapeutic privilege, and thus permitting the non-disclosure of certain risks because the doctor regards them as risks which would distress the patient or which might deter the patient from therapy, the doctor is in real terms given considerable discretion. Ultimately, the position is tautologous. If the patient is to be given the benefit of risk disclosure because he or she has a right to decide whether or not to accept therapy, it is strange indeed that the doctor may equally not disclose risks because they may put the patient off the therapy. The doctor may be shielded therefore by invoking therapeutic privilege so long as there was nothing else in his or her behaviour which was unreasonable or negligent. This is the case, despite the fact that the court did attempt to distinguish the purely medical aspect of the doctor-patient relationship from its other characteristics by noting that '[i]t is evident that many of the issues typically involved in non-disclosure cases do not reside peculiarly within the medical domain.'[45]

However, even under the 'prudent patient' test the reasonable-ness of the doctor's non-disclosure plays a significant part in esti-mating whether or not it is valid, and in this aspect also there is similarity to the 'prudent doctor' test. Just as the latter distances the need for disclosure from the instant patient, so too does the former. Not only does the patient have no immediate rights, therefore, but the assessment of what is a prudent patient will involve assessment of whether or not the therapy, in the eyes of the courts – and given the doctor's claims about the reasonableness of non-disclosure and the anticipated benefits of therapy – *should* have gone ahead.

To some extent, therefore, the 'prudent' patient will be someone who makes a medically (or legally) rational decision, and the group most likely to provide at least persuasive evidence in this assessment will, of course, be doctors thmselves. It is arguable, therefore, that the distinction between the 'prudent doctor' test and the 'prudent patient' test may not be as substantial as it is claimed to be. In the face of perceived difficulties of proof, and the undoubted value assumed in therapy, the patient becomes less of an individual whose own emotional and financial considerations are crucial to the information which they need, and more someone whose views, however strong, are susceptible to external 'objective' decision making.

## Conclusions

In summary, therefore, the American courts have remained relatively committed to a medicalized assessment of the limitations of reasonable risk disclosure. This, despite the fact that the court in *Canterbury* acknowledged the difficulties of using professional tests. As Robertson points out:

> Two reasons in addition to the patient's right to self-determination, were given by the court to justify this departure from the established view that the meaning of 'reasonable disclosure' was a matter for the medical profession to determine. First, it was thought that a standard of disclosure based on the custom of the medical profession could be a facade for non-disclosure. Secondly, the court felt that the question of what risks a person would regard as material was an issue which could be determined without special knowledge of medical science.[46]

It was suggested at the beginning of this chapter that American courts have traditionally shown overt concern for matters of human rights in general, and rights in medicine as a sub-species of this. Analysis of their actual formulation of the weight to be attached to the competing interests involved, however, tends to point to a conclusion that decisions are still considerably influenced by the evidence of colleagues of the professional whose behaviour is under scrutiny. To this extent, not even the 'prudent patient' test can succeed in vindicating any right of the patient to receive full information about risks, benefits and alternatives in therapy.

Equally, although paying lip-service – and in *Canterbury* perhaps even more than that – to the separation of the moral and technical aspects of medical practice, the position remains that, consciously or unconsciously there *is* a presumption that professional expertise can validly be drawn on in defence of limited or non-disclosure. Even in rights-conscious America, therefore, the trap is not avoided altogether even by the most progressive decisions.

In part, of course, this stems from the use of negligence analysis itself. Without the assertion of the priority of rights over duties – and in particular the right to receive information and the corresponding duty to provide it – negligence analysis continues to incorporate presumptions about the totality of behaviour which deny the constituent parts. A patient who is not told of risks or alternative therapies may well be helped by the recommended therapy, and may indeed have been made confused or anxious had these been disclosed, but the patient has also been denied the opportunity to learn from this experience, to weigh the stress or confusion appropriately, to ask for clarification and to make an autonomy-enhancing decision. That the law fails to recognize the value of this, and to compensate for invasion, is a clear and unequivocal sign that it is – to date at least – not truly prepared to give precedence to patients' rights, however impressive its rhetoric.

## Notes

1. For discussion of the role of defence organizations, see e. g. Harland, W. A. and Jandoo, R. S., 'The medical negligence crisis' 24 *Med. Sci. Law*, 123 (1984); Hawkins, C., *Mishap or Malpractice*, London, Blackwells, 1985.
2. Cf. Harris, P., *An Introduction to Law*, (2nd edn) London, Weidenfeld and Nicolson, 1984; Walker, D. M., *The Law of Delict in Scotland*, (2nd edn revised) Edinburgh, W. Green and Son Ltd., 1981, at pp. 8–9 'The social function of the law of delict is to give legal recognition and protection to certain valuable interests of the individual and of groups of individuals and corporate persons. Interests are those claims or demands or desires which human beings seek to satisfy, which the legal ordering of human relationships must take account of, and which are deemed by the law to be valuable, deserving of protection, and justifying retribution or compensation if interfered with.'
3. *Roe* v. *Wade* 93 S Ct 705 (1973); *Thornburgh* v. *American College of Obstetricians and Gynecologists* 476 US 747 (1986).
4. Cf. *Katz* v. *United States* 389 US 347 (1967).
5. Weir, T., *A Casebook on Tort*, (5th edn) London, Sweet and Maxwell, 1983 at p. 5.
6. Walker, op. cit., at p. 9.
7. Cf. *Chatterton* v *Gerson & Anor*. [1982] 1 All ER 257; *Natanson* v *Kline* 186 Kan 393 (1960). For a US history of the shift from assault to negligence, see Shultz, M. M., 'From informed consent to patient choice: a new protected interest' 95 *Yale Law J*. 219 (1985); see also Robertson, G., 'Informed consent to medical treatment' (1981) 97 LQR 102.

8.  For discussion, see Robertson, loc. cit; Skegg, P. D. G., 'Informed consent to medical procedures' (1975) 15 *Med. Sci. Law* 124; Brazier, M., 'Informed consent to surgery' (1979) 19 *Med. Sci. Law* 49; Strong, 'Informed consent: theory and policy' (1979) 5 *J. Med. Ethics* 196; Meisel, M., 'The expansion of liability for medical accidents: from negligence to strict liability by way of informed consent', 56 *Neb. Law Rev.*' 51 (1977); Kussman, R. S., 'Informed consent: new rulings, new concepts, new terms', *Legal Aspects Med. Pract.* 4 (1981); Picard, E., 'Consent to medical treatment in Canada' 19 *Osgoode Hall Law J.* 140, (1981).

9.  *Schloendorff* v. *Society of New York Hospitals* (1914) 105 NE 92.

10. loc cit, at p. 220.

11. 123 Va 113 (1918).

12. At pp. 133–134.

13. 154 Cal App 2d 560, 317 P 2d 170 (1957).

14. Ibid., at p. 578; 317 P 2d at pp. 180–181.

15. Montrose, J. L., 'Is negligence an ethical or sociological concept?' (1958) 21 MLR 259, at p. 263.

16. Supra cit. at p. 410 (350 P 2d at p. 1106) the court said that the doctor had a duty to make a 'reasonable disclosure . . . of the nature and probable consequences of the suggested or recommended . . . treatment, and . . . a reasonable disclosure of the dangers within his knowledge which are incident to, or possible in, the treatment which he proposes to administer.'

17. Cf. Mason, J. K. and McCall Smith, R. A., *Law and Medical Ethics*, (2nd edn), London, Butterworths, 1987, n. 11, p. 154 'Approximately three-quarters of the United States adhere to a professional standard.'

18. 464 F 2d 772 (1972); see also, Seidelson, 'Medical malpractice: informed consent in "full disclosure" juridictions' 14 *Duq. Law Rev* 309 (1976).

19. At p. 779.

20. At p. 781

21. At p. 782

22. At p. 784.

23. See note 17 supra; see also *Smith* v. *Auckland Hospital Board* [1964] NZLR 241, [1965] NZLR 191 (New Zealand); *Male* v. *Hopmans et al.* (1965) 54 DLR (2d) 592; *Kenny* v. *Lockwood* [1932] 1 DLR 507; *Reibl* v. *Hughes* (1980) 114 DLR (3d) 1 (Canada); *Battersby* v. *Tottman and State of South Australia* (1985) 37 SASR 524 (Australia); but see also, *Crichton* v. *Hastings et al.* (1972) 29 DLR (3d) 692; *Hopp* v. *Lepp* (1979) 98 DLR (3d) 464.

24. *Sidaway* v. *Bethlem Royal Hospital Governors & Ors.* [1985] 1 All ER 643 (HL)

25. At p. 779. 'The context in which the duty of risk-disclosure arises is invariably the occasion for the decision as to whether a particular treatment procedure is to be undertaken. To the physician, whose training enables a self-satisfying evaluation, the answer may seem clear, but it is the prerogative of the patient, not the physician, to determine for himself the direction in which his interests seem to lie.'

26. C.f. *Dessi* v. *USA* 489 F Supp. 722 (1980) 'Support for the subjective theory [of consent] derives from the broad principle underlying informed consent that a man is the master of his own body and may do with it whatever he wishes, however irrational. To inject a reasonable man standard into this determination arguably undermines the patient's right to make his own decision. *While this is a theoretically appealing rationale, it ignores the practical problem with reliability of proof.*' (emphasis added).

27. For discussion, see Walker, op. cit.; *Winfield and Jolowicz on Tort*, op. cit.; Atiyah, P. S., *Accidents, Compensation and the Law*, (3rd edn) London, Weidenfeld & Nicolson, reprinted 1984, ch. 4.

28. Supra cit.
29. At p. 247
30. E. g. in *Chrichton* v. *Hastings et al.* 29 DLR (3d) 692 (1972), Brooke, J. A. (dissenting) said, at p. 704: 'Mere failure to warn is not actionable negligence. It must be established that such failure caused or contributed to the respondent's injury and damage.'
31. 489 F Supp. 722 (1980)
32. Supra cit.
33. At p. 705.
34. Supra cit., note 31.
35. Supra cit.
36. Report of the Royal Commission of Inquiry on Compensation for Personal Injuries in New Zealand (Government Printer, New Zealand, 1967); for further discussion, see chapter 7, infra.
37. At p. 221.
38. See e. g. *Thake* v. *Maurice* [1986] 1 All ER 497, per Nourse, J, at p. 511: 'The function of the court in ascertaining objectively the meaning of words used by contracting parties is one of everyday occurrence. But it is often extremely difficult to discharge it where the subjective understandings and intentions of the parties are clear and opposed.'; on witness hindsight, see *Carmarthenshire C. C.* v. *Lewis* [1955] AC 549.
39. At p. 512
40. At p. 511
41. At p. 512
42. At pp. 786–7: 'Thus, the test for determining whether a particular peril must be divulged is its materiality to the patient's decision: all risks potentially affecting the decision must be unmasked.'
43. 'Informed consent to therapy' 64 *NWUL Rev.* 628.
44. Ibid. at p. 780.
45. At p. 782
46. Loc. cit. at p. 106.

# 7 Information disclosure – UK

British courts routinely pay less verbal attention to the language of human rights, but this is not to say that they do not recognize them, nor that they do not regard them as significant. Merely, their language differs from that of their American counterparts. Thus, it is equally fundamental to British law and legal process that basic rights are protected, and that remedies are made available to redress legitimate grievances. The form of the available remedy will, as in the United States, play a part in determining the ease with which redress can be obtained. Until recently British courts have apparently given little consideration to the question of what information must be disclosed before a medical consent is real and effective.[1] The negligence action has long been preferred and what is generally under consideration, therefore, is primarily whether or not the doctor acted in a professionally acceptable way. Robertson[2] suggests that there effectively was no doctrine specifically applying to the disclosure of information in British law until the 1970s, and the case of *Chatterton* v. *Gerson*.[3] This, of course, does not mean that such matters were not considered in the past, but rather that no special status had been accorded to the question of consent by British courts, even in those cases where it was central to the issue.

The leading cases which Robertson uses to substantiate this suggestion are the cases of *Hatcher* v. *Black*[4] and *Bolam* v. *Friern Hospital Management Committee*.[5] Both, according to Robertson, demonstrate that there was no comprehensive or comprehensible doctrine relating to 'informed' or real consent in medical cases.[6] Certainly in neither case was there an enunciation of a special doctrine of consent, and the emphasis on patient's rights which could be encapsulated in such a doctrine seems to be quite clearly lacking.

While their American colleagues struggled to find an acceptable test to measure the scope of necessary disclosure and the situations in which it must, could, or should be made, British courts tended to remain comfortable with a relatively simplistic professional model. The two significant characteristics of the application of the negligence action in medical cases in the United Kingdom have been the almost overwhelming weight placed on medical judgement and the deference shown to orthodox medicine and its therapies. Thus, even the Royal Commission on Civil Liability and Compensation for Personal Injury (Pearson Commission),[7] when considering problems of disclosure suggested that, '[a] balance has to be maintained between the possible consequences of treatment and the possible outcome if treatment is not carried out.'[8] In other words, what is weighed in the scales of justice when it is alleged that insufficient information has been disclosed, will inevitably bear in mind the potential benefit of therapy even where this conflicts with the perspective of the individual patient raising the complaint. This deference to the medical view has been identified by a number of writers and is by no means a trivial point. Klass,[9] for example, suggests that this attitude is one possible reason for the huge (and he considers excessive) prescription of drugs in the United Kingdom. Failure to challenge the practice of medical practitioners even in the routine situation has led, or may lead, to general societal unwillingness to challenge other aspects of medicine.

British courts, therefore, have seldom contemplated with any degree of seriousness a deviation from the professional test, which is in practice in medical cases often apparently definitive, rather than merely persuasive. Thus, the professional standard sets the initial pace, and when combined with a desire to protect and advance the 'good' of orthodox medicine, provides a strong disincentive to admit the validity of challenges to medical behaviour. There was, in the United Kingdom, therefore, neither the apparent desire, nor any recognized need, to consider the possible application of an equivalent to (or improvement on) the 'prudent patient' test.

It was said above that the use of the term 'informed' to qualify 'consent' was in many ways problematic, and that for this reason it would not routinely be used in this discussion. Indeed, it has been expressly stated in one English case that informed consent forms no part of the English law[10] – nor, one can reasonably assume, of Scottish law.[11] The difficulties inherent in the use of the concept of being 'informed' will be further discussed below, but for the moment it is necessary only to point out that although eschewing 'informed' consent, British courts do not deny the importance of a real or legal consent – merely they reject the terminology. As Robertson notes:

> It is firmly established in English law that, in the absence of exceptional circumstances, such as an emergency situation, a doctor must

obtain the consent of his patient before undertaking treatment involving physical contact with his patient.[12]

This, however, does not mean merely an overt consent, but rather entails a more complex assessment of the nature and extent of the information disclosed or withheld in order to decide whether or not the patient was both *sciens* and *volens*.[13] The significance of this relates to the fact that the defence of *volenti non fit injuria*[14] will apply where risks are in fact consented to. The doctor who obtains a real consent both protects him or herself against allegations of illegality, and safeguards the moral nature of his or her intervention. As the court said in *Bowater* v. *Rowley Regis B.C.*[15]:

> In regard to the doctrine *volenti non fit injuria*, I would add one reflection of a general kind. That general maxim has to be applied with especially careful regard to the varying facts of human affairs and human nature in any particular case, just because it is concerned with the intangible factors of mind and will . . . A man cannot be said to be truly 'willing' unless he is in a position to choose freely; and freedom of choice predicates . . . full knowledge of the circumstances upon which the exercise of choice is conditioned . . . [16]

However, as has been noted, interpretation of what amounts to a real consent to therapy depends on the assessment of the quality, nature and extent of information disclosure – ultimately, in cases of dispute, assessment by the law. Thus, the method by which challenges are made and the tests applied in decision making will play a crucial role in determining the amount of information disclosure that is legally necessary. They will describe the extent to which the patient has rights to information, and by implication, the extent to which the patient can expect his or her right to self-determination in medicine to be upheld by the law.

The earlier cases such as *Hatcher*[17] and *Bolam*,[18] did not distinguish the provision of information from any other aspect of the doctor's duty of care to his or her patient. No consideration was given to the possibility that there was a difference between technical skills and non-technical skills, nor that the interests protected by rules about disclosure might be of more significance than the possibility, or even probability, of cure or relief of suffering. Thus, although both cases discussed the question of disclosure, they also gave considerable credence to the kinds of arguments so successfully challenged by Buchanan.[19] In *Bolam*, for example, the judge suggested to the jury that where the doctor feels that the therapy in question is the only hope of cure or alleviation of symptoms, and fears that the patient may be put off the therapy if all the risks are made known, then they might not wish to criticize the doctor for failing to inform the patient of the risks – as indeed the jury did not.

The obligation to make disclosure was not denied, but the court chose to see it as defined not in terms of patients' rights, but rather – and very specifically – in terms of doctors' duties. The obligation of the doctor, therefore, was merely to act in a reasonably skilful manner in the exercise of his or her profession. Duties in respect of the provision of information and the exercise of technical skills, were not distinguished in any way, and '. . . the issue of whether this duty encompasses the giving of information relating to risks inherent in the treatment is a question, not of law, but of reasonable medical judgement'.[20]

Again, therefore, the central element in assessing the quality of information disclosure was deemed to be the evidence as to whether or not other doctors, as representatives of a responsible body of medical opinion, would or would not have made it. There are two vital points here. First, the court, of course, can reserve the right to decide that any professional practice is negligent, since professional practice is founded on criteria, and rooted in traditions, which are not necessarily those of the law. Negligence is a legal concept legally defined, and serves a purpose far beyond that which is sought by the development of professional practices and techniques.[21] The law can, and in some situations does, fly in the face of professional practice in the interests of justice.[22] In *Bolam*, however, the court seemed content to bind its own hands and feet to the professional standard, and to shut off the possibility that the law might set different standards. Indeed, there was no serious suggestion that medical evidence as to practice should be anything other than determinative of the issue. Nor was the possibility of deciding between the merits of individual practices seriously countenanced by the court.[23] The so-called *Bolam Test* which emerged from this case indicated that where a doctor acts in accordance with a school of thought accepted as reasonable by a responsible body of medical opinion, then he or she will not be negligent. The effect of this is that the assessment of what amounts to evidence satisfying the legal concept of negligence is determined substantially by the medical profession, and its boundaries are essentially set by medical practice. This is problematic enough in allegations of technical negligence, but how much more problematic when it is not the doctor's skills as a practitioner which are under scrutiny, but his or her response to, and respect for, patients' rights?

In setting this standard for decision making, *Bolam* was the landmark decision in British jurisprudence for some considerable time. The use of the professional test clearly provided the British courts with a manageable instrument, which fitted in well with the nature of the negligence action and with their own preconceptions about the impact of negligence litigation on the practice of orthodox medicine. Scant attention was paid to the claims of patients to have rights in this interaction. Not, that is, rights to a cure, but certainly rights to be respected as human beings and to make choices about their own therapy based on a sufficiency of information. Moreover, the *Bolam* test had found extensive support in subsequent cases, making it the cornerstone of decision making for some time.[24]

In *Thake* v. *Maurice*,[25] for example, the court held out the possibility that the surgeon in question could have provided himself with a legal excuse for his somewhat vague explanation had he claimed that it was not common practice to give any clearer an explanation. As Kerr LJ said:

> It would have been open to the defendant to qualify the answers which he gave either in cross-examination or re-examination, by saying that he did not believe that it was the general practice to give any such warning or that other surgeons might consider this to be necessary. He was given the opportunity of doing so in a later part of his cross-examination when it was suggested to him that he might not have given the warning because this might have caused worry or concern to the plaintiffs, but he did not accept this. Accordingly, . . . in the present case there was nothing to be placed in the balance against the need for the warning which the defendant himself recognised in his evidence.[26]

In sum, therefore, the British courts have made no real pretence at setting anything other than a professional test for disclosure. The emphasis is on the doctor's duty and not on the patient's rights, thus making the evidence of fellow professionals of similar significance in disclosure cases as it is in cases involving the application of technical skills. In fact, only Sir John Donaldson in the Court of Appeal judgement in *Sidaway*,[27] and Lord Scarman[28] in the House of Lords made any real attempt to override the dominance of professional evidence.

Courts, however, have laid down the rough tests to which they hold doctors accountable, and it is therefore possible to argue that there remains the possibility that courts will not place overriding emphasis on the evidence of the doctor and his or her fellow professionals. Also there is a possibility that they can and will consider the question of whether or not a doctor's non-disclosure was negligent in the light of alternative criteria. If this were indeed the case, then the concern generated by the use of the professional test might at best be misplaced, and at worst exaggerated. What, therefore, do the courts have to say about disclosure, independently of the medical profession?

## The duty to disclose

As has already been noted, the duty to make disclosure to a patient is, in British law, apparently an aspect simply of the doctor's general professional duty of care towards his or her patient. However, this need not mean that courts have no say in its definition. Despite the translation of patients' rights into doctors' duties, which seems to be a regular implication of the shift from assault to negligence, the courts could still play a substantial role in protecting patients' rights. In other words, the law could, by setting sufficiently clear and unequivocal standards, still assess the quality of disclosure with a relatively critical eye. Even where the professional test takes priority, this remains possible.

What then is the standard set by British courts? Accepting that neither *Bolam*[29] nor *Hatcher*[30] did any more than tell us that the courts would pay primary attention to evidence of other doctors and to the therapeutic imperative, the case of *Chatterton* v. *Gerson*[31] seems to have been the first to make a real attempt at defining what information should be disclosed in order to make the consent of the patient both technically possible and legally meaningful. *Chatterton* also made it clear that, save in cases of gross failure to disclose, the appropriate form of action lies in negligence. The court stated the doctor's duty of care thus:

> In my judgement there is no obligation on the doctor to canvass with the patient anything other than the inherent implications of the particular operation that he intends to carry out. He is certainly under no obligation to say that if he operates incompetently he will do damage. The fundamental assumption is that he knows his job and that he will do it properly but he ought to warn of what may happen by misfortune however well the operation is performed, if there is a real risk of misfortune inherent in the procedure.[32]

This statement poses a number of problems for the disaffected patient. As Robertson notes:

> The adoption of this standard negligence formula in the present context can be seen to imply that the doctor's duty to disclose the 'real risk' of the operation stems from his overall duty to exercise reasonable care in the treatment of his patient. The doctor is under a duty to take reasonable care to avoid exposing his patient to any foreseeable risk of injury, and, as the decided cases indicate, 'foreseeable risk' is equated with 'real risk'. Thus, it would follow that the source of the duty to inform the patient of the 'real' risk inherent in the proposed treatment is simply the overall duty of care arising from the doctor-patient relationship.[33]

Thus, even the apparent freedom of the court to decide what is 'real' risk, is none the less generally predicated on an assessment that is intimately linked with what is reasonable medical practice in the circumstances, since the obligation to disclose is merely one aspect of the doctor's overall duty of care. Clearly this has implications for patients' rights. Indeed, if this is the test applied, and *Chatterton* has consistently been referred to with approval by subsequent courts,[34] the:

> . . . . disclosure of risks inherent in the proposed treatment will be seen as a product of the doctor's duty of care rather than as a product of the patient's right to self-determination. Thus, since the doctor's duty of care is defined in terms of acting as a reasonable doctor, there is a danger that in the future English courts will see the duty to disclose inherent risks as stemming from the fact that reasonable doctors disclose such risks (which may be subject to rebuttal by medical evidence) rather than from the fact that the patient's rights to self-determination demand such disclosure.[35]

Although somewhat vague, therefore, it can be seen that the risks which British courts expect the doctor to disclose are those which a reasonable doctor would regard as 'real'. As noted in *Chatterton*, this does not include the possibility of negligent performance. The doctor has to show that his or her behaviour in not disclosing the risk was legitimate, either because the risk was not real or because his or her professional colleagues would not have disclosed it. Evidence of either of these would satisfy the court that there was no negligence. To deal with the latter first, it was noted in *Canterbury* v. *Spence*[36] that there are known difficulties in obtaining evidence from a doctor or group of doctors which would indicate that a fellow professional had been negligent. Moreover, taking into account the terms of the *Bolam* test, it is not necessary to show that *all* doctors would support your position – only that a reasonable body of medical opinion would. Thus, even if several groups of reasonable medical practitioners *would* have disclosed the information, the doctor who fails to make such disclosure will not be negligent if one other body of reasonable medical opinion would not have disclosed it. Since medical practice changes, and, as was said in *Thake* v. *Maurice*, '[o]f all the sciences medicine is one of the least exact',[37] it is not unlikely that there *will* exist a body of responsible opinion which does not regard the failure to disclose as being in any way reprehensible.

Moreover, the courts have imported a further refinement which moves the question of what information needs to be disclosed even further from the actual patients in question, and which makes allegations that they would have regarded the risks as 'real' or important subject to even more *caveats*. This further device equates broadly to the 'prudent' or reasonable patient test. In other words, not only is the doctor's behaviour judged in essence by what his or her colleagues have to say about what is acceptable medical practice, but there are further assumptions made both about what the reasonable patient would have known already, and about what he or she would have wished to know. In the case of *Thake* v. *Maurice*, Nourse, LJ, portrayed both the court's role and its dilemma, in this way:

> The function of the court in ascertaining objectively the meaning of words used by contracting parties is one of every day occurrence but is often extremely difficult to discharge it where the subjective understandings and intentions of the parties are clear and opposed . . . In the end, the question seems to be reduced to one of determining the extent of the knowledge which is to be attributed to the reasonable person standing in the position of the plaintiffs.[38]

In this case, the particular question hinged on whether or not the reasonable patient would have understood that tissues, once severed, as in a vasectomy, could regrow and rejoin, thus naturally reversing the effects of the sterilization. The court accepted that it would not be rational to suppose that:

> . . . a reasonable person standing in the position of the plaintiffs would have known that the vasectomy is an operation whose success depends on a healing of human tissue which cannot be guaranteed. To suppose that would be to credit him with omniscience beyond all reason.[39]

In this statement there seems to be some hope for the patient. The fact that the vast majority of medical acts involve technical information and skills about which the patient could not know without the implication of 'omniscience beyond all reason' might make it seem likely that failure to disclose such information would result in the doctor being liable. However, the court immediately qualified this statement, and in so doing considerably undermined its significance for the patient. Nourse, LJ continued:

> But it does seem to me to be reasonable to credit him with the more general knowledge that in medical science, all things, or nearly all things, are uncertain. That knowledge is part of the general experience of mankind, and in my view it makes no difference whether what has to be considered is some form of medical or surgical treatment or the excision, apparently final, of a section of the vas. Doubtless the general experience of mankind will acknowledge the certainty

that a limb, once amputated, has gone forever. Such has been the observation from time immemorial of a species to whom the spectacle of war and suffering is commonplace. But where an operation is of modern origin, its effects untried over several generations, would a reasonable person, confronted even with the words and demonstrations of the defendant in this case, believe that there was not one chance in ten thousand that the object would not be achieved?[40]

Clearly, this question could readily be answered in the affirmative, although the judge chose to answer it in the negative. It is surely stretching what the reasonable patient might know to suggest that it is common knowledge that, in effect, when parts of the body *are* cut to separate them, they can regrow – the example of the amputated limb which the judge himself introduced could, with respect, equally have pointed to the opposite conclusion. Moreover, it is not entirely clear at what point something becomes so routine or well tried that the reasonable patient knows or should know what are its chances of complete success. Indeed, the court may be thought to have introduced this as a rather unsubtle way of avoiding, or attempting to avoid, liability. Why, and indeed how, should the average patient have access to such information?

In this case, the judges seem to have become confused between whether or not a doctor guarantees the absolute success of therapy (which admittedly he or she does not, and cannot), and whether or not the risk of failure is known to the patient. There was no suggestion in this case that the parties would have rejected the therapy had they known the risk of failure, but rather that – had they been alert to this possibility – subsequent difficulties and grief could have been avoided. In other words, the plaintiffs' subsequent freedom to make decisions and to avoid hazard, was severely affected by the failure to give them adequate information – information which would be demanded out of respect for their moral autonomy. Damages were obtained but they were obtained rather on the basis of future limitation of freedom of choice and costs associated with this than on the basis of the failure to disclose.

*Sidaway* v. *Bethlem Royal Hospital Governors and others*[41]

The impact of the *Bolam* test on the development of a body of law supporting or defending patients' rights to information has been substantial. However, it was open to a superior court to modify or overrule this test and to substitute an alternative. Indeed, in an article preceding the *Sidaway* case, Robertson made what amounts to a plea for consideration of this very point, when he said:

> Given that the duty to disclose is regarded as part of the overall duty of care, it seems likely that courts will be willing to accept that a doctor may be justified in withholding information concerning the risks of proposed treatment if he reasonably believes the performance of the treatment to be in his patient's best interests and the patient is likely to refuse the treatment if warned of the risks. This is a potentially far-reaching proposition which militates against the basic premise that the decision to undergo medical treatment should ultimately be that of the patient and not that of the doctor. It is hoped that it is a proposition that English courts will accept only in the most exceptional circumstances.[42]

His hope, therefore, was that the courts would only rarely ally themselves too closely with the interests of the professional group involved. After all, it would be scarcely surprising if doctors were not often to regard therapy as almost inevitably a good thing, or to view disclosure of therapeutic alternatives as unnecessary. To accept this, however, is to ignore the potentially opposing view of the patient who may – if fully informed of likely risks or benefits, or alternative therapies – nevertheless wish to reject the recommended treatment or to opt for one which is not medically optimal, or for none at all.

The *Bolam Test* gives rise to the concern that the disinterested decision making, which can reasonably be expected in a court of law, will effectively be subject to control by the interested professional group, and that thereby the rights of the individual patient will take a poor second place to the protection of the doctor's exercise of clinical judgement. Whatever the motivation of the doctor, and no matter how potentially beneficial the therapy, the choice is that of the patient, and it is for the law to set a standard which clearly takes account of patients' rights. Clearly, the *Bolam Test* is more concerned with professional consensus and standards than it is with the rights of any patient. The therapeutic imperative was given substantial credibility by the court, as was the professional assessment of negligence.

The House of Lords, however, was recently given the opportunity in the *Sidaway* case to pronounce once and for all on the nature and extent of disclosure that is legally acceptable, and on the rationale of rules about disclosure. The *Bolam* test could, if found wanting, have been modified or overruled, and emphasis placed firmly on patients' rights. Indeed, the members of the court were well aware of the problems confronting them, having extensively consulted evidence from a number of jurisdictions and academic writings. Interestingly, the members of the court, while reaching the same conclusions as to liability, did so by different routes. Moreover, in the lower courts, the judgements were so varied that there was some difficulty in reconciling them to each other, and in reconciling some of the judgements to the ultimate decision.[43]

The *Sidaway* case presented unusual difficulties of proof, in that the physician whose behaviour was the subject of the complaint had died in the period between the source of the action and its resolution. Of necessity, therefore, the court was required to speculate on occasion, but this did not prevent Their Lordships from pronouncing clearly on the question of consent to medical treatment and the tests to be applied. From the perspective of the patient, the most supportive judgement was that of Lord Scarman, who – although not dissenting from the final conclusion – none the less was prepared to go considerably further towards the *Canterbury* test than were his colleagues. It is important, therefore, to consider the judgements in some detail since they now provide a clear statement of law for the United Kingdom as a whole. Courts may, of course, try to distinguish this judgement,[44] and Brazier[45] claims that *Sidaway* has not finally settled the law in this area. Merely, she says, *Sidaway* tells us that the 'prudent patient' test is rejected. However, this view is arguable, since the case does seem to settle a number of things unequivocally. First it makes clear that negligence is the appropriate form of action, and second it reinforces the view that medical evidence is highly significant in determining the adequacy of disclosure, thus failing to make a distinction between the technical and the non-technical aspects of a doctor's duty of care.

Interestingly, although the judges agreed on the question of liability, they reached their conclusions from different perspectives and by different means. Lord Scarman's judgement represents the most radical approach and was considered by some to be a sign that the courts were opening up to protection of patients' rights. Lords Diplock, Keith and Bridge, however, presented a different picture, and one which is more clearly in line with earlier decisions. It is to their judgements that discussion will turn first, and thereafter consideration will be made of the extent to which Lord Scarman's opinion, had it been that of the majority, would have given priority to the rights of the patient.

It is also worth, at this point, distinguishing two separate strands of concern. To date, this discussion has concentrated on the emphasis placed by negligence analysis on patients' rights. This is, of course, a very substantial part of the overall picture. There is, however, one further important characteristic of the shift from assault to negligence which has so far not been considered in much depth, and that is the question of causation. This omission has been deliberate, and will be rectified later.

For the moment, however, attention will be focused on the first of these – that is, the way in which the House of Lords described the balance between patients' rights and doctors' duties. It is from this that the first two aspects of the successful negligence action are firmed up – that is, the existence of the duty of care and the shape that duty takes. The causation element logically follows this.

In his judgement in the *Sidaway* case, Lord Diplock, in the first few sentences, seems to take the professional priority for granted. In his introductory remarks he seems to presume that decisions will be taken *by* doctors *for* their patients, noting that there are risks attached to all therapy, but that:

> All these are matters which the doctor will have taken into consideration in determining, in the exercise of his professional skill and judgement, *that it is in the patient's interests that he should take the risk involved and undergo the treatment recommended by the doctor*.[46] (Emphasis added)

The fundamental assumption, therefore, would seem to be that it is for the doctor to weigh in the balance what risks the patient *should* be prepared to take in the interests of the possibility of improvement.[47]

Lord Diplock accepted that it was not certain whether or not the doctor in this case had weighed up these risks or whether or not he had passed them on to Mrs Sidaway, but in any event these considerations were not regarded by him as having major importance or meriting serious consideration. In Lord Diplock's view there was one crucial piece of evidence on which he based his judgement, and this was, in line with the *Bolam Test*, the evidence of other doctors as to whether or not they would have disclosed the information of whose lack Mrs Sidaway subsequently complained. As he said, although the court did not know exactly what the particular doctor had done:

> What we do know, however, and this is in my view determinative of this appeal, is that all the expert witnesses specialising in neurology . . . agreed that there was a responsible body of medical opinion which would have undertaken the operation at the time the neurosurgeon did and would have warned the patient of the risk involved in the operation in substantially the same terms as the trial judge found on the balance of probabilities the neurosurgeon had done, i.e. without specific reference to risk of injury of the spinal cord.[48]

In other words, even although the trial judge was, in fact, in no position to decide what the doctor probably did, and even although his decision flew in the face of the evidence given by Mrs Sidaway, who was actually there to give evidence of what she had been told, the relevant factor was not whether or not the warning actually had been given, but the fact that the other expert witnesses would equally not have given it.

Interestingly, Lord Diplock was vociferous in his praise for the *Bolam Test* on grounds which were scarcely under consideration in this case, where what *was* under consideration was whether or not disclosure of information had been made, and whether or not any lack of disclosure was negligent. However, courts seem to find the spectre of defensive medicine an irresistible tool in their decision making in medical cases, and whatever its relevance (or lack of it) here, Lord Diplock asserted the importance of avoiding the 'American disease' in no uncertain terms. Moreover, he declined to draw any distinction between the exercise of technical skills and that of others. As he said:

> In English jurisprudence the doctor's relationship with his patient which gives rise to the normal duty of care to exercise his skill and judgement to improve the patient's health in any particular respect in which the patient has sought his aid, has hitherto been treated as a single comprehensive duty covering all the ways in which a doctor is called on to exercise his skill and judgement in the improvement of the physical or mental condition of the patient for which his services either as a general practitioner or as a specialist have been engaged. This general duty is not subject to dissection into a number of component parts to which different criteria of what satisfies the duty of care apply such as diagnosis, treatment and advice (including warning of any risks of something going wrong, however skilfully the treatment advised is carried out).[49]

There are a number of interesting features of this assertion, not least that it follows immediately after a passage in which one is reminded that medicine changes and that we should not seek to inhibit such change. Might the law not equally require to modify itself to deal with novel and important situations?

In any event, the judge's refusal to separate the two distinct aspects of the doctor's duty – that is, on the one hand the use of his or her professional skills in diagnosis and identification of the appropriate range of therapy, and on the other hand the more human, and less technical, duty to respect the autonomy of another, by honestly placing the choices before the patient – bodes ill for any serious consideration of patients' rights. Indeed, it seems – as did the *Bolam* case – to suggest that, if the patient has a right at all, it is the right to be treated if the doctor thinks this is a good idea – no more than that. Where it is impossible, however, to disagree with Lord Diplock, is in his somewhat scathing account of the use of the concept of 'informed consent' which – as has been noted above – is generally so beset with *caveats* as to be rather meaningless. As Lord Diplock asked, what is the purpose of a doctrine of this sort when it effectively introduces the notion of the 'objective' or 'reasonable' patient, thus making the assumption that some risks, but not all, need be disclosed? As he enquired:

> On what logical or juristic basis can the need for informed consent be confined to some risks and not extended to others that are also real and who decides which risks fall into which class?[50]

This, of course, is an excellent question, but as a reason for applying the *Bolam Test* it is scarcely convincing. The alternative for the House of Lords was not, and never was, the mere unthinking adoption of tests which Lord Diplock made quite clear were jurisprudentially foreign to English law. It is not beyond the capacity of the law to reject existing tests and come up with another, and yet the tone of his judgement seems to suggest that adoption of one or other of the established tests was indeed the sole option he perceived.

In any event, Lord Diplock was unimpressed by the suggestion that it was possible to differentiate aspects of doctors' behaviour into those which arise from their professional expertise, and those with which they are charged because they are the people with the expertise and therefore the only people in a position to make explanations. This distinction he dismissed.

> To decide what risks the existence of which a patient should be voluntarily warned and the terms in which such warning, if any, should be given, having regard to the effect that the warning may have, is as much an exercise in professional skill and judgement as any other part of the doctor's comprehensive duty of care to the individual patient and expert medical evidence in this matter should be treated in just the same way.[51]

However, merely to assert that this is so does not make it so. Distinctions can be, and have been, drawn, to which Lord Diplock was apparently disinclined to attend.

Moreover, hidden in these words is more than just a simple statement that the disclosure of information is a technical matter. The decision whether or not to disclose information can be regarded as merely the professional exercise of the doctor's skills *qua* doctor, only if it is thought likely to have a significant impact on the patient's choice as to whether or not to accept the recommended therapy; and in fact, only if it is thought likely that the patient would not agree with the professional assessment made by the doctor that therapy, or particular therapy, should be undertaken. When seen in this light, the statement in effect is suggesting that, when the doctor thinks – in the exercise of his or her professional judgement – that the patient should undergo a particular therapy, then the patient should not be given the opportunity to decline. In other words, the perceived value of therapy takes precedence over the patient's rights to reject it (however medically irrational this may seem) and to exercise his or her self-determination knowledgeably and in a calculated fashion. The same is true of choices in respect of therapeutic alternatives.

Equally, it is submitted with respect, that the opinions of Lords Keith and Bridge failed to distinguish between the exercise of technical and other aspects of the doctor's role. In referring with approval to the judgement in *Hunter* v. *Hanley*[52] that, '[i]n the realm of diagnosis and treatment there is ample scope for genuine difference of opinion and one man clearly is not negligent merely because his conclusion differs from that of other professional men . . .',[53] and in applying this to the disagreement among the experts in this case as to whether or not the information would have been disclosed by them, the learned judges arguably mistook the role of information disclosure.

The test in *Hunter* v. *Hanley* (that of failing to act as a doctor of ordinary skill acting with ordinary care) may be a sound basis for deciding technical matters, but it scarcely applies to non-technical ones. This is not to say that Lord Bridge, for example, does not recognize that alternative positions are tenable. There are, he noted, several possible options to be considered. As he said:

> It could be argued that if the patient's consent is to be fully informed, the doctor must specifically warn him of all risks involved in the treatment offered, unless he has some sound clinical reason not to do so. Logically, this would seem to be the extreme to which a truly objective criterion of the doctor's duty would lead.[54]

To dismiss this possibility, as Lord Bridge does, because it is not a feature of any jurisdiction to which the court was referred, seems somewhat disingenuous. However, neither was Lord Bridge prepared, at least overtly, to support what he saw as the opposite side of this extreme – that is, that doctors should not disclose information merely because to do so would alarm the patient. Unfortunately, not only does he fail to make a distinction between the technical and non-technical impact of a doctor's practice, even while accepting the importance of the patient's right to self-determination, but he then makes the fundamental mistake of assuming that the nature of the information to be disclosed is of a technical sort.

There is a certain ambivalence in his judgement, which, paradoxically perhaps, makes it clear which of the interests under consideration is seen as being more valuable. Lord Bridge agrees that the prime matter for consideration is patient autonomy, and acknowledges its value, but considers its attainment to be served best by the clinical judgement of the instant doctor and his or her colleagues. None the less, he has some sympathy with the court in the Canadian case of *Reibl* v. *Hughes*,[55] and expressly refers to what is perhaps one of the best known statements of the rights of patients in this area. In this case, Laskin CJC said:

> To allow expert medical evidence to determine what risks are material and, hence, should be disclosed and, correlatively, what risks are not material is to hand over to the medical profession the entire question of the scope of the duty of disclosure, including the question whether there has been a breach of that duty. Expert medical evidence is, of course, relevant to findings as to the risks that reside in or are a result of recommended surgery or other treatment. They will also have a bearing on their materiality but this is not a question that has to be concluded on the basis of the expert medical evidence alone. The issue under consideration is a different issue from that involved where the question is whether the doctor carried out his professional activities by applicable professional standards. What is under consideration here is the patient's right to know what risks are involved in undergoing or foregoing certain surgery or other treatment.[56]

In his judgement, Lord Bridge apparently fully appreciated the force of this reasoning, but then introduced a *caveat* which in effect so dilutes the reasoning purportedly accepted as to make it significantly different. This *caveat* is that of 'clinical judgement' and is described by Lord Bridge as '. . . a decision what degree of disclosure of risks is best calculated to assist a particular patient to make a rational choice whether or not to undergo a particular therapy . . .'[57] Thus, he concludes, the *Bolam Test* is the appropriate basis for decision making.

This can only be the case if two pre-suppositions are accepted, which at no stage appear in the reasoning of Laskin CJC. First, it is necessary to accept that when assessing the acceptable level of disclosure the issue is the exercise of solely technical professional skills. If the argument presented by Laskin is in fact accepted, then, although medical evidence may contribute to the test of materiality, it is the patient's right that is definitive of it.

Further, Lord Bridge assumes the necessity of making a rational

choice. It has been said above that rationality need not be a definitive criterion when the patient's right to self-determination is being
protected, and this need not be rehearsed again here. However, it
is worth considering the extent to which 'rational' in this context,
and subject to these tests, means 'personally rational' or 'medically
rational'. If clinical judgement can be used to withhold information,
then one must ask why? Presumably because it might distress the
patient, or might put him or her off the therapy which the doctor
regards as being appropriate.

But the self-determining patient might well regard his or her
distress at certain types of possible risk as being highly relevant to
the making of a personally rational decision. Yet the court seems
to be suggesting that, rather than this being an important aspect of
the patient's decision, it should simply be avoided. Equally, if the
risks associated with the medical choice are such that they might
deter the patient from undertaking the therapy, then it is not
necessarily irrational to choose not to undertake them. What is
referred to as being 'rational', then, would seem to be what is
*medically* rational – in other words, what has been referred to earlier
as the therapeutic imperative. Thus, in this judgement apparent
sympathy with Laskin's viewpoint merely serves to disguise the
underlying value given to medical choice and medical judgement.

Lords Diplock, Keith and Bridge were in substantial agreement
that the *Bolam Test* – presuming as it does the supremacy of medical
judgement, and assuming the disclosure question to be one which
is merely an aspect of the doctor's overall duty of care to his or
her patient – was the appropriate test to use in such cases. Lord
Templeman reached substantially the same conclusion, but by a
somewhat different route. He placed considerable emphasis on the
fact that the reasonable patient could be expected to know that
major surgery was potentially risky, and also on the skill of the
doctor in balancing the risks and benefits and coming up with a
recommendation which was in the patient's best interests. He
accepted that the ultimate decision was that of the patient, but
emphasized that this did not mean that the patient should be told
of all the risks. As he put it:

> The relationship between doctor and patient is contractual in origin,
> the doctor performing services in consideration of fees payable by
> the patient. The doctor, obedient to the high standards set by the
> medical profession, impliedly contracts to act at all times in the best
> interests of the patient. No doctor in his senses would impliedly
> contract at the same time to give to the patient all the information
> available to the doctor as a result of the doctor's training and experi-
> ence and as a result of the doctor's diagnosis of the patient. An

obligation to give a patient all the information available to the doctor
would often be inconsistent with the doctor's contractual obligation
to have regard to the patient's best interests.[58]

It is submitted that this last sentence is both an overstatement, and
a serious misunderstanding of the best interests of the patient. It
may be true that, on occasion, information may cause the patient
more suffering, and indeed one writer has suggested, that in such
cases, disclosure of that information could itself amount to a kind
of negligence.[59] However, to suggest that this is often or routinely
the case is to translate mere speculation into legal principle, and is
also to reinforce the suggestion that distress caused to the patient
by the possibility of the occurrence of a particular risk is not relevant
to the decision, when in fact in some cases it may be the crucial
and legitimate determinant of the patient's choice. Moreover, Lord
Templeman also seems to imply that the best interests of the patient
will 'often' be impeded by disclosure, apparently assuming that the
medical choice will generally be in the patient's best interests – but
how can this be so if a risk occurred which would have deterred
the patient from therapy in the first place?

Although couched in slightly different terms from his colleagues,
Lord Templeman's judgement also introduces a particular view of
the nature of the choice that the patient is *entitled* to make. As Lord
Bridge referred to 'rational' choices, so Lord Templeman considered
that information disclosure should be constrained by the need to
obtain 'balanced' choice.[60] But, this 'balance' seems heavily
weighted in favour of medical choice, although it is conceded that
the patient *may* make a choice which is not 'balanced'. In viewing
the issue from the perspective of the doctor's duty it is, of course,
not illogical to suggest that the major criterion should be the exercise
of the doctor's skills in restoring, or seeking to restore, health.
However, if seen from the perspective of patient autonomy, then
the choice as to whether or not the *chance* of restoration of health
is worth the risks entailed by therapy is not a medical one but a
highly personal one, which cannot effectively be undertaken
without information.

However, in the nature of the negligence action, it is the doctor's
duties which are under consideration, and the patient's rights seem
to play a secondary role. Lord Templeman, regarding the primary
good as the restoration of the patient's health, put the test to be
applied thus:

> In order to make a balanced judgement if he chooses to do so, the
> patient needs to be aware of the general dangers and of any special
> dangers in each case, without exaggeration or concealment. At the

end of the day, the doctor, bearing in mind the best interests of the patient and bearing in mind the patient's right to information which will enable the patient to make a balanced judgement, must decide what information should be given to the patient and in what terms that information should be couched.[61]

While not expressly approving the *Bolam Test*, this latest formulation of the doctor's duty does nevertheless countenance deliberate non-disclosure of information, and indeed justifies it. Moreover, the clinical judgement of the doctor will seldom be readily open to challenge, and therefore his or her view of what information is necessary for the patient to make a balanced judgement will necessarily be given considerable weight. This test, therefore, also implies that the doctor is the primary guardian of what would be a balanced judgement by a given patient and effectively precludes argument as to the doctor's assessment, since if it is made in good faith, and in what the doctor (and his or her colleagues) believe to be the best interests of the patient, the fact that the decision *for* therapy subsequently turns out to have harmed the patient – and, it could be argued, was therefore not in his or her best interests – is not relevant.

From the patient's perspective, perhaps the most reassuring judgement was that of Lord Scarman, who although agreeing with the final decision of the court on this particular set of facts, none the less took a radically different view of the fundamental issue for concern. While Lord Templeman did not expressly accept the *Bolam Test*, neither did he expressly reject it, and it could be argued that the effect of his approach would, in any event, be roughly similar. Lord Scarman, in urging his colleagues to an acceptance of the *Canterbury Test*, seemed, however, to be giving primacy to the rights of the patient rather than being prepared to accept conventional medical wisdom as determinative of the issue. Although his view did not prevail, his reasoning is none the less worthy of consideration.

Lord Scarman started from the question as to whether or not the professional test, which is used in assessing matters of professional skill, was indeed the appropriate test in matters of disclosure. He indicated that, if the professional test was deemed appropriate, then:

The implications of this view of the law are disturbing. It leaves the determination of a legal duty to the judgement of doctors . . . It would be a strange conclusion if courts should be led to conclude that our law, which undoubtedly recognizes the right of the patient to decide whether he will accept or reject the treatment proposed, should permit the doctors to determine whether and in what circumstances a duty arises, requiring the doctor to warn his patient of the risks inherent in the treatment which he proposes.[62]

Moreover, and in direct contrast to Lord Diplock's view, Lord Scarman could see no reason why novelty should be a bar to contemplating legal change. As he said:

> The common law is adaptable. It would not otherwise have survived over the centuries of its existence . . . It would be irony indeed if a judicial development [that is, the negligence action] for which the opportunity was the presence in the law of a flexible remedy should result now in rigidly confining the law's remedy to situations and relationships already ruled on by the judges.[63]

Lord Scarman, in approving the *Canterbury Test*, and rejecting the *Bolam Test*, provides his own formulation of the nature of the enterprise. He concluded that if it was a denial of rights to fail to disclose risks, and if those risks did occur and did cause harm, there was no reason 'in principle' why the law should not enforce these rights and pay out compensation.[64] He continued by making the important point that there are non-medical factors which influence the life of a patient – factors which the doctor should take care not to ignore. The doctor's duty, therefore was to:

> . . . advise as to medical treatment but also to provide his patient with the information needed to enable the patient to consider and balance the medical advantages and risks alongside other relevant matters, such as, for example, his family, business or social responsibilities of which the doctor may be only partially, if at all, informed.[65]

Throughout this entire case this remains the single direct assertion that there are matters other than the purely medical which might be of sufficient weight to affect decisions about therapy, and is the only proffered standard which values the patient's personal considerations equally with the medical. To this extent, it represents a radical departure from the views of previous courts, and indeed from those of his colleagues.

This is not to say, however, that Lord Scarman would decide the issue entirely without reference to medical opinion, merely that he would not give it the primacy that it seems otherwise to have. Again, this view is very much in line with the *Canterbury Test* which, in his view, provides a good standard, since:

> Without excluding medical evidence they set a standard and formulate a test of the doctor's duty, the effect of which is that the court determines the scope of the duty and decides whether the doctor has acted in breach of his duty.[66]

Indeed, Lord Scarman was fulsome in his praise for the *Canterbury* test referring to it as, '. . . a legal truth which too much judicial reliance on medical judgment tends to obscure.'[67] And he continues, differentiating the technical from the non-technical:

> In a medical negligence case where the issue is as to the advice and information given to the patient as to the treatment proposed, the available options and the risk, the court is concerned primarily with the patient's rights. The doctor's duty arises from the patient's right. If one considers the scope of the doctor's duty by beginning with the right of the patient to make his own decision whether he will or will not undergo the treatment proposed, the right to be informed of significant risks and the doctor's corresponding duty are easy to understand, for the proper implementation of the right requires that the doctor be under a duty to inform his patient of the material risks inherent in the treatment.[68]

Unfortunately, this seemingly unequivocal assertion of the patient's rights is, as in *Canterbury* itself, here too subject to the exception of therapeutic privilege which can effectively limit the nature and extent of the disclosure which the doctor must, in practice, make.

Equally, Lord Scarman recognized that the decision as to what is a material risk should ideally be based on what was material to the given patient. This, however, he ultimately rejected as being Utopian, preferring the equivalent of the 'prudent patient' test. While accepting that this permits considerable opportunity for the reintroduction and re-emphasizing of medical evidence, Lord Scarman none the less maintained the view that the ultimate decision remains legal and not medical. The extent to which it is Utopian to regard it as a possibility or a probability that medical evidence would be discounted in these circumstances, and that the court would effectively condemn an established medical view, remains open, since unfortunately Lord Scarman was content to rest there.

In any event, even if the court did make such a radical departure from its general practice, Lord Scarman holds out one further possible defence for the doctor. That is, '. . . the defence that he reasonably regarded it to be against the best interests of his patient to disclose . . .'[69] Thus, from an apparently definitive commitment to the rights of the patient, what remains is a vague rule with a series of exceptions which render the general rules significantly less meaningful.

*Summary*

The *Sidaway* case has been considered in considerable detail for the main reason that it highlights the problems of adhering to the view that information disclosure is a technical matter, best left to the discretion of professionals and adequately judged by their evidence.[70] What then are the implications of this judgement for the claim, accepted by all of the judges, that the patient does indeed have rights in the medical enterprise to decide on whether or not therapy recommended by his or her doctor should be accepted? It is submitted that the adoption at the highest level of the *Bolam Test* (even in modified form) renders it virtually impossible for patients to succeed in claiming damages where the assertion is that their decision was based on inadequate disclosure of information. Part of this submission relates to the kind of proof demanded of the patient in such cases, and part to the question of causation.

In terms of the *Bolam Test*, the patient, in order to succeed, would need to establish that no responsible body of medical opinion would have withheld the information which was withheld in the present case. Not, it should be noted, that there *is* a body of responsible medical opinion which would support the patient's claim that the information should have been disclosed, a task – given the differences of opinion demonstrated in the *Bolam* case itself – in which it would by no means be impossible to succeed. The test, on the contrary, demands only evidence that there *is* a responsible body of opinion which would have supported non-disclosure, and if this can be found the patient's case falls. Given the fact that cases are seldom defended unless there is expert evidence to support the doctor, the patient will almost inevitably be faced with just such a body of opinion.

Moreover, the difficulties of finding professionals who would be critical of their colleagues is well known. The patient may have difficulty in finding a doctor willing to say in a court of law that he or she would have acted in a manner different from his or her professional colleague. The emphasis on clinical judgement, and the primary assumption that the doctor will inevitably act in good faith and in the best interests of the patient, renders the difficulty of proof even more substantial. In fact, only those cases which amount to a gross failure to disclose, and which would, in any event, following *Chatterton* v. *Gerson*,[71] have the potential to be raised in assault, would be likely to be susceptible of the kind of proof which the patient is required to lead.

## Causation

Even assuming that such evidence could be made available, and that the case continues to be heard under the aegis of the negligence action, there remains one further test. As in all allegations of negligence, it must be shown that the negligent act caused the harm complained of – that is, there remains the question of causation. At first sight, this may seem relatively unproblematic. In general, causation is established by the fact that had the person not been negligent then the harm would not have occurred. In questions relating to disclosure, however, it can be extremely problematic.

If a risk is inherent in a given therapeutic or diagnostic procedure, then its disclosure to the patient may render the doctor non-negligent, but it could not by definition be avoided. Conversely, the negligence of the doctor who does not disclose the risk is less clearly capable of correlation to the harm which occurred, since it could have occurred in any event. Indeed, the only clear link here would be if the disclosure resulted in every case in the patient rejecting the therapy – a situation which is clearly ridiculous. In other words, therefore, the link between non-disclosure and the eventuation of harm is somewhat tenuous.

For this reason, the patient must rely on showing that he or she *would* in fact have rejected the medical act had the information been disclosed and this may be extremely difficult to do. The patient may well allege that had he or she been informed of the possibility of the risk which in fact eventuated then the therapy would have been rejected. However, as the court noted in *Canterbury* v. *Spence*,[72] there are difficulties in deciding against what kind of test such an assertion should be measured. It is thought to be too easy for the patient to act with hindsight, and in the face of what could amount to a severe disability, and therefore to claim that he or she would not have consented. Therefore, yet one more test has to be imposed, whether or not overtly, in assessing not merely the credibility of the witness, but also the likelihood of disclosure of the risk actually having deterred the patient from proceeding with the therapy. As Robertson notes:

> In testing the plaintiff's credibility and reliability (since the patient himself may have difficulty in deciding retrospectively whether he would have undergone the treatment despite the risks) the court will have to introduce a certain degree of objectivity. Thus, the extent to which the treatment was truly 'elective' and the magnitude and nature of the risk involved are likely to be crucial factors in determining whether or not the patient would have consented to the treatment had he been informed of the risk.[73]

Consequently, the court will not address itself to the issue of whether or not *this particular patient* would have agreed to therapy knowing the risks, but rather to the question of whether or not it would have been *reasonable* for him or her to attach significance to them. In making such judgements the court will, of course, have some concern for the credibility of the witness/patient, but since the court is also charged with establishing the duty of the doctor, it will necessarily also be interested in an assessment of whether or not the doctor was negligent in his or her assumptions about the need for disclosure. In other words, there is a clear Catch 22.

On the one hand, courts allow that the doctors can, in the exercise of clinical judgement, decide (without being negligent) that a particular risk may deter a patient from therapy or cause unnecessary distress, yet on the other, it purports to make an objective assessment of whether or not the risk would have been relevant to the patient's decision and therefore should have been disclosed. In other words, if the doctor acted in good faith, and in accordance with a professionally acceptable standard, in not disclosing the risks, how – in terms of the negligence action, as limited in particular by the *Bolam Test* – could the court subsequently agree that the patient would not have gone ahead had the risk been disclosed, thereby establishing the element of causation? Given the combined use of therapeutic privilege and clinical judgement, the patient seems to be in an impossible position.

Quite apart from this problem, of course, if the *law* did really set the standard and was not dominated by the medical evidence, the court – which is as removed from the patient as is the doctor – only substitutes its own view of what the 'reasonable patient' would have regarded as an acceptable risk for the view of the doctor or the patient. Thus, whatever the *patient* says, if the judge in question would not have regarded the risk as unacceptable (and this calculation may be based on statistics, or on a judicial view of the patient's position, or mere personal bias) then it is unlikely that the link between non-disclosure and the ultimate damage will readily be established. Of course, if the likelihood of the risk actually occurring is particularly remote (statistically) then it may be difficult to claim that it is more than a mere fluke, thus rendering a common sense view of what causation is rather more difficult to satisfy. In any event, it can be seen that the use of the *Bolam Test* makes it unlikely that courts will have to consider this question, since the difficulties of establishing that the duty of care was in fact breached are on their own almost insurmountable. Whatever the problems with the *Canterbury Test*, it at least permits of the possibility, if not the probability, of success.

Moreover, establishing causation is further complicated by the fact that harm must be shown. Where the treatment did not harm the patient, and the patient is rather complaining about the denial of a right to make a choice, this last must be a recognized and distinct right, breach of which is understood as causing legally recognized harm.[74] The patient who has sustained damage (physical) will at least be able to point to this – it is measurable and undeniably equates to legal harm. However, the patient who complains of an insult to integrity is claiming compensation for a harm which will only be recognized if the right to self-determination in medicine is accepted as a legally vindicable interest. Of course, physical harm is not the only basis on which compensation may be successfully sought. As Winfield and Jolowicz put it:

> In the law of tort, there is a growing body of case law where negligent defendants have been held liable even though they have not injured the plaintiff or his property by any positive act and where their conduct seems most naturally expressed in terms of failure to ensure the receipt of expected benefits.[75]

Although an intensive analysis of the heads of damages is not within the scope of this discussion, the point that legal recognition of the type of harm is crucial to the availability of compensation, cannot be ignored. This serves to distinguish yet again between the value of actions in trespass/battery/assault and those raised in negligence. As Winfield and Jolowicz further note:

> Whereas most torts require damage resulting to the plaintiff which is not too remote a consequence of the defendant's conduct, a few, such as trespass in some, or perhaps all, of its various forms and libel, do not require proof of actual damage.[76]

## The enquiring patient

It is clear, therefore, that adherence to the professional test poses considerable difficulties for patients who are aggrieved at a shortfall in information which prevents them from being able to act in an autonomous manner.

There is, in addition, one further complication which arises from the emphasis on doctors' duties, and which is worthy of brief consideration here. If the issue is the exercise of professional skills then the doctor is entitled to fail to make disclosure where that omission is carried out in good faith. This exercise of clinical judgement is justified *because* the doctor possesses certain skills and information which are denied to the lay person. Paradoxically, however, there is a growing body of case law (unlike *Hatcher* v. *Black*)[77] which seems to suggest that patients may have their right to information satisfied if they know the appropriate question to ask the doctor.

In the recent case of *Blyth* v. *Bloomsbury Health Authority*,[78] the patient – a trained nurse – was said to require less careful warnings than other patients since she might be presumed to know of the medical indications of an adverse reaction to therapy. Whether or not she *actually* knew this information was apparently less relevant than the fact that she *could* have. Has the position now been reached where there is a 'specialist patient' test?

In any event, if it is true that the withholding of information can be in the patient's best interests, then would this not be true whatever the situation of the patient? In particular, would it not remain true whether or not the patient asks for the information? Here the fallacy of this justification for non-disclosure becomes clear. Paradoxically the most internally consistent judicial statement is to be found in the judgement of Lord Denning in the case of *Hatcher* v. *Black*,[79] a decision which is so open to criticism as to be routinely rejected. In this case a doctor deliberately answered a direct and straightforward question about a particular type of risk, falsely. Lord Denning held the doctor to be entitled so to do 'in the best interests of the patient', on the assumption that had the risk been disclosed, and had the doctor then been forced to disclose the existence of alternative therapy which did not carry this risk, the patient might have rejected the doctor's choice of treatment. While morally open to question, this decision is at least consistent with the contention that the doctor is entitled to withhold information on the basis that it would distress the patient, or deter him or her from therapy – whether or not questions are asked.

However, the majority of American and British decisions do make a distinction between the patient who asks questions and the patient who does not. It is paradoxical that there seems to be more concern about the doctor actively lying to the patient than there is about the doctor who presents a false picture by omission. *Blyth* ties the 'specialist patient' intimately to the enquiring patient. As was said:

> As the plaintiff was in my judgement, seeking information and as she was someone with nursing qualifications who could be trusted not to act irrationally because of what she was told, she was, in my opinion, entitled to be given such information as was available to the hospital.[80]

There are a number of interesting and interlinking strands to this statement. In the first place it would seem that it was the qualification of the patient (herself medically oriented) which entitled her to the information, presumably on the assumption that she would none the less have opted for the medical recommendation. Equally, the fact that she asked a straight question (which might, of course, be possible only where some medical information is already known) meant that she acquired rights, even to potentially distressing information, which would be denied in other circumstances. The view that the enquiring patient should be answered honestly by the doctor, and should be given the information which the doctor would otherwise have been legally and professionally justified in withholding, is paradoxical. Yet, it also has received wide support. Although dismissed out of hand in *Canterbury*,[81] it is generally accepted as an exception to the rule that the doctor is the master of the instance.

While it may seem morally satisfying that a patient who asks questions should be told the truth and not a lie, this merely begs the fundamental question. If courts would otherwise have upheld non-disclosure, as seems almost certain, then there must presumably be good grounds for so doing. These grounds are legally accepted as being that it is not in the patient's interests to know this information. How, then, does it become in the patient's interests merely because the question occurs to him or her, perhaps fortuitously? In truth, of course, the 'average' patient consults a doctor because he or she does not have access to certain information. In view of this, it is unlikely that the patient will know what questions to ask of the doctor, and yet if he or she does stumble on the right question, there is an immediate (albeit extremely random) attribution of rights to which their fellow patients are not entitled. Of course, it could be said that to ask a particular question about a possible risk is not dependent on medical knowledge. This would be in line with the argument that the information to be disclosed is personal rather than technical. Thus, if it is true that the patient should be told of risks, and that these risks are not merely technical risks, then the ordinary patient *will* ask the right questions because no medical knowledge is necessary to the formulation of the question. However, this argument is somewhat naïve, since in truth the likelihood of, for example, drug therapy resulting in brain damage or paralysis is scarcely within the contemplation of the patient, although it may be known to the doctor. The patient can, of course, appreciate the impact on his/her life of the risk of brain damage, but it would take some technical skill or knowledge for him or her to think of asking the question. Technical knowledge may therefore be necessary to formulate the right question, but not necessarily to understand the answer.

In any event, the patient is under no duty to question, since the doctor is the party with duties in the medical enterprise. Patient distress, so convenient a reason for non-disclosure, is a more valid issue when concerned with whether or not the patient, who has no medical knowledge and may be suffering from a distressing illness, should also be expected, if his or her rights are to be vindicated, to ask the right question. To insist on this would certainly be morally unacceptable, and would be to discriminate between the aggressive or assertive patient and the patient who is cowed by involvement in the medical enterprise, or by the fact of illness. Verbal acuity or personal confidence scarcely seem sound bases for the attribution of specific and significant rights. Yet, courts seem happy to make the assumption that the patient does become entitled to more (even distressing or deterring) information, merely because they have the nous to have asked for it.

In the *Sidaway* case, for example, enquiring patients were singled out for special consideration by some of the judges, as they were in the *Bolam* decision, where MacNair J said:

> Having considered [the evidence on this point], you have to make up your minds whether it has been proved to your satisfaction that when the defendants adopted the practice they did (namely, the practice of saying very little and waiting for questions from the patient), they were falling below a proper standard of competent professional opinion on this question of whether or not it is right to warn.[82]

In *Sidaway*, Lord Diplock also draws such a distinction:

> . . . when it comes to warning about risks, the kind of training and experience that a judge will have undergone at the Bar makes it natural for him to say (correctly) it is my right to decide whether any particular thing is done to my body and I want to be fully informed of any risks there may be involved of which I am not already aware from my general knowledge as a highly educated man of experience, so that I may form my own judgement whether to refuse the advised treatment or not. No doubt, if the patient in fact manifested this attitude by means of questioning, the doctor would tell him whatever it was the patient wants to know . . . [83]

Leaving aside the question as to whether or not only 'highly educated' people can correctly say they have a right to make choices about what is to be done to their bodies, there remains no justification for distinguishing between the person who asks and the person who doesn't. If rights are attributed because the person is entitled to respect for his or her self-determination, then only stringently applied and compelling reasons would justify invasion. Failure to ask a question, which in any event lack of technical

information may preclude one from having the capacity to formulate, can scarcely be regarded as a legitimate basis for the withholding of information which may have a significant impact on
the capacity to exercise the right of self-determination. Although
differing in the basis of his decision from the majority, Lord
Templeman also drew a similar distinction.

> Mrs Sidaway could have asked questions. If she had done so, she
> could and should have been informed that there was an aggregate
> risk of between 1% and 2% of some damage either to the spinal cord
> or to a nerve root resulting in injury which might vary from irritation
> to paralysis.[84]

It is arrogance indeed to claim on the one hand that the patient is
likely to act irrationally if all information is disclosed, or that the
doctor should avoid telling the patient of risks which might upset
him or her, and yet, on the other hand, to demand that, in order
to maintain his or her capacity to make self-determining choices,
the patient is virtually under an obligation to ask relevant and
specific questions. But it is not altogether unusual to find courts
demanding just such standards from patients. This point was raised
approvingly in, for example, *O'Malley-Williams* v. *Board of Governors
of the National Hospital for Nervous Diseases*,[85] and the same distinction
was drawn in *Lee* v. *South West Thames A.H.A.*[86]

At least one Canadian case has further refined this test, and since
it seems to be completely in line with the attitude of British courts
it is worthy of brief consideration. In describing the doctor's duty
of disclosure in the case of *Lepp* v. *Hopp*,[87] the court explained it
thus:

> The law draws a distinction between the general duty of disclosure
> imposed on a surgeon when he is obtaining a patient's consent to
> surgery and the duty of disclosure he is under when he responds to
> specific questions from his patient . . . When specific questions are
> directed to the surgeon he must make a full and fair disclosure in
> response to them. This duty requires the surgeon to disclose risks
> which are mere possibilities if the patient's questions reasonably
> direct the surgeon's attention to risks of that nature *and if they are
> such that the surgeon, in all of the circumstances, could reasonably foresee
> would effect the patient's decision.*[88] (emphasis added)

In other words, not only the non-enquiring patient, but, to a lesser
extent perhaps, even the enquiring patient, will be subject to the
doctor's assessment of whether or not a risk would be material.

In any event, as Robertson points out,[89] both this and other
similar decisions (such as *Smith* v. *Auckland Hospital Board*)[90] rely on

an arguable interpretation of the rule in *Hedley Byrne & Co. Ltd*. v. *Heller & Partners Ltd*.,[91] which permits the person who is asked questions the option of silence. Robertson argues, however, that the doctor-patient relationship differs from the standard contractual one in a significant and determinative manner – that is that there is a pre-existing duty of care on the doctor which 'deprives the doctor of the "option of silence" and which requires him to answer the question with reasonable care.'[92]

It is, therefore, a highly dubious proposition that the patient who asks questions is entitled by this mere fact to additional autonomy-enhancing information. Were the truth or dishonesty of the doctor the central issue, then failure to answer a direct question might well take on a major significance. However, what is at issue here is a far greater consideration – that of the patient's right to self-determination, and this cannot be dependent on the patient having sufficient preliminary knowledge, or even plain courage, to ask the right question, nor on his or her capacity to challenge or question medical authority. As Robertson says, '[t]he law should seek to ensure that, in relation to disclosure of risks inherent in proposed treatment, the onus lies with the doctor and not with the patient.'[93] To this end, the view of the court in *Canterbury* v. *Spence* bears repetition. The court said:

> We discard the thought that the patient should ask for information before the physician is required to disclose. *Caveat emptor* is not the norm for the consumer of medical services. The duty to disclose is more than a call to speak merely on the patient's request or merely to answer the patient's questions; it is a duty to volunteer if necessary, the information the patient needs for an intelligent decision.[94]

However unsatisfactory it may be that the enquiring patient is in these cases said to be entitled to additional information, the subsequent hearing of the *Blyth* case in 1987 added a further refinement which effectively denies even this. The court at this hearing was unwilling even to concede that a straight answer should always be given to a direct question. As Kerr LJ said in the Court of Appeal:

> . . . I am not convinced that the Bolam test is irrelevant even in relation to the question of what answers are properly to be given to specific enquiries, or that Lord Diplock or Lord Bridge [in *Sidaway*] intended to hold otherwise. It seems . . . that there may always be grey areas, with differences of opinion, as to what are the proper answers to be given to any enquiry, even a specific one, in the particular circumstances of any case.[95]

## Conclusions

It has already been said that the *Bolam* test was effectively reinforced by the *Sidaway* case. Brazier[96] has suggested that the different approaches of the judges in both the Court of Appeal and the House of Lords leaves scope for a re-interpretation and that the *Bolam* test need not inevitably form the basis of decisions about information disclosure and consent. Clearly she was right to suggest that the possibility of taking an alternative approach existed, but it seems unfortunately not to have materialized.

In *Gold* v. *Harringey Health Authority*[97] it was quite clearly inferred that the *Bolam* test applies to the provision of information and advice, even where the proposed treatment is non-therapeutic. In *Venner* v. *North East Essex Health Authority & Anor.*[98] the court also reinforced the *Bolam* test, describing it as having been 'amplified' by the House of Lords in *Sidaway* – amplified, not modified or discounted. In *Blyth*[99] the *Bolam* test was extended even to answering direct questions. In *Palmer & Anor.* v. *Eadie*[100] the court suggested that the apparent differences between the approaches of the judiciary in *Sidaway* were in any event not important, since whether one followed Lord Bridge, Lord Diplock or Lord Templeman the outcome would be the same. And in *King* v. *King*[101] the *Bolam* test was again applied. Emphasis on the importance of not choosing between expert and reasonable bodies of opinion – the central characteristic of *Bolam* – was further validated in the case of *Maynard* v. *West Midlands RHA*[102] where Lord Scarman said:

> It is not enough to show that there is a body of competent professional opinion which considers that theirs was a wrong decision if there also exists a body of professional opinion, equally competent, which supports the decision as reasonable in the circumstances.[103]

It is clear therefore that there are a number of difficulties attached to the negligence action in general – difficulties which relate in part to the attitudes of the courts, and in part to the interpretation of the action itself. In medical cases the inclusion of the duty to disclose information in the doctor's general duty of care may prove to be the most problematic hurdle for the aggrieved patient. If it is the case, as Robertson suggests, that the development of the concept of informed consent by American courts was primarily a device to expand the liability of the medical profession,[104] then even here it can be seen to have been, relatively speaking, a failure.

The extensive use of the professional test in the United States, as in the United Kingdom, makes successful challenge of non-disclosure unlikely, unless the failure to disclose was so great as to amount, in any event, to an assault, or to trespass against the person. Even the development of other tests, such as the 'prudent patient' test, is not a complete answer. The nature of the proof required of the patient, and the rationalization of behaviour inherent in the negligence action, remove the matter for consideration far from the individual aggrieved patient and render it subject to tests which are designed to be objective. However, as with all so-called objective tests, there remains the potential to incorporate policy, personal and professional prejudice and subjective assessments by courts and experts. That the finder of fact in the 'prudent patient' test is the court rather than the doctor, will be small comfort if it is borne in mind that courts have in the past demonstrated their own bias in favour of medicine as a 'good', and through this assessment have often deferred to doctors as a group and as individuals.

Of course, the use of an 'objective' test is an inevitable outcome of the use of the negligence-based action. This action is neither designed nor equipped to deal with purely subjective information, nor is it used other than to assess rationalized duties, and to decide on a reasonable basis what the duty is, and whether or not it has been breached. Even in those cases where there are clear statements to the effect that the law, and not the medical profession, sets the standard of care to be followed, there is little doubt as to the weight given to medical evidence. Moreover, the use of therapeutic privilege, advocated even in the most radical judgements,[105] sufficiently reduces the impact of any theoretical attention to patient's rights so as to render it merely rhetorical.

With the notable exception of the court in *Canterbury* v. *Spence*, and the limited number of cases following it, emphasis in the United States has concentrated on 'informed consent' – a term much used even in cases in the United Kingdom. However, the use of this terminology can be misleading and gives rise to its own difficulties. What is really the important issue is observance of the duty to disclose, which is a necessary precondition of real consent, and this duty can be separated from the question of 'informed' consent. For example, as we have seen in respect of children and the mentally handicapped, a duty to disclose information may be thought to exist even in a situation where there is doubt as to the recipient's legal capacity to offer a real consent.

It is argued here that the duty to disclose information arises independently of considerations such as clinical judgement, and is a clear and unequivocal vindication of the. patient's rights. However, if seen merely as an aspect of a general – and loosely defined – duty of care, then the negligence action is ill-equipped to deal with something as contentious and potentially abstract as individual rights. As a means of protecting individual freedoms, given that individuals are idiosyncratic, the negligence action cannot, as currently applied, be satisfactory.

In addition, there is the fundamental difficulty that, not content with imposing one level of objectivity – that is the 'reasonable doctor' test – courts are willing to impose yet one more test – that of what information the 'reasonable patient' would have regarded as being of significance. Since apparently the individual's statement of what he or she would have found significant is not convincing,[106] the actual outcome is unlikely to be based on direct attention to individual rights. Given the current application of negligence analysis, with its emphasis on doctors' duties, it is difficult to see how it could.

In any case, the reluctance of the judiciary in the United Kingdom to expand the liability of the medical profession makes it less than likely that – even were significant changes possible - the position will be radically altered. As Robertson says:

> It is to be regretted that the law should seek to restrict the doctrine of informed consent in this way, since this belies the importance to be attached to the patient's fundamental right to decide whether to undergo proposed medical treatment. For this to happen, much less emphasis would have to be placed on concepts such as 'accepted medical practice' and 'best interests of the patient' as reasons for excusing non-disclosure. However, regardless of the importance of the patient's right in relation to the decision to undergo medical treatment, one cannot avoid the fact that the doctrine of informed consent, expanding as it does the liability of the medical profession, is the servant of judicial policy regarding such expansion. It is the judicial policy, rather than the importance of the patient's right to determine his own medical treatment, that will dictate the future development of the doctrine of informed consent in this country.[107]

Although this writer has not used the term 'informed consent', Robertson's argument is no less applicable to the argument for information disclosure.

The development of the legal recognition of information disclosure will, as Robertson says, depend on the willingness of the judiciary to expand the liability of the medical profession, and recognize the rights of patients. In the United Kingdom, however, the situation would seem to be that the judiciary, who themselves developed the concept of negligence, have also kept a tight control on its expansion. In medical cases, fear of extra-legal consequences such as the spread of defensive medicine, and consideration of extra-legal factors such as the good of medicine as a discipline and the impact of a finding of negligence on the doctor's position, are routinely used to deny liability. In the specific case of consent, the *Bolam Test* sets hurdles for the patient which, it is submitted, make it relatively certain that no claim will succeed unless the failure to disclose information is so gross as in any event to merit consideration under assault analysis.

If the important issue is patients' rights, however, then the relevant question is not whether or not the patient would have rejected therapy, but whether or not the doctor is entitled to use the defence of *volenti*. For this to apply, the patient must have been informed of the type of risk(s) to which exposure was possible, and must have agreed to accept them. This is a test much more readily susceptible of proof, and in a sense much less objectionable, than that of reasonable or accepted medical practice. However, to consider the question from this perspective seems to be beyond the imagination of current decision makers in the United Kingdom or in the United States. Moreover, the apparent sanctioning of the *Bolam Test* by the House of Lords[108] and in subsequent cases renders its use in the future even less likely.

It can be concluded, therefore, that as presently applied the negligence action is unsuited to a vindication of patients' rights. Its lack of suitability is as much a matter of judicial attitude as it is an aspect of the nature of the action itself, although both contribute to the problems faced by the disaffected patient. The current description of medical negligence lacks the capacity for subjective decision making which an adherence to individual rights would demand, and judicial fears and attitudes, however, well or ill-founded, serve merely to increase the distance between the claimant and possible compensation. As Skegg notes:

> At present some English judges are likely to treat such evidence [of a common and approved practice] as conclusive, if the patient brings an action in which he challenges a doctor's failure to provide him with adequate information about a proposed procedure.[109]

One can only agree with him that it would be

> . . . regrettable, if in future the English courts did not play a more important role in protecting the interests of patients who wish to be able to reach an informed decision about whether to consent to medical procedures . . . [110]

even if one does not necessarily agree that it would also be 'surprising'.[111]

The last two chapters have gone into some detail in order to demonstrate the considerable risk to patient autonomy represented by a failure to look closely and analytically at the provision of advice and information as opposed to the execution of technical skills. Recognition that the doctor's duty of care to the patient is an amalgam of independent although linked duties rather than a vague, and professionally definable cohesive, whole would go a long way to resolving the difficulties outlined in preceding chapters.

Before taking this point further, however, it would be remiss not to explore one further option. It has been conceded that one major obstacle to the protection of patient autonomy is the way in which liability is currently assessed. This might be thought to point inexorably towards a need for major change in the system of liability – a suggestion which seems increasingly to have gained the support of many groups and individuals.[112] It is now relatively common to read and hear apparently unquestioning support for a system of liability which does not depend on proof of fault, and the power of the lobby for this makes it important that some consideration is given to the impact of such a scheme on patient autonomy.

## Notes

1   Cf. Robertson, G., 'Informed consent to medical treatment' (1981) 97 *LQR* 102.
2.  Loc. cit.
3.  [1981] 1 All ER 257.
4.  *The Times* 2 July 1954.
5.  [1957] 2 All ER 118.
6.  Loc. cit., at p. 114: 'Although it is clear that, in order to obtain a valid consent from his patient, a doctor is required to explain the "nature and purpose" of proposed treatment, until recently it was not clear whether the doctor is also under a legal duty (independent of the *validity* of the patient's consent) to inform him of the risks inherent in the treatment, i.e. a duty corresponding to the doctrine of informed consent . . .'
7.  Cmnd 7054/1978.
8.  Para 1315.
9.  Klass, A., *There's Gold in Them Thar Pills*, Harmondsworth, Penguin, 1975.
10. *Hills* v. *Potter* [1983] 3 All ER 716.
11. Although Scots and English law differ, the likelihood is that the Scottish courts would be equally likely to eschew the transatlantic doctrine of 'informed consent', in particular since it has developed in a common law system.
12. Loc. cit., at pp. 112–113; *Cull* v. *Butler* [1932] 1 *Br. Med. J.* 1195; *Hamilton* v. *Birmingham R.H.B.* [1969] 2 *Br. Med. J.* 456; *Chadwick* v. *Parsons* [1971] 2 Lloyd's Rep. 49 (QB), [1971] 2 Lloyd's Rep. 322 (CA).
13. That is, both knowledgeable and willing.
14. Roughly, there is no injury if something is lawfully agreed to.
15. [1944] 1 KB 476.
16. At p. 479.
17. Supra cit.
18. Supra cit.

19. Buchanan, A., 'Medical Paternalism' 7 *Philosophy and Public Affairs*, 340 (1978).
20. Robertson, loc. cit., at p. 115.
21. Cf Rogers, W.V.H., *Winfield and Jolowicz on Tort*, (12th edn), London, Sweet and Maxwell, 1984, at pp. 1–2: 'At a very general level, however, we may say that tort is concerned with the allocation or prevention of losses, which are bound to occur in our society. It is obvious that in any society of people living together numerous conflicts of interest will arise and that the actions of one man or group of men will from time to time cause or threaten damage to others.'; Walker, D.M., *The Law of Delict in Scotland*, (2nd edn, revised), Edinburgh, W. Green & Son Ltd., 1981, at pp. 8–9.
22. Cf. *Paris* v. *Stepney Borough Council* [1951] AC 367; *General Cleaning Contractors* v. *Christmas* [1952] 2 All ER 1116; *Barkway* v. *South Wales Transport* [1950] 1 All ER 402; *Lloyd's Bank* v. *E. B. Savory & Co.* [1933] AC 233; *Hunter* v. *Hanley*, supra cit.; *Markland* v. *Manchester Corporation* [1934] 1 KB 566.
23. Cf. Montrose, J. L., 'Is negligence an ethical or a sociological concept?', (1958) 21 MLR 259 discussing the judgement of McNair, J., in *Bolam* supra cit., at p. 261: 'From the premises of McNair, J it does indeed follow that in "a situation which involves the use of some special skill or competence", and where there are diverse practices followed by those possessed of that skill, then conformity with one of those practices cannot be negligent.'
24. Cf. *Sidaway* v. *Board of Governors, Bethlem Royal Hospital* [1985] AC 871, [1985] 1 All ER 643 (HL); *Hills* v. *Potter*, supra cit. For a criticism of the professional standard test, see Robertson, loc. cit.; see also, Howie, R.B.M., 'The standard of care in medical negligence' *Juridical Rev* 193 (1983); McLean, S.A.M., 'The right to consent to medical treatment' in Campbell, et al., (Eds), *Human Rights: From Rhetoric to Reality*, Oxford, Basil Blackwell, 1986; McLean, S.A.M., 'Negligence – a dagger at the doctor's back?', in Robson, P., and Watchman, P. (Eds), *Justice, Lord Denning and the Constitution*, Aldershot, Gower, 1981; Robertson, G., '*Whitehouse* v. *Jordan* – medical negligence retired' [1981] 44 MLR 457; *Winfield and Jolowicz on Tort*, supra cit., at p. 102: 'Failure to conform with general practice may raise an inference of negligence against the defendant and it has been held at first instance that it reverses the burden of proof and requires the defendant to justify his conduct. However, it is certain that a showing of conformity with general and approved practice will generally lead to a decision for the defendant.'
25. [1984] 2 All ER 513, [1986] 1 All ER 497 (CA)
26. [1986] 1 All ER 497, at pp. 506–507.
27. Supra cit., at p. 1028, where he said that a practice must be '. . . *rightly* accepted as proper . . .'
28. Even here, however, Lord Scarman pointed out, at p. 654, that even so: 'The "prudent patient" test still calls for medical evidence.'
29. Supra cit.
30. Supra cit.
31. Supra cit.
32. At p. 266.
33. Loc. cit., at p. 117.
34. E.g. *Sidaway*, supra cit.; *Eyre* v. *Measday* [1986] 1 All ER 488; *Lee* v. *South West Thames R.H.A.* (1985) *New Law J* 438; *Gold* v. *Harringey Health Authority The Times* 17 June 1986.
35. Robertson, loc. cit., at p. 117.
36. 464 F 2d. 772 (1972).
37. Supra cit., at p. 512.
38. Supra cit., at p. 511.

39. Per Nourse, J, at p. 511.
40. Id.
41. Supra cit.
42. Loc. cit., at p. 122.
43. See *Sidaway*, supra cit., [1984] 1 All ER 1018 (CA).
44. E.g. *Blyth* v. *Bloomsbury A.H.A. The Times*, 24 May 1985 – but here the decision was based on the fact that the treatment (sterilization) was carried out for convenience rather than on 'therapeutic' grounds; *Gold* v. *Harringey*, supra cit.
45. Brazier, M., *Medicine, Patients and the Law*, Harmondsworth, Penguin, 1987.
46. At p. 656.
47. This is clearly in line with the *Bolam* test described supra.; for further discussion, see chapter 5, supra.
48. At p. 656.
49. At p. 657.
50. At p. 658.
51. At p. 659.
52. 1955 SC 200.
53. At p. 217.
54. At pp. 660–661.
55. (1980) 114 DLR (3d) 1.
56. At p. 13.
57. At pp. 662–663.
58. At p. 665.
59. Cf. Brazier, M., 'Informed consent to surgery' 19 *Med. Sci. Law* 49 (1979).
60. At p. 666: 'The duty of the doctor . . . subject to his overriding duty to have regard to the best interests of the patient, is to provide the patient with information which will enable the patient to make a balanced judgment if the patient chooses to make a balanced judgment.'
61. Id.
62. At p. 649.
63. At p. 650.
64. Particularly at p. 651.
65. Particularly at p. 652.
66. At p. 653.
67. At p. 654.
68. Id.
69. Id.
70. Although Brazier, op. cit., maintains that this is not the end of the debate, it is submitted that, given the narrowness of the distinction between the prudent doctor and the prudent patient tests, and the dependence on the professional test for the purposes of this approach to consent, the debate is substantially, if not definitively, over.
71. Supra cit.
72. Supra cit.
73. Loc. cit., at p. 122.
74. For discussion, see *Winfield and Jolowicz on Tort*, supra cit.; *Street on Torts*, (7th edn), London, Butterworths, 1983; as Walker, op. cit., says at p. 9: 'It does not necessarily follow from the assertion of some right as a natural right or a human right, or as an individual or social interest, that the law will protect it and enforce legal rights and duties arising therefrom. Whether or not to recognize some interest is a policy decision for the law . . .'
75. Op. cit. at p. 7; see *Ross* v. *Caunters* [1980] Ch 297; *Junior Books Ltd.* v. *Veitchi Co.* [1982] 3 WLR 477.

76. Op. cit. at p. 43; see also, Walker, op. cit., at p. 489: 'The claim for damages [in assault] is not merely for damage sustained, but *in solatium* for affront and insult, and it is not discharged by the application of criminal sanctions. Hence solatium can be claimed even where no actual injury is or can be proved.'

77. Supra cit.

78. *The Times* 24 May 1985; *The Times* 11 Feb. 1987.

79. Supra cit.

80. Supra cit.

81. Supra cit.; the court said (n. 36) 'We discard the thought that the patient should ask for information before the physician is required to disclose. Caveat emptor is not the norm for the consumer of medical services. Duty to disclose is more than a call to speak merely on the patient's request, or merely to answer the patient's questions; it is a duty to volunteer, if necessary, the information the patient needs for intelligent decision.'; but see also the Canadian case of *Lepp* v. *Hopp* (1979) 98 DLR (3d) 464, at p. 470: 'In my view, the law draws a distinction between the general duty of disclosure imposed upon a surgeon when he is obtaining a patient's consent to surgery and the duty of disclosure he is under when he responds to specific questions from his patient . . . When specific questions are directed to the surgeon he must make a full and fair disclosure in response to them.'; see also, *Hatcher* v. *Black*, supra cit.

82. Supra cit., at p. 124.

83. At p. 659.

84. At p. 664.

85. (1975) 1 *Br. Med. J.* 635.

86. Supra cit.

87. Supra cit.

88. At p. 470.

89. Loc. cit., at pp. 118–120.

90. [1965] NZLR 191.

91. [1964] AC 465.

92. Robertson, loc. cit., at p. 119.

93. At p. 120.

94. Supra cit., n. 36.

95. *The Times* 11 Feb. 1987.

96. Op. cit.

97. [1987] 2 All ER 888.

98. *The Times* 21 Feb. 1987.

99. Supra cit.

100. May 1987, CA, unreported.

101. 1987, CA, unreported.

102. [1985] 1 All ER 635.

103. At p. 638.

104. Loc. cit., at p. 109.

105. E.g. *Canterbury* v. *Spence*, supra cit.; see also the judgement of Lord Scarman in *Sidaway*, supra cit.

106. Cf. *Cobbs* v. *Grant* 104 *Cal. Rptr.* 505 (1972) 'Subjectively he may believe [that he would have declined treatment] with the 20–20 vision of hindsight but we doubt that justice will be served by placing the physician in jeopardy of the patient's bitterness and disillusionment.'; see also, McNorrie, K., 'Informed consent and the duty of care' *Scots Laws Times* 289 (1985); Mason and McCall Smith, op. cit., at p. 151: 'The obvious difficulty . . . is one of discounting the wisdom of hindsight. It will be only too easy for a plaintiff,

once he has suffered damage, to allege that he would not have given his consent to the procedure, when, in reality, he may well have been prepared to do so, even with full knowledge of the risks entailed . . .'

107.  Loc. cit., at p. 126.
108.  *Sidaway*, supra cit.
109.  Op. cit., at p. 86.
110.  Id.
111.  Id.
112.  For example, in *King* v. *King*, supra cit., the judges expressed their deep sympathy for the claimant, and indicated that this was the kind of case which might well have attracted compensation had the system been different.

# 8 Liability without fault

It must be conceded at the outset that there are considerable attractions in the notion of no fault liability. The reasons given for seeking change from the fault based system are, for many, compelling. The expense, the uncertainty, the delay and the anxiety which can be, and often are, associated with personal injury litigation are roundly criticized by victims and lawyers alike. In addition, it is asked, how can it be fair that some people who are damaged can claim substantial awards in compensation while others who are equally damaged receive nothing, simply because they can find no one to blame?

In medical litigation other factors are also relevant – for example, fears of defensive medicine if litigation spirals. And of course account must be taken of the assertion that the majority of harm suffered by patients is the result of medical accident rather than medical negligence. Under the current system, this, if true, can attract no compensation. In response, therefore, there is increasing interest in changing the basis on which compensation is sought in order that doctors (and courts) are no longer afraid of the consequences of litigation and that the apparent majority (i.e. those suffering because of medical accident) can receive compensation based on their needs.

Making such a move, of course, would involve a number of deep-seated changes to current law. Instead of the individual who caused the harm being liable to pay compensation the state would take over responsibility. Instead of having to identify a wrongdoer, mere evidence of harm would suffice. And, inevitably, if the state has to pay, the current trend towards massive compensation awards would be reversed. In addition, the prospective litigant could be assured that an impecunious wrongdoer would not affect the availability of compensation. Rather, all of those harmed and qualifying under whatever test of eligibility were devised, would receive some form of compensation, most probably based on needs.

Currently, most developed legal systems have a variety of mechanisms for awarding compensation. The negligence action is but one of them, and a relatively recent one at that. Liability in some situations may be strict, depending therefore on proof of causation alone, but compensation in this system is still paid by the individual or group who generated the risk which caused the harm and awards of damages may still be substantial. Two countries have, however, made radical changes to their scheme of liability – Sweden[1] and New Zealand. Since the New Zealand scheme is the more wide-ranging, it is to this system that attention will be turned in this chapter.

Analysis of the efficacy of this scheme will be undertaken from the perspective of the value placed on the right of the patient to receive information which permits the making of an autonomy-enhancing decision and to receive compensation for the invasion of this right.

## An introduction to no fault in New Zealand

Before proceeding further, however, it is useful to look briefly at the details of the system. The Accident Compensation Scheme was established by the Accident Compensation Act 1972, following the Report of the Royal Commission of Inquiry into Compensation for Personal Injury in New Zealand (Woodhouse Report).[2] A description of the system, amendments and eligibility, can now be found in the Accident Compensation Act 1982. Eligibility is based on evidence of harm resulting from 'personal injury by accident', which includes 'medical, surgical, dental or first aid misadventures' but excludes damage caused by sickness, disease or the aging process.[3]

The exclusion of sickness from the scheme is often desribed as a major inconsistency, although it is a direct translation into legis-lation of the recommendations of the Woodhouse Report.[4] Not only does it seem to sit ill with the scheme as a whole, but it is arguably at odds with Woodhouse's own statement that 'all injured persons should receive compensation from any community financed scheme on the same uniform method of assessment, *regardless of the causes which give rise to their injury.*'[5] Obviously for the patient the exclusion of sickness may be particularly problematic, since many of them are by definition already ill. Clearly if an ill person is involved in a street accident the fact of pre-existing illness will generally be irrel-evant, but if the cause of the harm is an event arising in the course of, or as a result of, therapy then it will be very much more difficult to decide whether or not the damage was 'personal injury by acci-dent' or merely a consequence of the illness.

Even in non-medical cases it has been claimed that:

The meaning of 'accident' for the purposes of the Act has been a fundamental problem which has not been simplified by legislative definition. However, it is clear that merely because an injury is unexpected and caused by negligence it will not necessarily be covered by the Act.

As with most permissive legislation, and in particular where the central definition is relatively vague, interpretation may serve to limit or expand eligibility. It would seem that the Accident Compensation Scheme has tended to adopt a restrictive rather than a liberal interpretation of what amounts to 'accident' and has thereby limited the availability of cover under the scheme.[7] The interpretation of 'accident' was taken from the definition in the English case of *Jones* v. *Secretary of State for Social Services*.[8] In these terms an 'accident' is an unlooked-for or undesigned event. The Accident Compensation Corporation advised the medical profession that '[a]s a matter of general principle *personal injury by accident* means any form of damage to the human system which is unexpected and which was not designed by the person injured'.[9]

Eligibility for compensation results generally in the rapid payment of needs-based compensation amounting to a percentage of lost earnings (periodically assessed to take account of inflation and changing needs), and on occasion limited lump sum payments can be made. Failure to establish that harm was the result of 'personal injury by accident' leaves the victim with the option of raising an action in the traditional manner. But the ultimate arbiter of what amounts to 'personal injury by accident' is the Accident Compensation Corporation itself, and claimants must first seek their judgement before courts will entertain an action for personal injury.

Evidently, there are many aspects of the system which are open to interpretation, leaving the residual anxiety that the attitudes of decision-makers may play a considerable part in assessing eligibility, just as they can and do in fault based schemes. Equally, a state funded scheme may be under further pressures which can reflect on decisions about eligibility. Financial resources and political will or ideology cannot be entirely separated from the working of such a system. Initially in New Zealand there was evidence of financial reserves,[10] but it would seem that this position has now changed. It is said, however, that there is evidence of a high success rate in claims made to the Accident Compensation Corporation,[11] but this is by and large true of the common law systems also [12] with the apparent exception of medical litigation.[13] None the less the no fault system must directly confront the spectre of state financial constraints, since '[w]hen the Accident Compensation Commission decides whether there has been personal injury by accident it is making a decision about its own money and resources.'[14]

The definition of accident, which incorporates an unexpected event, automatically excludes anything which is a process, such as illness.[15] In some cases the decision that something was an accident and not a process will be straightforward. But in others the distinction will be much more difficult to draw. This potential difficulty was explicitly recognized in one case where it was said that:

> The boundary line between an accident injury and a disease injury may be hard to discern at times but there is no doubt that the legislature requires the line to be drawn and the interpreter of the Act must take cogniscance of this.[16]

But given that the effect of the Accident Compensation Scheme will be to deny the traditional right to sue in some cases, it is particularly important that clarity and consistency of interpretation and operation are maintained. The question posed by Klar, therefore, is of particular concern:

> The challenge presented to tort lawyers by the program's abolition of common law rights for personal injury victims is obvious: can the cause of action be eliminated without any appreciable harms to the society and in fact with benefits to the society as promised by tort law abolitionists.[17]

To some extent the answer to this question will hinge on the capacity of a given society to come to terms with an entirely new concept of compensation. In addition, of course, if the claims *are* more likely to succeed then the community may be prepared to sacrifice large lump sum payments in occasional cases for smaller but more regular awards. What is clear is that the society in question would have to disabuse itself of the notion that compensation awards would be calculated on the same basis as they are in the common law systems. Less money, but perhaps more equitable distribution of financial redress, would be the net result.

More problematic, however, is the situation of those who do not manage to establish eligibility for the new scheme. Not only will they doubtless feel badly as a result of this rejection but they may also be reluctant to pursue an action in the civil law having already tried and failed in one system. One commentator, however, has claimed that:

> It is clear from the attempts made by victims who have been intention-

ally or recklessly injured to use the common law rights of action, that the social justice aimed for by the Woodhouse proposals has resulted in grave injustice to some. This ought not to be a feature of social reform.[18]

However, there is no real or systematic evidence of a mad rush to the courts. Indeed, as Mahoney notes:

> A public that has been told for a decade that the drunk driver and the rapist are immune from civil suit can hardly be expected to learn by osmosis from a few legal journals the possibilities of suing a doctor where medical treatment does not turn out as expected or promised.[19]

Common law advocates have also pointed to additional problems with the New Zealand scheme. The Woodhouse Report levelled its attack particularly at the negligence action – an action which is in general not without its critics. But the institution of the Accident Compensation Scheme did more than merely remove this action from the forefront of litigation. Except when forced to take advantage of the residual rights of action, the common law board was swept clean. This, in effect, means that actions which were not open to the scathing indictment of negligence analysis also vanished into legal limbo. As Klar notes:

> . . . the legislation bars all civil proceedings which relate to damages arising directly or indirectly from personal injury and death by accident, and not merely actions which would have been based on negligence law. This includes actions in occupier's liability, product liability, nuisance, strict liability, intentional torts, and so on. Causes of action which have never been the subject of criticism from tort law opponents and which do not share the same defects as negligence law, have been eliminated.[20]

This brief review of the New Zealand system was designed to outline the world's most comprehensive no fault compensation scheme and to highlight some of its major problems. Most notably, perhaps, there remains considerable room for discretionary decision-making in this, as in the traditional, system. From the point of view of patients, therefore, interpretation of 'accident', 'disease' and 'medical misadventure' will be vitally important to their capacity to obtain compensation under the new, more accessible, scheme and will predict whether or not they are thrown back on to the common law action, with all its problems. Some analysis of the scope given to these terms is therefore appropriate.

## Accident compensation and the patient

One area of particular interest in jurisdictions retaining common law actions has been that which relates to medical negligence. In some countries there is said to be an explosion in medical litigation, and patients and others have sometimes been disaffected by the attitudes adopted by courts. In Woodhouse's terms, medicine might be seen as an area in which his justification for state compensation is particularly clear. The practice and development of medicine are clear examples of society's desires for progress, and medicine is an inherently risky process. Therefore, one might think, this an area in which claims would be frequent, whatever the skills of the doctor, and deserving claims would be equally regular.

Policy factors in common law countries have been used to expand the liability of some individuals and groups, but there is a recurring suggestion that '[t]here has been a surprisingly strong emphasis on policy, not so much to expand, but rather to limit, the application of negligence to doctors.'[21] The Pearson Commission in the United Kingdom apparently acknowledged this trend in noting relative success rates in personal injury actions.[22] While the general success rate was high, in medical cases it was considerably lower, and although there may be a number of factors involved in this finding (in particular that settlements are often made out of court) it would none the less at first sight seem likely that the victims of medical accident (which the Pearson Commission felt to be the largest group) would be considerably benefitted by a system such as the accident compensation scheme. No longer would the medical profession be subjected to ever-increasing public allegations of negligence in their high-risk practice, nor would patients find themselves dissatisfied with the legal process, if claims were heard privately, need not depend on allegations of professional fault and were settled relatively quickly.

Courts in the United Kingdom have frequently referred to the problems generated by a *laissez-faire* attitude to medical claims, and condemned the impact of readily available compensation on health care. Substantial awards of damages have come under fire as having an impact on the profession and on the provision of health care.[23] Under the New Zealand scheme such problems would, in theory, be things of the past. Doctors would pay no more in terms of insurance were the patient to be compensated, reputations would remain intact, patients would receive some (periodically reassessed) assistance, and since awards are designed to cushion rather than to replace loss there would be no need for the huge lump sum awards increasingly made in some countries.[24]

The Woodhouse Report was critical of the underlying philosophy of the negligence action, and therefore was at pains to use alternative and potentially more wide-ranging terminology. The term selected – 'misadventure' – was designed to cover the unlooked-for side-effects of medical treatment thus avoiding the value judgements inherent in the terminology of negligence. Theoretically, as Blair points out:

> It is plain that 'medical misadventure' is broader in meaning than *medical negligence* and that to qualify for compensation . . . it is sufficient for a claimant to show a causal relationship between a medical mishap amounting to medical misadventure and his injury.[25]

Misadventure, therefore, need not include negligence although clearly it could. Rather it is an 'event arising out of medical treatment which causes undesigned injury to a patient which may not be regarded as an illness flowing naturally from the treatment'.[26] The Accident Compensation Corporation itself gives to doctors an apparently straightforward account of what is meant by medical misadventure:

> The effect of the definition is that it is not necessary to show that there has been negligence on the part of a medical practitioner before a claim will lie for medical misadventure. The definition embraces the cases where the correct procedures were carried out but where a mischance or accident, unexpected and undesigned, occurred.[27]

This seems quite straightforward, and if there is no need to establish negligence then the assumption must be that patients are more likely to receive compensation under the accident compensation scheme. But is this so?

What anyone has to establish in order to be compensated under the scheme is that the relevant damage was the result of personal injury by accident (an unexpected or unlooked for event) and that it did not therefore amount to sickness or disease. In the case of the patient, one possible way of showing this is to demonstrate that the injury was the result of medical misadventure, which is an example of what could be termed personal injury by accident. Medical misadventure, therefore, is not an alternative definition of personal injury by accident. Merely, it is one species of personal injury by accident and it was not intended that establishing it should impose a further evidential burden on the victim.

An analysis of some of the cases which have been decided under the accident compensation scheme will serve to demonstrate whether or not the patient is more likely to be compensated within the framework of these determining factors. While the two elements (personal injury by accident and medical misadventure) were not necessarily intended to be different and distinct, it is intended in this section to deal with them in a separate manner in as much as this is possible. Consideration will first be made of personal injury by accident in the context of its relationship to sickness and disease, and second of medical misadventure, and in particular the unexpected nature of the event.

## Accident and disease

> The difficulty [of defining accident] is especially apparent in the area of response to medical and surgical treatment. People differ widely in their inherent attributes, their life styles, their dietary habits and so on. The reaction therefore to particular medical or surgical treatment is likely to differ widely from individual to individual.[28]

This statement makes clear some of the difficulties particularly associated with distinguishing between 'accident' and sickness. Further, it points to the special problems which occur when the accident arises as a part, or as the result, of medical treatment. Nowhere is it more difficult to make such a differentiation than in this context, where injuries or damage may arise spontaneously in the course of treatment. When reviewing the cases, there are two points to bear in mind. First, that a distinction has been made between accident and disease, and that this will be maintained by the decision makers. Second, that accident must be an unlooked-for and unexpected event (according to Woodhouse, unlooked-for and unexpected by the person to whom it happens) arising from an external cause.

The difference between accident and disease is made clear in one case, in which it was held that the development of an embolus after surgery was not an 'accident' even although the patient did not expect it.[29] Rather it is by its nature a process of sickness or disease – not an accident. Not only is it a progressive condition, but it is also a known possibility of surgery and therefore not accidental. The second point will be considered later. The distinction between accident and disease is particularly problematic in medical cases, primarily because the results of badly or inadequately administered treatment, or of a failure to treat, may often manifest themselves as a complication or continuation of the pre-existing disease.

Under the common law, it is possible, although rare, for doctors to be held liable for a failure in diagnosis if this is negligently done. The responsibilities of doctors include a duty to treat reasonably, which may include accurate assessment of condition. Although failure to diagnose is not always negligent, it may be, depending on the circumstances of the case. One immediate problem of the accident compensation scheme (as far as the patient is concerned) is that there is almost no way (even where there is negligence) that a failure to treat or diagnose can be deemed to be personal injury by accident. The reasoning is as follows: whatever harm has been caused as the result of failing to make an accurate diagnosis or omitting to treat is harm which resulted from the original illness itself. Because illness is not accident it cannot be compensated under the scheme. Although there remains a residual right to raise a common law action, only rarely will the courts be prepared to hold a doctor liable in these circumstances. The patient is, therefore, pratically denied redress for what may be major disabilities. As one Appeal Decision put it '. . . one must be satisfied that the omission by the doctor to either diagnose the disease or to discover the condition during the operation process materially contributed to the death.'[30] The test is, therefore, very stringent, and difficult to meet. As one Review Decision points out:

> . . . a failure to diagnose leading to the true ailment not receiving medical treatment can rarely, if ever, be the foundation for a claim under the Act, in that the patient's condition remains attributable to the ailment alone.[31]

Although the outcome is achieved by a different route, the impact of the new scheme is much the same as that of the common law. Failure to treat or diagnose will virtually never be compensable under the Accident Compensation Acts. In fact, it may be the case that the patient has a relatively better chance of success under the common law, an outcome surely not designed or predicted by the proponents of the accident compensation scheme.

Nor are problems solely associated with clear failures to treat or diagnose. Where the patient involved has a pre-existing condition which comes to light or is exacerbated by an event in the nature of an accident, there may be further difficulties in assessing what actually is the cause of the harm. It is worth noting that only in cases such as these is cause actually relevant to the assessment of eligibility, a situation which patently results from the problematic distinction between accident and disease. A clear example is the case of a person with a pre-existing back condition which is exacerbated by a fall. Now, vast numbers of people, especially among the older groups in the community, will have some back problems as the body begins to wear down. The fall is an accident within the meaning of the Act, but the actual harm is the result of the pre-existing back condition. Thus the person will not receive compensation under the scheme because the damage is caused by illness and not accident.

What then is medical misadventure? It is not disease, and it is not failure by the doctor to make an accurate diagnosis or to treat. In fact, the circumstances which would entitle the patient to compensation under this scheme relate very closely to those which would be compensable under the fault based system. The authoritative definition of medical misadventure is contained in one review case, and is as follows:

> Medical misadventure is when (a) a person suffers bodily or mental injury or damage in the course of, and as part of, the administering to that person of medical aid, care or attention, and (b) such injury or damage is caused by mischance or accident, unexpected and undesigned, in the nature of a medical error or medical mishap.[32]

This statement equates medical misadventure to situations where there is medical error or medical mishap. It is worth noting that the word 'negligence' is never used in this context. Indeed it is clear that the intention of the legislators was that misadventure should amount to more than just negligence. As has been said:

> It is plain that medical misadventure is broader in meaning than medical negligence. If Parliament had intended that cover for this kind of injury was to be restricted to that resulting from negligence, it would have used the well understood word 'negligence' rather than invent the phrase 'medical misadventure'.[33]

If the term 'medical misadventure' is broader in meaning than medical negligence then one would anticipate that this would inevitably mean that more cases would fit within its terms. The fact that fault need not be proved might also encourage liberal decision making within the system since the doctor's reputation, so often raised as an issue under the common law, would not be damaged where no attribution of fault is made. However, it has been seen that the term may in fact not be significantly wider than medical negligence, and it is submitted that – in reality – the two correspond rather closely. Indeed, Palmer has noted that in these cases there is a clear similarity between the tests used for medical misadventure and those used for medical negligence.[34]

Medical misadventure, then, is certainly not intended to be the same as medical negligence, although there is a certain similarity in the tests used to establish them. Moreover, it may even be that in some cases the interpretation of misadventure is narrower than the interpretation of negligence. Misadventure is defined in terms of medical error or mishap, terms which have been authoritatively reviewed in one leading decision.

> 1.  *'Medical error'* means the failure of a person involved in the administering of medical aid, care or attention to observe a standard of care and skill reasonably to be expected of him in the circumstances. Medical error can relate to the correctness, the propriety, the adequacy, and the quality of the medical aid, care or attention given. Error may arise either in the performance of that aid, care or attention, or in the diagnosis, judgement, or preparation that leads to it. It arises only if the service to the patient is of a lower standard than was reasonably to be expected in the circumstances . . . *The test may be considered similar to the test of negligence in the common law system, but it is not intended that they should necessarily coincide.* (emphasis added)
>
> 2.  'Medical mishap' . . . as a generalisation, but not as a definition, 'medical mishap' normally describes the situation when there is the intervention or intrusion into the administering of medical aid, care or attention of some unexpected and undesigned incident, event or circumstance, of a medical nature, that has harmful consequences to the patient.[35]

Ultimately, then, medical misadventure can be described in terms very similar to those which would describe medical negligence. The above definitions explain circumstances in which – even under the common law – a claim for damages has a reasonable chance of success, the latter by the use of the doctrine of *res ipsa loquitur*.[36] Clearly, 'medical error' relates very closely to the accepted view of negligence, and 'medical mishap' seems to envisage situations where, for example, a swab is left behind in a patient or a surgical instrument breaks and causes harm.[37]

Indeed, in many of the accident compensation decisions in medical cases there is a striking similarity between the kinds of tests used for medical misadventure and those used in assessing negligence under other systems. However, there is a further problem for the claimant under the accident compensation scheme in that the damage caused has to be in the nature of an accident and not a continuation of the existing ill-health. In many cases, as has been seen, it may be that the necessary distinction will be hard to make. Damage may not readily be attributable either to accident or to the pre-existing complaint, and where there is doubt as to attribution, the scales will weigh in favour of disease. As Blair puts it:

> If the medical evidence is in such terms as to leave the Commission with the impression that, as between accident and disease, the scales are evenly balanced, then it cannot be sucessfully contended that the

condition laid down by the statute has been met, and the claim for compensation is therefore not established.[38]

Narrow decision making is sometimes claimed to be a feature of medical negligence cases and seems to be not uncommon in the accident compensation scheme. It seems clear that by making the distinction between accident and disease, the intention of the legislators and the Woodhouse Commission was to limit the availability of compensation to certain groups. It has already been pointed out that this distinction is philosophically illogical and pragmatically problematic. In the case of the injured patient these problems would seem to be exacerbated by the apparent reluctance of decision makers to award compensation in medical cases. As Hughes says:

> . . . it is suggested that there has been an unfortunate tendency to restrict the concept of 'medical misadventure' rather than approaching it in a liberal way so as to incorporate an expanded 'injury' element in the definition of 'personal injury by accident.[39]

The disaffected patient is, then, unlikely to be more readily compensated under the accident compensation scheme than under the negligence action, and indeed may sometimes be in a worse position given the range of qualifications which apply to medical cases.

## Summary

The Woodhouse condemnation of the negligence action coupled with the desire to include more people within the ambit of accident compensation demanded the use of a less narrow and value laden terminology than that of negligence. To confine the award of compensation to circumstances equating to negligence, with the implication of fault, runs completely contrary to the ideology of the scheme. Equally, in theory at least, no special allowances are made for any group whose behaviour may contribute to the occurrence of harm to others. Certainly doctors are given no special status under the Accident Compensation Acts, and the patient may therefore expect to be treated in the same way as any other potential claimant.

Unlike the tort or delict systems, which concern themselves with factors extraneous to the actual harm, the accident compensation scheme should be indifferent to them. While judges, and indeed some commentators, in the common law jurisdictions of the world have expressed disquiet about the impact on the practice of medicine of a finding of negligence in respect of a doctor, theoretically such concern is foreign to the New Zealand scheme and should not contribute to the assessment of eligibility for compensation.

However, there is some evidence that: '[t]he Commission has interpreted the new phrase [medical misadventure] cautiously with the result that doctors remain at common law risk to some extent if the interpretation be correct.'[40] Indeed, the evidence tends to suggest that 'medical misadventure' has been interpreted not merely as an example of personal injury by accident, but almost as a further test to be met in establishing eligibility for compensation under the scheme.

Statements from decision makers in the accident compensation scheme and in cases relating to it are remarkably similar to those used by some judges in the tort or delict system. For example in *ACC v. Auckland Hospital Board*[41] the judge almost echoes the words of Lord Denning in the case of *Roe v. Ministry of Health*[42] by saying that '[i]t is the nature of medical and surgical treatment that unexpected and abnormal consequences may follow . . .'[43] The expectation that adverse consequences may follow medical treatment is deemed to have an impact on their status as 'accidents' or 'misadventure' for the purposes of compensation. For example, the judge continued:

> Where there is an unsatisfactory outcome of treatment which can be classified as merely within the normal range of medical or surgical failure attendant upon the most felicitous treatment, it could not be held to be a misadventure.[44]

There is, as Palmer says, 'a ring of the old tort law'[45] in such a statement – almost as if the impact of the occurrence of the risk on the patient is less significant than the interests of medicine or the protection of the reputation of the doctor. Under the accident compensation scheme such factors should be irrelevant. Nonetheless '[t]he Commission by its restrictive interpretation seems concerned to avoid sliding down the slippery slope and compensating illness or death every time medical treatment fails.'[46]

Since the outcome of failed or risky medical treatment may be illness, then the distinction between accident and disease becomes particularly relevant. While this distinction has been described as illogical, it may be less problematic if consistently applied. Thus the patient may seem to be in no worse a position than anyone else whose disability or loss flows from sickness rather than accident. However the patient *is* in a different position, partly because he or she is almost by definition already ill and the problems of distinguishing between illness and accident are therefore exacerbated. As

Klar points out there is a kind of rough and ready distinction drawn by the Corporation, but this distinction is not without problems.[47]

## Information disclosure and no fault liability

This somewhat lengthy discussion of the replacement of 'medical negligence' by 'medical misadventure' is relevant as setting the basic standards to be applied in comparing the two systems. Since alleged failures to make adequate disclosure to patients are now generally dealt with by the negligence action, its counterpart in the no fault system is of considerable interest. The problems associated with the interpretation of 'medical misadventure' are therefore of concern to all patients alleging that they were denied relevant information. For these patients, however, there are even further hurdles to be overcome.

The effect of medical intervention (or lack of it) may be that the patient's illness continues unabated – this will remain uncompensated. In addition, there is no pretence at developing an ideology in relation to patients' rights to receive and use relevant information, since it would seem that the only person whose ignorance of risk is irrelevant is the patient. The calculation of unexpectedness, said to be so central to eligibility, in this situation alone seems not to relate to the person who suffers the harm. Yet the Woodhouse Commission related unexpectedness directly to the person who suffers harm, with the implication that if something unexpected and caused by an external event happens then compensation logically follows. In the run of the mill case this is precisely what happens, but there would seem to be a difference in approach when dealing with those injured in the course of medical treatment. Consider this statement:

> It is against human experience that the results of medical treatment will always be favourable . . . There must be few significant medical treatments that do not contain some risk of the results being contrary to hopes and expectations and some risks of developments adverse to the patient's condition. The likelihood of the risk eventuating, the gravity of the possible consequences, and the balance struck between these attendant risks and the advantages that might be gained, are factors influencing the decision as to whether the treatment should be given and accepted. But if adverse developments or results are known to reasonably informed medical opinion to constitute a known risk of the treatment, and that risk then materialises, can it be said that those adverse risks are personal injury by accident? In my view a person who accepts (or in some cases is deemed to accept) medical treatment is to be regarded as accepting the possibility that the known

risks may eventuate. It is not to be considered as an 'accident' to him if the consequences that are at risk do in fact occur.[48]

There are a number of interesting points about this statement. First, it seems to say that only those risks which are unexpected will be covered by the scheme. This, of course, is entirely in line with the Woodhouse view and the routine interpretation of the Acts. However, what is different, is the apparent presumption that the unexpectedness element is linked to the knowledge of a third party. At no point is it suggested in any of the cases that the patient's lack of knowledge is the crucial factor. In other words, if the doctor knows of a risk the occurrence of that risk will not be compensable, whether or not it was known to the patient.

There is a further difficulty with the concept of 'unexpectedness'. To say that adverse side-effects are not 'unexpected' rather than not known may be to stretch the unexpectedness factor considerably. Even where the patient is informed of possible risks, it may, in cases where the risk factor is small, be stretching common sense too far to suggest that because they are known they are also expected. In fact, if one looks at other types of claim it can be seen that foreknowledge of possible risk is not held to render the harm 'expected'. For example, the well-known risk to participants in certain contact sports does not preclude compensation in the event of that risk occurring. One can only hypothesize that the perceived difference between the two cases is the involvement of a third party, that is the doctor. If this is so, then there would seem to be – even under the accident compensation scheme – an apparent reluctance to attribute responsibility for harm to medicine, perhaps because it is seen as itself a social 'good'.

In medical cases, some relatively sophisticated interpretation of language has been indulged in to avoid the admission that the damaging event was an accident and therefore compensable. For example, in one Review case it was said:

In relation to many forms of medical or surgical treatment there are known complications or consequences and some of them may, when they occur, be unexpected by the patient although anticipated by the doctor or surgeon . . . that degree of unexpectedness, however, does not mean that the complications or consequences must not only be adverse to the patient's well-being but must also have been unexpected by the doctor or surgeon giving the treatment.[49]

It is open to question why such an interpretation should be adopted by the Accident Compensation Corporation. Moreover there is no necessary implication in any other type of claim that a risk has been accepted, whether or not the person was aware of its existence, merely because someone else knew of the possibility of the risk eventuating. What such an interpretation seems to do is to reinforce the notion that patients tacitly accept the risks of treatment whether or not these are fully or partially explained to them. In other words, this is remarkably similar to the interpretation often adopted in common law systems. One further possible explanation for narrowing the scope of liability in this area is the desire (again apparent in other jurisdictions) to avoid the ascription of liability in medical cases.

It should be noted, however, that the accident compensation scheme is not in theory concerned with the ascription of liability but rather with the amelioration of loss and harm. The concept of personal liability, which is central to the tortious or delictual action, is not of relevance in this system, except, it would appear, in medical cases. If this is the case, then it seems that in cases involving patients the decision makers *are* considering 'blame' or 'fault' and taking account of factors extraneous to the claim itself in assessing eligibility. This leaves the patient in a vulnerable position. Denied access to the accident compensation scheme, he or she is left only with the option of using the residual common law action. Yet Woodhouse was highly critical of this action which is not notoriously successful in medical cases.

In one case a rule of thumb was given which is worthy of note. Normal risks of medical treatment (whether or not expected by the patient) will not constitute personal injury by accident. But:

> . . . it is possible that some adverse consequences of medical treatment might be so rare or so grave that they should fairly be regarded as constituting personal injury by accident. I would consider that entitlement would be granted in such circumstances only if the following qualifications are met:
> (a) the risk that eventuated was a rare and remote one;
> (b) such risk would not reasonably be taken into account when considering the wisdom of the treatment proposed;
> (c) the consequences were grave and totally disproportionate to the significance normally attached to the treatment;
> (d) such consequences were clearly beyond the extent of adverse consequences that would normally and reasonably be contemplated as included within the risk.[50]

The impact of this view is clear. First, there is a requirement that if a risk eventuates which *will* be classified as 'personal injury by accident' it must be grave, rare and remote. So rare or remote, in fact, that it would not normally be taken into account – in fact, not even disclosed to the patient, since it would not normally be taken into account (by the physician). The patient, therefore, *may*, but only may, have a right to receive certain information (although New Zealand Courts are unlikely to be more radical than others) but certainly has no right to receive information about risks which doctors regard as rare or remote, and as unlikely to be taken into consideration. This test, in fact relates fairly closely to the 'reasonable doctor' standard applied in many other jurisdictions, since the tenor of the judgement clearly suggests that there are risks which need not and would not be disclosed. If this is the case then the phrase 'reasonably taken into account' must relate to the doctor and not to the potential sufferer of the risk.

There is, therefore, no real incentive for doctors to tell patients any of the risks, since failure to disclose risks known as possible by the doctor means only that the patient is not permitted the option of choosing in a rational manner not to have the therapy. If the risk is sufficiently 'normal' and it occurs, this is not 'personal injury by accident' and the patient cannot successfully claim under the Accident Compensation Scheme. The fact that a residual right of action remains is scant comfort.

## Conclusions

Many of the criticisms which can legitimately be levelled at negligence analysis manifestly do not apply in the no fault system. But the New Zealand system does incorporate its own set of difficulties, such as the exclusion of disease (leading to the drawing of fine and arguable distinctions). In addition, the system is equally vulnerable to the vagaries of interpretation, and the importation of extra-legal factors, which critics of the fault based system would argue make it essentially unpredictable and ultimately unfair. Clear guidance as the meaning of 'medical misadventure' is one requirement which could help to minimize these problems.[51]

In fact, the New Zealand system seems paradoxically to have placed the patient in a situation remarkably similar to his or her counterpart in other, less radical, systems. As Mahoney[52] points out:

> The restrictive interpretation which has been placed upon the phrase 'medical misadventure' has resulted in many deserving claimants being excluded from the aegis of the definition of 'personal injury by accident' and thereby from receipt of compensation under the Act.[53]

He does, however, see the possibility of improvement following the judgement of Bisson J in the case of *MacDonald* v. *The Accident Compensation Corporation*[54] but admits that it is by no means certain that this one case will set a pattern for future decision making. Indeed, cases which preceded *MacDonald* by only a short space of time were decided on the basis that '. . . unless the patient asks the doctor specifically about the risks the doctor is under no obligation to inform the patient.'[55] In any event, it does seem likely that the very existence of the scheme might discourage people from raising an action in the courts where they have failed to have their damage recognized by the Accident Compensation Corporation.

The New Zealand system, therefore, both presents novel problems for the patient who was not informed of risks or alternatives in therapy, and may be said to compound some of the old ones. Admittedly, not all of the problems are insurmountable, since they depend on attitudes and these can change. Others, however, such as the definition of 'accident' are more central to the structure of the system, and less readily susceptible of change. What current decision making in New Zealand shares with the fault based tradition is an apparent reluctance to award damages in cases where what is under challenge is the professional practice of physicians. This attitude is perhaps even more acute in cases relating to information disclosure. Both the traditional and the radical systems appear unprepared to value what could be seen as abstract rights over the preservation of the practice of medicine. Indeed, the radical system almost *could* not value such things because of resource limitations and eligibility requirements, and certainly any argument which led to the conclusion that the human and the technical can be, or should be, separated in decision making seems doomed to failure. Perhaps the fault based system, by concentrating on personal liability, could encourage an approach that relates to rights and duties, but this is foreign to the no fault approach.

As a result, therefore, of the attitudes of the decision makers in the accident compensation scheme, some people, by virtue of their already vulnerable position, become even more vulnerable. They cannot claim successfully where no treatment is given or where the wrong treatment is provided. They must face the inherently tricky task of showing that their injuries result from accident and not disease. Without resorting eventually to the tort based action they cannot claim in respect of a lack of real consent to treatment, and they are forced to accept risks which may never have been disclosed to them. In many cases they will be thrown back on the much-maligned negligence action. The aims of Woodhouse to support and rehabilitate the work force cannot be achieved in this way.

There are further implications flowing from this interpretation which also have serious repercussions for all patients. There is clearly no incentive within the scheme to protect the patient's right to make knowing choices about the desirability of treatment from his or her point of view if consent (or at least acceptance of risks and benefits) is implied from acceptance of the treatment. Problems of information disclosure will be left to the common law with the possible exception of those cases where consent was given to one treatment but another was actually undertaken. Even under systems which use the traditional approach such cases are given special protection, but they will amount to only a very small proportion of the total.

In any event, failure to disclose the existence of a known risk which may have affected a patient's choice, but which did not in fact eventuate, can never be compensable under the accident compensation scheme, since it does not and cannot meet the tests for eligibility. Evidently, if the insult is to integrity and does not result in incapacitation from work, then there is no basis for compensation in Woodhouse's terms. Changes in interpretation of 'accident' or 'medical misadventure' could offer compensation in cases where harm resulted, but could never provide a vindication of the abstract right, since the kind of harm caused is not legally recognized.

A broad interpretation of pesonal injury by accident and medical misadventure would include negligence as well as other accidental mishaps which occur in medical practice. It would also minimize the common law risks to the doctor and ensure compensation for the patient who is damaged whether or not by anyone's fault. However a review of decisions would suggest that in fact only limited categories of medical events are deemed to be included in the cover offered by the accident compensation scheme. These are roughly as follows:

1. situations where the doctrine of *res ipsa loquitur* would have been applied under the common law;
2. accidental damage to, or breaking of, implements used in the medical transaction; and
3. acts of operational negligence.

The situations excluded would be:

1. failure to treat or diagnose accurately;
2. the occurrence of risks known to the doctor but not necessarily to the patient; and
3. failure to make disclosure of sufficient information to permit a morally satisfactory decision by a patient.

Thus, the new scheme neither covers all aspects of what might have been negligence under the pre-existing system nor does it cover all situations which would equate to a common sense view of what amounts to 'accident'. As Cripps says:

> The proposition that personal injury caused by negligence is not synonymous with personal injury caused by accident, and hence may not be covered by the Act, has been accepted by the Authority and by the Courts. Although such acceptance appears at first sight to run contrary to the intention of the legislation to abolish the negligence proceeding for personal injury, it illustrates yet again the difficulties involved in clearly defining the term 'accident' for the purposes of the Act.[56]

Misguided attempts to protect the conventional practice of medicine and the unfortunate distinction between accident and illness conspire to leave both doctor and patient in a vulnerable position. In this area, accident compensation decisions bear a striking resemblance to their counterparts in common law jurisdictions and only enlightened decision making will alter this unsatisfactory situation. Effective cover will only be available when a wide interpretation is used and the distinction between accident and sickness is removed.

Admittedly, were a no fault system to be adopted in other countries, it need not, and probably would not, be in exactly the same terms as that which exists in New Zealand. The problem is, however, that there would still have to be tests for eligibility which would inevitably bear in mind the potential cost to the state. Limitation on availability of compensation is inevitable, and even if the distinction between accident and illness were not a feature of, say, a British scheme, it seems unlikely that insult to integrity would play an important role in the hierarchy of compensable harms, since it does not seem to at the moment even under the traditional systems.

It might be said, of course, that this is just the luck of the game, and that it is scarcely an important enough point to merit a denial of, or resistance to, the no fault ideal. This is a point which may be well taken, since – if it is the case that more and speedier compensation is available – there need be no major problem in leaving information disclosure cases to the traditional court forum. In fact, most people would probably support a move to no fault, even with its drawbacks, and any change in the basis of liability would meet with approval particularly where a residual right of action remains. The problems, therefore, are back in the court of negligence analysis. Unless and until courts concede the importance of self-determination in medicine, the patient who is insulted by the unwarranted assumption of authority over his or her body or mind, will remain uncompensated and, perhaps even more importantly, unsupported. These patients can derive no comfort from a radical change in liability for personal injury and will continue to be forced into a system which pays scant attention to their claims. The answer, if there is one, seems then to lie in the analysis currently most commonly used.

## Notes

1.  For discussion of the Swedish system see Royal Commission on Civil Liability and Compensation for Personal Injury (Pearson Commission) Cmnd 7054/1978
2.  Accident Compensation Act 1982 s. 2 (ii)
3.  Ibid., s.2 (*b*) (i) and (ii)
4.  Compensation for Personal Injury in New Zealand (Woodhouse Report), Wellington 1967, esp. at para 289, p.113.
5.  Ibid., para 55, p. 39
6.  Cripps, C. R., 'Medical practitioners' liability for personal injury caused by negligence' *N.Z. Law, J.* 83 [1978], at p. 84.
7.  For discussion, see Mahoney, R., 'Informed consent and breach of the medical contract to achieve a particular result: opportunities for New Zealand's latent personal injuries litigators to peek out of the accident compensation closet', 6 *Otago Law Review* 103 (1985).
8.  [1972] All E R 145.
9.  *Medical Information Bulletin*, No. 13, Oct. 1981.
10. Mr Justice Woodhouse noted, for example, that '. . . the Accident Compensation scheme, in the five years of its operation to 1979, has been able to make savings for reserves of no less than $172.9 million.' Kennedy Elliott Memorial Lecture reproduced in *N.Z. Law J.* [1979] 395.
11. See, Sandford, K. L., 'Personal injury by accident' *N.Z. Law J.* 29 [1980] at p. 30 'The percentage of claims declined is less than 4 percent, and in a proportion of those the reason for declinature is some matter irrelevant to the present subject (e.g. that the accident happened before 1 April 1974).'
12. The Pearson Commission, supra cit., noted a success rate in personal injury litigation of 86% – para 1326.
13. In medical cases the success rate was 30–40%.
14. Black, Tony, 'What is Personal Injury by Accident?' *N.Z. Law J.* 465 [1979], at p. 42.
15. From *Jones* v. *Secretary of State for Social Services*, supra cit.
16. Appeal Dec. No. 9 (1976).
17. Klar, L. N., 'New Zealand's Accident Compensation Scheme: a tort lawyer's perspective' 33 *Univ. Toronto Law J.* 80 (1983), at p. 80.
18. Klar, loc. cit., at p. 88.
19. Mahoney, loc cit., at p. 137.
20. Loc. cit., at p. 86.
21. Gamble, A. J., 'Professional liability', in McLean, S.A.M., (ed), *Legal Issues in Medicine*, Aldershot, Gower, 1981, at p. 89.
22. Para 1326.
23. Cf. *Lim Poh Choo* v. *Camden & Islington A.H.A.* [1979] 1 All ER 332; for further discussion, see Brazier, M., *Medicine, Patients and the Law*, Harmondsworth, Penguin, 1987, chapter 6.
24. Blair, A. P., *Accident Compensation in New Zealand*, Wellington, Butterworths,

1978, at p. 9: '. . . the Act is not controlled by restitution principles, and in fact does not purport to provide full compensation, but rather attempts to minimise the accident victim's loss by providing both monetary and other practical help which will aid the claimant not only as regards the immediate difficulties caused by the accident, but also as regards the long term effects.'

25. Op. cit., at p. 43.
26. Id.
27 *Medical Information Bulletin No. 14* (Wellington, Accident Compensation Corporation) October 1981.
28. *Application for Review 74/R00186* (1974), at p. 3.
29. *Review No. 74/R00408* (1974) '. . . in the absence of original injury by accident I cannot accept that the development of an embolus can itself be regarded as an accident any more than many other physiological changes and reactions within the body.'
30. *Appeal Decision No. 9* (1976) at p. 6.
31. *Review No. 74/R00432* (1974).
32. *Review No. 77/R1352*, at p. 7.
33. Blair, op. cit., at p. 43.
34. Palmer, G. W. R., 'Accident compensation in New Zealand: the first two years' 25 *Am. J. Comp. Law* (1977) 1, at p. 38.
35. *Review No 77/R1352* (1977) at pp. 7–8.
36. I.e. the facts speak for themselves.
37. E.g. *Mahon* v. *Osborne* [1939] 2 KB 14.; *Cassidy* v. *Ministry of Health* [1951] 2 QB 66; Kilner Brown, J in *Ashcroft* v. *Mersey Regional Health Authority* [1983] 2 All ER 245, at p. 246: 'Where an injury is caused which should never have been caused, common sense and natural justice indicate that some degree of compensation ought to be paid by someone.'; *Grant* v. *Australian Knitting Mills* [1936] AC 85.
38. Op. cit, at p. 33.
39. Hughes, J, 'Accident compensation and childbirth' *N.Z.Law J.* 79 [1981] at p. 85.
40. Palmer, loc. cit., at p. 38.
41. [1981] NZACR 9.
42. [1954] 2 QB 66.
43. At p. 13.
44. Id.
45. Loc. cit. at p. 39.
46. Id.
47. Loc. cit.
48. Review No. 74/R00408 (1974) at p. 3.
49. Review No. 75/R0236 (1975) at p. 2.
50. Review No. 74/R00408 (1974) at p. 3.
51. For further discussion see Mahoney, loc. cit.; McLean, S.A.M., 'Liability Without Fault – The New Zealand Experience' [1985] *J.Soc. Welf. Law* 125
52. Loc cit.
53. At p. 105.
54. Unreported, High Court Administrative Division, Hamilton, 25 July, 1985, 55/85.
55. *Re Priestly* [1984] NZACR 787, per Willis J, at p. 789.
56. 'Medical practitioners liability for personal injury caused by negligence' *N.Z.Law J.* 83 [1978] at p. 83.

# 9 Conclusions

The question of patients' rights in medicine is one of increasing scholarly interest. It is, however, much more than a mere academic concern. Patients, doctors and lawyers are closely and sometimes painfully involved in the fight to assert and vindicate them. As medicine outstrips the lay person by its incredible capacities, so patients redefine their involvement with it. But medicine too has to rethink its aims and priorities. As Pellegrino and Thomasma have said:

> A philosophy of medicine is needed to help clarify medicine's goals in relationship to those of the technological civilisation. Medicine suffers from an abundance of means and a paucity of ends.[1]

The contention here has been that there is at present a certain ideological tension about the way in which certain patients' rights are dealt with both by physicians and by the law. In fact, there are some important paradoxes in the legal response to patients' rights in general and the right to receive and use information in particular. Although this right is justified by its capacity to facilitate autonomy-enhancing decisions it seems clear that many patients will be denied adequate information and that this denial will apparently be upheld by courts of law. Whatever physicians and lawyers may *say* they are doing, and however benign their motivation, the stark truth is that legally sanctioned behaviour is actively denying the autonomy of sane, adult patients.

Of course, if the rights we are talking about are about autonomy then at first sight it seems plausible to argue that they are only of limited value. Because we might choose to regard some groups as lacking the characteristics of autonomy they would surely be excluded. For this reason, two groups with particular legal disabilities were considered, and the conclusion was reached that the law is – in certain circumstances – currently prepared to extend to them the status of patient with all the attendant rights which

162

this implies. While conceding that there may be some circumstances where extending the right to information would be without value beyond the symbolic it was also contended that there is no clear rationale for a blanket denial of rights in health care to these groups.

Examples of the legal response to special groups in fact seem to show that importance *is* attached to the facilitation, where possible, of their autonomy. In other words, for many of them the position is the same as that of the sane adult. Not only does this bring with it the benefits of such a status, however, but it also imports the drawbacks. If even the sane adult is not routinely provided with adequate information, then neither are they. There would seem to be two main reasons for the uneven distribution of rights.

In the first place, the law is not required to recognize every interest as meriting legal protection. Thus, if the law *never* did recognize the need for information disclosure, then it could simply be said that it does not feature in the hierarchy of interests. Manifestly, however, this is not so. Although protection is sporadic it is none the less there. This leads to the second point, that the failure to respect rights in all cases stems from the unwillingness of the law to distinguish between the human and the technical aspects of medicine. Clearly, patients are not in a position to reach technical conclusions, but they evidently *are* in a position to make personal choices about their lives, including their health care. As Shultz says:

> . . . although patients may be incapable of supervising the quality and administration of care, they are capable, indeed uniquely so, of balancing ultimate costs and benefits of care decisions. Moreover, they are capable of determining the extent to which they wish to allocate decision making authority to their doctors.[2]

Ideally, of course, the good practice of medicine would not distinguish between the technical and the human, but this is no reason why the courts cannot or should not do so. Patient concern for a technically competent medical act is obviously very important but their interest in autonomy is equally important. Society as a whole has a genuine and legitimate interest in ensuring not just that medicine is practised competently, but also that it is carried out ethically. The ethics of medicine however cannot and should not be determined simply or solely by reference to professional etiquette or accepted practice. They demand standards which are set by reference to more wide ranging concerns. But if the law fails to make this distinction and fails to validate patients' claims for respect then the ethics of medicine will continue to be those set by the profession itself.

It can be said that the law does invest information disclosure with a significance which makes it worthy of consideration. That significance relates not only to respect for persons but also legit-imates medical behaviour. A knowing choice is the precursor of a medical act for which consent has been truly (and therefore legally) given. But this recognition, unfortunately, stops short of a real commitment. No legal system as yet has evolved a process of sufficient sophistication to deal sensitively with the complex and subtle issues of freedom of choice in medicine. Or at least, the process may exist but it is not currently used in this way. Reluctance to initiate decision-making practices which respect patients' rights even in the face of competing professional interests, may stem from two distinct sources.

On the one hand is the perception of general beneficence. That medicine is a benign discipline is not disputed, but there is a real question as to whether or not this justifies the kind of special status apparently accorded to it. Eminent judges and scholars have been prepared to accept, apparently without question, two main impli-cations as flowing from this status. First, that litigation is to be discouraged since it will adversely affect the practice of medicine, and second that arguments for non-disclosure or limited disclosure, based on medical opinion, are legitimate bases for reaching conclusions which affect the rights of patients. Both of these have already been challenged but it may be worth briefly restating the basis for rejecting them.

If litigation is discouraged then wrongs go unrecognized and unrectified. Moreover, if finding a negligent doctor to be negligent has adverse effects on other non-negligent doctors then this tells us something about the professional group itself. It is certainly not logical, and is not an argument adduced to discourage litigation in respect of, for example, solicitors. Further, if it is accepted that respect for patient autonomy is a matter of much wider importance than the description of (medically) acceptable medical practice then it is equally clear that the law has a role to play in delivering independent judgements about how autonomy can be respected. The relevant information is not derivative from the accepted wisdom of the profession, yet all too often this is the basis of the courts' decisions.

A further barrier to recognition of patients' right is erected by the failure to distinguish between the technical and the human or moral aspects of medicine. This has resulted in an unhappy dependence on the evidence of 'experts' and leaves the patient with a theoretical right of action which in practice seems doomed to failure. Moreover, this approach prioritizes the duties of the doctor when the real issue is the rights of the patient from which these duties are derivative. In any event, if the adequacy of information disclosure is tested against medical criteria then it is easy to validate non-disclosure or limited disclosure by reference to fears of deterring patients from accepting therapy or likely patient distress.

If the law is to accord respect to the patient, and to set appropriate standards for medicine, then a mechanism must be found which permits it to do so. It is important, therefore, that decision makers proceed from the presumption that rights exist and should be vindicated, but it is also important that vindication is feasible within the system of liability pertaining at any given time. The radical system in New Zealand has been shown to be inadequate in this respect, and paradoxically it is to the much-maligned negligence action that we may turn for satisfaction. One other possibility which must, however, be touched on briefly is the possibility of raising an action based on contract.

## A remedy in contract?

One option not so far considered in detail would be the raising of an action on the basis of the existence of a contract between doctor and patient. In the United Kingdom, cases based on contract have indeed been raised,[3] and it is fair to say that the patient who is involved in private health care may find him/herself with access to significantly improved rights of choice since freedom of choice is central to the nature of a contract. Deceit, fraud or inadequacy of information can render any contract null and void,[4] and the patient is theoretically in no different a position from that of any other contracting party. Further, as the court pointed out in *Edgar* v. *Lamont*[5] the private nature of an agreement may well provide a remedy in contract but does not deny the existence of delictual or tortious liability. In *Thake* v.*Maurice*[6] the existence of a private arrangement between doctor and a patient was taken at first instance to introduce an implied warranty into the agreement that the service would fulfill the purpose for which it was undertaken, and a failure to indicate that success was not inevitable could then be taken as sufficient to lead to an award of damages.

The fact that an additional protection may be offered by the existence of a contractual agreement, however, serves to emphasize, not solely the value of the contract itself, but rather the importance of information disclosure to a valid agreement. Vindication of access to information is facilitated by the nature of a contractual arrangement, but is not generated by it. Since the majority of health care provision in the United Kingdom is undertaken through the National Health Service, the theoretical availability of contractual redress is, however, of limited relevance. In any event, there is no clear rationale for legal rules which permit some patients access to vital information, but deny it to others, merely on the grounds of their capacity to pay for the service or on the strength of their ideological or political commitments to health care provision as a whole.

In some jurisdictions, however, the availability of a contractual remedy will have considerably more significance, for example in the United States, where health care is essentially a private agreement between patient and doctor, for a fee. However, the availability of contractual remedies depends on the classification made of the event under scrutiny. Issues of professional malpractice in the United States are routinely dealt with on the basis of the negligence action, and if failure to disclose information is perceived as an aspect of professional duties, rather than as a free-standing interest, then the temptation will be to deal with this matter also in terms of professional negligence, as has substantially been the case. As Schultz notes:

> Because patients have been deemed incapable of individual bargaining about expert services, duties undertaken through a contract for professional care have been given content and specificity through negligence policy rather than through contract analysis . . . although patients may be incapable of supervising the quality and administration of care, they are capable, indeed uniquely so, of balancing ultimate costs and benefits of care decisions. Moreover, they are capable of determining the extent to which they wish to allocate decision making authority to their doctors. Thus, the rationale for adopting a standardized tort analysis does not extend to issues of decision making and allocation of authority; these matters could appropriately be analyzed under contract doctrine. Were such an approach adopted, the entire analytic paradigm would be reversed. Rather than an invasion of patient choice being one sub-type of injury causation within a professional negligence framework, professionally negligent care would constitute one species of breach of contract.[7]

In Shultz's view, therefore, the use of contract analysis would sharpen the focus on patient's rights or interests, and provide direct protection rather than the rather indirect protection offered by the negligence framework. Furthermore, such a specific form of action would recognize the power of the consumer of health care to dictate specific terms, and prevent the usurpation of authority which is currently common in the doctor-patient relationship. In her argument, the presumption therefore should be that 'where no explicit term [in the agreement between doctor and patient] is agreed to, patient control of decision-making should be the term implied into the contract.'[8] This, she claims is no significant infringement on the medical profession's role since at this stage their function is to advise and not to determine. Nor does it presume that all patients would wish to exercise this right. Merely it indicates that involvement should be the norm and not the exception. Legal regulation in this way would protect the rights of those who wish to be involved, and, she claims, '[g]iven the tradition of medical paternalism, patients who wish to opt out of such responsibility could easily do so.'[9] From the British perspective, however, a contractual remedy will have only a limited role to play.

## The common law remedies

Traditionally, common law offered a number of options in personal injury litigation. Remedies based on civil assault (trespass, battery, etc.) were competent in medical as well as other cases. This type of action had considerable benefits for the patient who need show only that information disclosure fell short of the required standard in order to succeed. However, the action also has many drawbacks, not least that it does not, and cannot, cover cases where the failure to have proper regard for the right involves the provision of no therapy, or failure to disclose therapeutic alternatives. The terminology of assault is stretched beyond credibility when appealed to in such circumstances. In any event, there is a marked, and understandable, reluctance on the part of the judiciary – and one suspects the general public – to classify medical intervention as an assault, even if this is in law what it amounts to. This distaste stems from recognition of the value of medical treatment, as well as from a general belief that the intention of the doctor is not to be equated with the kind of attitude which satisfies the concept of assault. Connotations of criminal or malicious intent cling to the use of the terminology of assault, and have resulted in its rejection as the appropriate form of action unless the failure to disclose was so gross as to remove the assumption of beneficence and to substitute the implication of deliberate and aggressive deceit.[10]

The trend, therefore, in most jurisdictions has been to treat a failure to make adequate disclosure as remediable only under the negligence framework, an action which has come to dominate the law of reparation.[11] While this removes some distaste from the picture, the shift to the negligence action – as currently interpreted – has been shown to have numerous disadvantages for the disaffected patient. The action itself ensures that concentration is on doctors' duties and not patients' rights, thus facilitating the importation of professional standards into what is in fact a question of respect for human dignity. Moreover, even where attempts have been made to re-emphasize the rationale which underlies the existence of the right of action, they have consistently fallen short of a vindication of full information disclosure, since negligence analysis, apparently unavoidably, demands that some weight be given to the quality of professional practice.[12] The reluctance of courts to condemn established medical behaviour results in a significant shortfall of success in litigation, even where it is admitted that information was not disclosed. Thus, emphasis is placed on the professional justifications for non-disclosure, and the right to information is watered down in the face of competing, but arguably scarcely equivalent, values.

Moreover, the general evidential requirements of the negligence action mean that the patient must demonstrate that he or she was harmed by the alleged breach of duty, a task which will generally be met with failure where the therapy has either not worsened the patient's medical condition, or has provided some relief for it. Inevitably, therefore, the basis of the patient's right is subjugated to the capacity of therapy to improve physical or mental health. By implication, the refusal of therapy takes on the taint of unreasonableness and is thereby disvalued as a self-determining act. A final, and supremely difficult, hurdle faced by the patient in the negligence action is that it is also necessary to convince the court that, had the information been disclosed, therapy would have been rejected.[13] As this is essentially unproveable, and in view of the presumption in favour of potential relief of ill-health which arises in part from concentration on doctors' duties, the patient is unlikely to succeed.

The current use of the negligence action, it is concluded, is apparently antipathetic to the vindication of fundamental rights. This is particularly true when decision makers are impressed by the admittedly high standards of a respected profession and the value of therapeutic intervention. Just as courts are hesitant to admit that non-existence could ever be preferable to existence,[14] so they are reluctant to place a value on continued ill-health, even where freely and knowledgeably chosen, when therapy has the potential to alleviate symptoms or to cure. There are, of course, further problems associated with the negligence action which apply in all cases, not merely those concerning information disclosure in medicine. Most notably, these relate to what has been called the 'forensic lottery'.[15] Lack of certainty bedevils the law in this area. Proceedings are expensive, often protracted and beyond the means of many.[16] Given that, in the case of a patient who was improperly or inadequately informed but who was nevertheless not physically harmed by the therapy, the award of damages in the event of a successful action would be minimal, few will have either the financial or the emotional capacity to undertake the uncertain, expensive and ultimately unsatisfactory task of suing.

The development of the doctrine of 'informed' consent by American courts, seen by some as an attempt to widen the liability of the medical profession,[17] has proved insufficiently weighty or rigorous to defeat the inherent problems of the fault based system. As Tancredi[18] says: '[a]s a legal doctrine, informed consent has hardly fulfilled its promise. It may have created a facade of patient involvement and control, when, in fact, the power still remains with the medical decision-maker.'[19]

What, then, if any, are the options available to secure, through legal mechanisms, this important right? Only if the right is accorded overt respect will it be adhered to rather than breached, and only through legal process can redress be obtained where the deterrence of the law has failed. As Shultz says:

> The law is not the only relevant tool for achieving such a relationship between doctor and patient. But ultimately the law is about line-drawing, and some basic division of authority is essential both for purposes of norm-setting and of dispute resolution. The fact that practice, time and complexity will embroider nuance and qualification upon the basic structure does not alter the need for such a framework.[20]

However, the capacity for change will depend substantially on the jurisdiction concerned, since different legal systems develop and follow distinct legal traditions. The ease with which any jurisdiction is capable of vindicating patients' rights depends on its history and jurisprudence as much as it does on willingness to make appropriate modification or enthusiasm for change. Moreover, the very nature of the health care provided in any state may significantly affect the type and quality of available actions for redress.

In general terms, it can be said that current legal provision for redress, where the interest invaded is the right of the individual to make autonomous choices in health care matters, is at best inadequate and at worst inappropriate to the value of the interest to be protected. A review of assault based actions, negligence based actions and actions based on no fault serves to demonstrate that the interest argued for is sporadically protected. Where it is protected it is often in an indirect fashion, rather than assuming centre-stage in the resolution of disputes. Yet patients should be in a position to avail themselves of professional services without inevitably rendering themselves vulnerable to denial of autonomy.

Any action which satisfactorily recognizes the significance of the right to consent to medical treatment, after adequate and sufficient disclosure of information, and which seeks to provide compensation when breach of this right occurs, must overcome the hurdles already outlined. In fact, the provision of compensation is perhaps of less significance than the symbolic effect of the existence and success of a right of action. Admittedly, where little practical harm has been caused, little will be anticipated in the way of financial restitution. However the rights and interests which patients have are not minimized by the fact that the award of compensation will not necessarily be substantial. One must agree that '[a]n interest is not delegitimated because in a particular instance its invasion produced little demonstrable harm.'[21] Nor is it invalidated because financial compensation is minimal. Interests are routinely protected by law, even although the average financial award, for example in personal injury cases, remains low.[22]

The harm resulting from the failure adequately to involve the patient in important, and sometimes vital, therapeutic decision making, while not inevitably, or even routinely resulting in obvious damage, is none the less a major infringement of a basic right, toleration of which should not be countenanced by a rights-conscious society. In any event, most developed legal systems protect other intangible rights which broadly equate with liberty, privacy and self-determination.[23] The argument for protection in this area can therefore be equated with the claims of the individual to liberty and privacy in other intimate areas of life. As Shultz, for example, says: '[t]he opportunity for maximum feasible control of medical fate would certainly seem to be as important an interest as control of name or likeness, reputation or seclusion.'[24]

In addition to this evaluation of the interests involved, there remains one further point to be made. Intrusion into the lives of citizens is sometimes made, and generally requires strong justification. However, this intrusion, by means, for example, of restrictions on freedom of speech, is generally undertaken by the state and for reasons which are thought to enhance the general social good by the advancement and vindication of other valued rights. Thus, intrusion into the right of freedom of speech can be justified by the impact which non-intervention would have on the rights of other citizens, and by the responsibility that the state has to all of its citizens.

In the case of medical practice, however, and except in situations which concern the control of diseases which threaten society as a whole,[25] the limitation of rights is undertaken by one professional group rather than by the elected representatives of a community, and on grounds and in circumstances which make effective review both of the basis of the practice and of its effect, extremely difficult to achieve.

Yet medical practice is not undertaken in a vacuum, and thera-peutic choices involve a number of moral and social factors.[26] While it is accepted that the physician is the more competent to make the clinically appropriate decision, the patient remains the person who alone can take account of this clinical recommendation, evaluate it, and ultimately make the satisfactory personal decision. The rights and interests to be balanced are both of major significance – that is, professional competence and self-determination – but the latter is argued here to be the more fundamental and wide-ranging of the two. Analysis of the doctor-patient relationship indicates that the doctor's professional standing and competence to act are deriva-tive from, rather than descriptive of, the standing to be accorded to the patient.

While the vindication of rights is not inevitably the province of the law, and given that not all interests are legally protected, it remains none the less the case that in situations where professional practice is challenged the most effective mechanism available to the aggrieved party is access to legal redress. In fact, there is no dispute that the law has a concrete interest in matters of information disclosure in medicine – an interest which has resulted from recog-nition of the potential invasiveness of therapy and the inequalities inherent in professional-client relationships. However, the argu-ment here has been that, while recognizing the abstract value of patient involvement in therapeutic decision making, courts have been influenced by a number of other factors into effectively mini-mizing the impact of this principle. Moreover, it is argued, the nature of the legal procedures applied to cases of this sort has proved to be an effective block to the adequate balancing of rights between the parties to the medical act.

The final question, therefore, is whether, accepting the signifi-cance of the right here described, the law *can* be modified to provide a more equitable solution to the problems illustrated in this discussion. The question as to whether or not the law *should* take account of them is, it is submitted, answered both by the fact that the law already purports to deal with them and therefore clearly regards them as valid objects of legal consideration, and by accept-ance of the value of the right to receive and use information about therapy and therapeutic alternatives. As has been noted, however, merely to say that the law *should* deal with these dilemmas is not to identify a mechanism whereby it *can*.

Only recognition of adequate information disclosure as a legally protected prerequisite of a legal and moral medical act will suffice to vindicate the rights of the patient who seeks self-determination in medicine as in other aspects of life. If this were done then even the much abused negligence action could offer hope of restitution.

The duties of the doctor would have to include a duty to tell patients all relevant and available information about risks, benefits and alternatives. Coupled with a professional recommendation, the patient is then, and only then, in a position truly to make a free and real decision. Judgements as to whether or not this duty has been adequately carried out would not depend on whether or not it was standard practice to disclose that information but on the *fact* of whether or not it actually *was* disclosed.

As for the need to show that harm resulted from a breach of duty, recognition of the value of self-determination would also facilitate the recognition of the insult to integrity which results from a failure to make disclosure. Inevitably, such an hypothesis will be objected to by some, and certainly there would be some difficulties associated with its implementation, but there are already much more fundamental problems intimately linked to its non-implementation. Certainly, it is the case that agreement on this hypothesis and its routine validation in courts would affect the practice of medicine, but it cannot be unquestioningly assumed that this will be for the worse.

The fact that current medical practice does not favour full disclosure will mean that many doctors will take time to change their practice. Inevitably, therefore, it can be assumed that litigation would, in the first instance, increase. If surveyors, solicitors or accountants deliberately withheld information so that their clients unknowingly embarked on a course of action important to their lives few would quibble if they were sued. The threat of defensive medicine equally doesn't work here, because defensive medicine in this case would result in full disclosure – which is the intended outcome.

A legal difficulty which can be easily dispensed with is the question of reliability of witnesses. In disputes between the doctor who claims to have disclosed something and the patient who claims that no disclosure was made, courts will simply have to depend on their regular responsibility to assess witness credibility.

Demanding full disclosure would enhance the medical act, rendering the patient a true participant in matters relating to his or her own health care. The medical enterprise would become truly voluntary and the moral standing of medicine would thereby be enhanced.

Ultimately, of course, the adherence of the courts to a consistently applied standard of this sort would alter the shape of medical practice. As doctors become aware of legal expectations they, like any other group, will develop practices which are consistent with them. Patients and doctors alike will eventually accustom themselves to a medical model which truly shares respect between the professional and the client.

Therefore, although the current practices of medicine and law seem to offer scant hope for the inadequately informed patient, the shift of emphasis argued for here would serve to improve the position of patients and to enhance the reputation of medicine and its practitioners. The right described, therefore, is taken to be a fundamental one and access to it is seen as vital to the human being's exercise of control over his or her own life and health (physical and mental). Logically, therefore, information relevant to the risks and benefits of the proposed therapy and its alternatives must be disclosed in order that the patient can make a choice as to whether or not to participate, even where failure to accept risks is potentially harmful.

Although the right to withhold consent is encountered most often by implication in British cases, there is a wealth of American jurisprudence on this matter, validating the claim made here that the right described is dependent on the quality of the information disclosure and not on the outcome. That is, it is not definable by the nature of the patient's choice, but by the fact that a choice was available and was made. In cases such as *In Re Quackenbush*[27] and *Superintendent of Belchertown* v. *Saikewicz*,[28] American courts have explicitly recognized that, although information disclosure may lead to refusal of therapy which is potentially beneficial, the value of the competent person's right to make such choices supersedes the unfortunate consequences of the withholding of consent. As Gostin says:

> Ethically, a patient should be free to make a decision which may be against his medical interests so long as he is able to understand the implication of that decision; the common law places no legal obstacle to a patient's decision to live in great pain or even to risk his life rather than to accept unwanted medical treatment.[29]

Moreover, observance of the patient's right to information about therapy and therapeutic alternatives far from threatening the doctor-patient relationship could effectively enhance it. Trust between doctor and patient depends not just on the patient's confidence in the doctor but on the doctor's respect for the patient. This necessarily denies the therapeutic imperative in favour of the therapeutic alliance.[30] As Picard points out '. . . a breakdown in the doctor-patient relationship often occurs when there is little or no communication between the parties.'[31] He reflects ruefully on the causes of a failure in communication which has such serious consequences for what Pellegrino and Thomasma[32] would call a 'good and proper' medical act.

It is a sad irony that the circumstances of each party militate against clear, thorough communication in a relationship of serious conse-quence. The doctor is likely balancing commitments to other patients, colleagues and committees. His medical education has prepared him to treat the disease but not necessarily the person, and the day-to-day demands on him may make getting to know the patient and his concerns seem impossible or unimportant.[33]

## Conclusions

Whatever the reasons, and however understandable they may be, it remains self-evident that the patient's right to information is often minimized or ignored in the current practice of orthodox medicine and in courts of law. This may be explicable but it is none the less unjustifiable in the vast majority of cases. Special groups such as children and the mentally handicapped may require, and have been given, special consideration, but even here it has been shown not only that lack of competence need not be presumed but also that courts in both Britain and the United States have in fact adopted a more *ad hoc* approach to decision making as to competence, at least in part recognizing the importance of the voluntariness of medical intervention. As Gostin argues '. . . forming categories of people in which the law automatically dispenses with the requirement of seeking consent is fraught with conceptual inconsistencies and practical difficulties.'[34] He concludes that '[t]here can be no greater intrusion on a competent human being than to compel him to receive physical treatment which he does not want.'[35]

Recognition of the scale of this 'intrusion' demands also that the apparent distinction between the unknowing patient and the unwilling patient is reassessed. Few, if any, would argue for the compulsory imposition of treatment,[36] yet the converse must also be true – that is, that the only therapy which *would* be argued for is that which is voluntarily undertaken. In other words, acceptable therapy is that which is entered into freely, in knowledge of the possible risks and benefits and with information as to possible alternatives where these exist.

The significance of this issue, therefore, is substantial, and the claim that information disclosure and the right to use that infor-mation should be legally recognized and protected is not defeated by the fact that on occasion its realization may be impossible, for example in extreme cases of mental incapacity or in the case of the very young child who has no method of expressing an opinion. Where therapy is, therefore, selected by others – either parents or otherwise authorized adults – its imposition is, except in rare cases, justified by the capacity of that therapy to enhance the likelihood of the *incapax* individual being capable in future of acting in a self-determining manner. In other words, the ends – of self-determination – may sometimes, albeit unusually, be realized by the use of means which would otherwise be unacceptable. However, recognition that there may be some problematic cases does not detract from the importance of the assertion of self-determination. The primary purpose, in these cases, of asserting the right to information disclosure facilitating the choice whether or not to accept therapy, is to ensure that the decision as to the competency of an individual patient is made against a background which demands respect for the right, and a correspondingly weighty and compelling justification for its denial.

Mere definition of the right, however, even when combined with justifications for its vindication, is not taken to be a sufficient step. As in the case of many other human rights, emotional or moral appeal does not guarantee respect. Yet if the right is of significance then respect for it must be sought, and failure to respect it must involve the imposition of sanctions and/or the compensation of the person whose right is infringed. In other words, the *law* must recognize and protect the right by giving it appropriate status in the hierarchy of legitimate interests.

Since ethical or professional codes are notoriously vague and relatively easy to ignore, proper vindication of the right, and sanctions for its breach, will therefore be the province of the law. As Gregory says:

> It is generally accepted among scholars in ethics that the human race, in the course of its cultural development, has described certain 'ideals' of behaviour; one hopes that all would conform to these high standards of behaviour without the need for a 'reward or punishment' scheme. But mankind has become realistic enough to know that, although these standards might be accepted as ideal, they will rarely generate uniform compliance by individuals faced with the mundane, everyday problems of life . . . The law steps in in such cases to fill the recognized vacuum. . . . to assure wherever possible, conformity to the ethical and moral ideal.'[37]

However, in reviewing the attitude of the law to this matter, it is noted *ab initio* that merely 'stepping in' indicates little about the effect of, or rationale for, legal control. Thus, considerable emphasis has been placed on the *nature* of the legal remedies available to vindicate this right, since the type of action which legal systems make available has a great impact on the balance of power between litigant (patient) and defender (physician). This balance is reflected by the nature and type of proof required by the form of action itself and by the capacity for subjectivity in decision-making tribunals, and is measurably related to the value which is placed by these tribunals on the right itself.

Certainly the law recognizes the value of autonomy in medicine, otherwise *no* remedy would be available, but adequate protection demands a form of decision making suited to the issue. It is not merely *recognition* of the importance of information disclosure that matters. Appropriate redress for grievances must also be available and clear legal standards laid down – standards which are set with a view to maintaining rights and not to the protection of a particular professional group, or even a valued enterprise. The cumulative effect of this will be the improvement of the doctor/patient relationship and the enhancement of the beneficence of medicine.

This seems to point to the need to re-evaluate the nature of the medical enterprise. Most appropriately, it has been argued, this can be done by distinguishing between the information required to agree (or not) to participate in diagnosis or therapy and the way in which that diagnosis and/or therapy is conducted. Professional assessment of technical behaviour may be relatively unexceptionable, but is inappropriate when the behaviour of the professional person is related to obtaining the agreement of an individual to participate.

The decision whether or not to accept risks is the personal and important right of the patient, and can be, and often is, independent even of medically optimal advice. Hedging bets, for whatever reason, is not acceptable when what is at stake is a matter of such significance. The law can and must adequately recognize this by respecting and enhancing the status of the patient as an autonomous human being, even if an ill one. On what basis can it be rational that the wishes of a deceased person will be respected, even where these wishes may deny life to someone else by means of organ transplantation,[38] and yet the person who is alive, and whose own life or well-being may be at stake, is denied that same respect? The formation of a therapeutic partnership, recognized and vinicated by law, can do nothing but good for the practice of medicine. Accepting that patients have a 'right to know' is the unequivocal path towards its generation.

# Notes

1. Pellegrino, E. and Thomasma, D., *A Philosophical Basis of Medical Practice*, Oxford, OUP, 1981, at p. vii.
2. Shultz, M.M., 'From informed consent to patient choice: a new protected interest' 95 *Yale Law J.* 219 (1985).
3. E.g. *Thake* v. *Maurice* [1984] 2 All ER 513, but see also [1986] 1 All ER 497; *Eyre* v. *Measday* [1986] 1 All ER 488.
4. For discussion of contractual obligations see Walker, D. M., *The Law of Delict in Scotland*, (2nd edn. revised). Edinburgh, W. Green & Son Ltd., 1981; Weir, T., *A Casebook on Tort*, (5th edn), London, Sweet & Maxwell, 1983.
5. 1914 SC 277.
6. Supra cit.
7. Loc. cit., at p. 281.
8. At p. 282.
9. Id.
10. *Chatterton* v. *Gerson & Anor.* [1981] 1 All ER 257.
11. Weir, T., op. cit., at p. 267: 'It was barely fifty years ago that the tort of negligence was born, or synthesised, but it has thrived so mightily and grown so lusty that one could be forgiven for wondering whether there was room left for any other tort at all.'
12. Since the essence of the negligence action is the concept of 'duty of care'.
13. C.f. *Sidaway* v. *Bethlem Royal Hospital Governors & Ors.* [1985] 1 All ER 643 (HL).
14. *McKay* v. *Essex A.H.A.* [1982] 2 WLR 890; for discussion of the problems in 'wrongful life' actions, see e.g. Liu, A.N.C., 'Wrongful life: some of the problems' 14, *J. Med. Ethics* 69 (1987); Symmons, C. R., 'Policy factors in actions for wrongful birth' (1987) 50 MLR 259.
15. Ison. T. G., *The Forensic Lottery*, London, Staples Press, 1967.
16. Even despite the availability of legal aid; for recent discussion, see *The Independent* 17 March 1987, under the headline 'How to remove financial insult from injury'.
17. E.g. Robertson, G., 'Informed consent to medical treatment' (1981) 97 LQR 102.
18. Tancredi, L., 'Competency for informed consent: conceptual limits of empirical data' 5 *Int. J. Law Psychiat.*, 51 (1982).
19. At p. 51.
10. Loc. cit. at p. 299.
21. Shultz, loc. cit., at p. 291.
22. For discussion, see Royal Commission on Civil Liability and Compensation for Personal Injury, (Pearson Commission) Cmnd. 7054/1978.
23. For an analysis of rights see Campbell, et al. (Eds) *Human Rights: From Rhetoric to Reality*, Oxford, Basil Blackwell, 1986.
24. Loc. cit. at p. 278.
25. Thus, societies may intervene on classical utilitarian lines if the exercise of someone's right threatens the rights of others, in line with J.S. Mills's classic statement '. . . the sole end for which mankind are warranted . . . in interfering with the liberty of action of one of their number, is self-protection . . . The only part of the conduct of anyone for which he is amenable to society, is that which concerns others.' 'On Liberty' 6 (1873).
26. Cf. Illich, I., *Limits to Medicine. Medical Nemesis: The Expropriation of Health*, Harmondsworth, Penguin Books, 1985 edition; Kennedy, I., *the Unmasking of Medicine*, London, George Allen & Unwin, 1981; Shultz, loc. cit.

27. 156 NJ Super 181 (1978); the court in this case permitted an elderly patient with a good prognosis to refuse life-saving therapy.
28. 370 NE 2d 417 (1977); the court held that the common law right to bodily integrity and the constitutional right to privacy protected a competent person's right to refuse medical treatment. For further discussion, see Davis, S.M. 'The refusal of life saving medical treatment vs. the State's interest in the preservation of life: a clarification of the interests at stake' 58 *Wash. Univ. Law Q.* 85, at p. 101: 'The right to bodily integrity involves the right to make decisions affecting one's body but also reflects a concern for avoidance of pain and indignity. Many believe that much of modern technology strips the patient of all human dignity, and that when treatment offers no real benefit a patient should not be subjected to it. Conscious but incompetent patients should be able to avoid medical treatment that causes pain or indignity without countervailing benefit. Although unconscious patients sense neither pain nor indignity, the right to bodily integrity should also extend to them, to protect competent persons' interests in assurance of proper treatment should they become incompetent'; see also, Jackson, D. L., and Younger, S., 'Patient autonomy and "death with dignity": some clinical caveats' 301 *New Engl. J. Med.* 404 (1979).
29. Gostin, L.O., 'Compulsory treatment in psychiatry: some reflections on self-determination, patient competency and professional expertise' 7 *Poly Law Rev* 86 (1982), at p. 86.
30. Cf. Teff. H., 'Consent to medical procedures, paternalism, self determination or therapeutic alliance' (1985) 101 LQR 432; Calman, K.C. and McLean, S.A.M., 'Consent, dissent, cement' 29, *Scottish Med.* J. 209 (1984).
31. Picard, E., 'Consent to medical treatment in Canada' 19 *Osgoode Hall Law J.* 140 (1981), at p. 140.
32. Op. cit.
33. Loc. cit., at pp. 140–141.
34. Loc. cit. at p. 86.
35. Loc. cit. at p. 89.
36. Although see Koldar, V.E.B., Gallagher, J., and Parsons, M.T., 'Court-ordered obstetrical interventions' 316 *New Engl. J. Med.*, 1192 (1987).
37. Gregory, D.R., 'Informed consent: an overview' 9 *Legal Aspects of Medical Practice* 4 (1981) at p. 4.
38. Human Tissue Act 1961.

# Index